Jullian –

Thanks for everything!

Best of luck

2003

Anchoring America

Anchoring America

The Changing Face of Network News

By Jeff Alan

With James M. Lane

BONUS BOOKS
Chicago and Los Angeles

07 06 05 04 03   5 4 3 2 1

Library of Congress Cataloging-in-Publication Data

Alan, Jeff.
  Anchoring America : the changing face of network news / by Jeff Alan with James M. Lane.
      p. cm.
Includes bibliographical references and index.
  ISBN 1-56625-194-X
  1. Television news anchors—United States—Biography.
I. Lane, James
Martin, 1959- II. Title.
  PN4871.A43 2003
  070.92′273—dc21

                                        2003013035

Bonus Books
875 N. Michigan Ave.
Suite 1416
Chicago, IL 60611

Printed in Canada

To my father

Contents

Contents

Preface

For all of us who grew up with the evening news anchors in our living rooms and family rooms five nights a week, it's fair to say that we saw more of the anchors than we saw of most of our neighbors, and even some of our close friends and relatives. It's also fair to say that most of our parents placed more trust in the evening news anchormen and women than they placed in politicians, astrologers, generals, newspaper columnists, mystics, religious leaders, and other types of public personalities who held the faith of earlier generations of Americans.

These newsmen and women were appointed to anchor news programs, but, in terms of our relationship with them, especially between 1960 and 1980, they anchored America, too. Successful anchors invariably were major public personalities and were sought after for public positions, from the Federal Communications Commission to the United States Senate. The most successful anchor of all time, Walter Cronkite, routinely was voted "the most trusted man in America" in a survey of the American public. He held the title even after he left the anchor desk for semi-retirement.

The anchors have been admired, reviled, criticized, threatened, lauded, hated, loved, and emulated by different sections of the public, but they never have been ignored. They have been the subject of countless books and articles—sometimes as the sole focus, sometimes as a group—but they never have been surveyed as a whole before, not only for their impact on the news landscape, but also for their impact on us, the public.

It was that simple thought—to examine our relationships with the anchors and the concept of anchoring in a series of profiles of the anchors—that led to this book. We set out to examine who they were, why we watched them, how the news affected them, how they affected the news, and how they affected us as we took in the events of the day they related.

The first and most difficult task was to define exactly what we meant by an *anchor*. The term itself dates to the 1950s, but it has come to stand not only for a device—a person serving as focal point of a news program—but for a singular personality who serves as the focal point for an entire network news operation. That person embodies the culture of the network and comes, in a few cases, to be held in the highest esteem by the public. An anchor is a fixture of the evening television experience, a subject of endless debate among viewers as to who's the best, and, in many cases, thought of as a keeper of the public trust.

In the broadest sense, almost every news broadcast has an anchor, someone who is anything from a simple presenter whose job it is to read the words on the Teleprompter convincingly, to a formidable journalist who combines the roles of reporter, commentator, and presenter. But, for most people, the anchors are the men and women who, for lengthy periods, sat at the anchor desk on the network evening news.

When we defined the anchors to be profiled in this book, we selected nineteen men and women, from Edward R. Murrow to Connie Chung. There was no hard and fast rule that led us to include Murrow, who never anchored a network evening news, but not Rod Cochran, who anchored the fifteen-minute ABC evening news in the early 1960s. It seemed to us that in many ways, Murrow exemplified and established the anchoring tradition—although he did so in radio.

Tom Wolfe, in his book, *The Right Stuff*, which is the story of the astronauts of the Mercury program, began with a profile of Charles Yeager, the "dean" of the test pilots. Yeager personified what it meant to be a test pilot, to have "the right stuff". Though Yeager never went into space, his profile is essential to the story of the space program. That is especially true when it comes to articulating the triumph of those who saw that to popularize the space program, astronauts had to be thought of as heroes, rather than simply as passengers perched on top of a rocket.

Murrow, in his own way, is the Chuck Yeager of this book. The "right stuff" he exemplified—his commitment to truth, candor, authentic reporting, and the public trust—eventually became part of the culture of the network evening news in the United States. Several of the early anchors were hired or served under him; later anchors continue to be ardent admirers of his uncompromising news standards. Although he never served as a network anchor, it is impossible to understand the culture of the news, and the news culture of CBS in particular, without a profile of his astonishing career.

We also included the three original anchors at the major networks—Douglas Edwards, John Daly, and John Cameron Swayze. All are great stories in their own right and lend themselves to providing a clear understanding of the early days of the news. None of the three had Murrow's stature, and there were other correspondents who were more highly regarded during their heydays in the 1950s. But Edwards, Daly, and Swayze were hired not only for their talents, but because more highly regarded journalists were hostile to the new medium. Nevertheless, it fell to those three to establish the format and style of the news and to wade through a thicket of logistical and technical questions, including remote coverage, live coast-to-coast feeds, the Teleprompter, lighting, and set decoration. They began at the absolute beginning of television news, when there were no established practices at all. By the time the last of them left (Edwards in 1962), the news had a recognizably modern shape.

The next generation of anchors included Walter Cronkite at

CBS and the team of Chet Huntley and David Brinkley at NBC. They were, perhaps, the preeminent anchors of all time, achieving widespread popularity, consistent ratings, critical acclaim, and immense public trust that grew through the years of the Vietnam War. They also provided the classic form of the thirty-minute broadcast, which was introduced during their time, with its combination of commentary and reporting from a distinguished set of national and international correspondents.

A succession of short-lived anchors at ABC between 1961 and 1969 was not included in the book because, except for Frank Reynolds and Peter Jennings, the anchors lacked ratings and longevity. Both Reynolds and Jennings later achieved great distinction in their respective second tours at the ABC anchor desk, however, beginning in 1978.

With the end of the 1960s, a new seriousness at ABC and Huntley's 1971 retirement from NBC sparked a new focus on anchoring formats. ABC tried a number of experiments in the 1970s, finding some success with the two-anchor format of Howard K. Smith and Harry Reasoner. ABC also introduced a number of firsts, with female anchor Barbara Walters and later a three-anchor format including Max Robinson, Jennings, and Reynolds. Longtime NBC veteran John Chancellor was at the helm of a distinguished program at NBC, where he was teamed for a time with David Brinkley, while Cronkite continued to win the ratings war from his desk at CBS.

In the 1970s, the news product was strongly influenced not only by the newsmen, but also by a pair of visionary producers: Don Hewitt and Roone Arledge. Arledge's moves at ABC not only reshaped the ABC network news programming, but he put a new emphasis on anchors as marketable stars. He made overtures to Tom Brokaw and Dan Rather that were instrumental in persuading NBC and CBS, respectively, to name the two as anchors of their own broadcasts. Hewitt, a former CBS *Evening News* producer, established the first highly successful, long-running news magazine hit with *60 Minutes*. His own correspondents, including Reasoner and Rather, became stars in their own right on the first program to rival the network evening news for ratings and prestige.

With the 1980s came the current trio of Jennings, Rather, and Brokaw. It was a close decision to include Connie Chung for her two-year stint as CBS co-anchor in the 1990s, but not to include Roger Mudd for his co-anchor role with Brokaw from 1982 to 1983. In the end, Chung was chosen not only for her anchoring service, but the unique example she represents today as a star journalist "anchoring" a non-news program on CNN.

Also during the 1980s, CNN arose, the first of many twenty-four–hour cable news networks that have contributed to a complete realignment of the network evening news. We included a chapter not only on CNN, but on the *MacNeil-Lehrer NewsHour*, which provided, along with CNN, an alternative to the networks throughout the 1980s and early 1990s.

Since the departure of Connie Chung in 1995, there have been no new network evening news anchors. Yet the proliferation of news magazine programs and twenty-four–hour cable news networks and the challenge of the Internet has given the network evening news its greatest ratings struggle since the 1940s. Consequently, we made the decision to profile the changes since 1995 in a single, focused chapter that examines the changes not only at the networks, but in our culture.

Putting the story together, we realized that there was an underlying theme to the book, which is the decline in the importance of the Murrow tradition and the classic network news anchor's role. We believe that there is no better way to demonstrate these changes than by contrasting the coverage of Pearl

Harbor, when the country thirsted for a national news leadership, with the coverage of September 11, 2001, when there seemed to be such comprehensive coverage from local and cable news that network evening news looked much like an anachronism. We decided to include a detailed chapter on each, showing what we, as the public, experienced in terms of information gathering.

In between Pearl Harbor and September 11, 2001, are portraits of our greatest anchors and some of our weakest. The profiles are designed to answer why we liked them, as well as what were they like. With a focus on the anchors and a close eye on America, we present the men and women in this book as a memory of times past. This is a look at their successes and failures so that we may find indications of how we will watch our news in the coming years and generations.

Acknowledgments

When you start out on a project the size of this one, you never know how many twists and turns it's going to take. I called upon my friends in the business and many scholars to help me out. The task was not easy, as I wanted to create a book that is not only a written documentary of those legendary men and women we watched on the evening news every night, but a work that will be part of America's historical archive. What happened was truly remarkable. The book took on a life of its own and is not only historical, but also entertaining.

The inspiration for this book came directly from the headlines that television news anchors may be going the way of the dinosaurs, and an evening news Ice Age may be in the offing.

James Lane felt the same way. So, together, we forged what you are holding in your hand. We also discovered the underlying premise that the evening television news anchors will never achieve the type of legendary status they had through until the 1980s. So, accordingly, my first thanks and my undying gratitude goes to James.

As I did in my first book, *Responsible Journalism*, I thank my first news director, Jack London, for setting me off on the right road. And I thank all my peers and employees over the years who spent more than fifty thousand hours of my life with me in a newsroom somewhere in America. For the good times and the not so good times, I thank each and every one of you. The learning experience has been invaluable.

I could not have written this book without the foresight of Jeff Stern at Bonus Books, who knew the importance of the material. A special thanks to our editor, Kelley Thornton, who had no idea that her life was to be cast into the world of television news.

To the person who shares my name (and everything else for that matter), Susan Alan, who endured my slaving over a computer for hundreds of hours.

I called upon some extraordinary people to be contributors to this book. So, a very special thanks to Walter Cronkite, Peter Jennings, Tom Brokaw, and Dan Rather, who gave me their time and words to make this book as good as it could be. Many names in this book will be recognizable, and there are many that readers will see for the first time. I thank all of them, if only in spirit, for their belief in their craft and their stories, which make up a great deal of this book.

Thanks also to all the people at ABC, NBC, and CBS, who helped me to obtain materials and photos. Special thanks to the Associated Press, Media Watch, the Radio Television News Directors Association, and CNN for generously providing text and guidance. And, thank you for picking up this book to read! Please enjoy *Anchoring America*.

How We Experienced December 7, 1941

Courtesy of CBS

At Pearl Harbor, Pharmacist's Mate Second Class Lee Soucy, a crewman aboard the USS *Utah,* heard about Pearl Harbor before the first bombs fell.

He had just finished breakfast and was looking out a porthole in sick bay. He recalls:

> Someone said, "What the hell are all those planes doing up there on a Sunday?"
>
> Someone else said, "It must be those crazy Marines. They'd be the only ones out maneuvering on a Sunday."

When I looked up in the sky, I saw five or six planes starting their descent. Then when the first bombs dropped on the hangers at Ford Island, I thought, "Those guys are missing us by a mile."

Practice bombing was a daily occurrence to us. It was not too unusual for planes to drop bombs, but the time and place were quite out of line. We could not imagine bombing practice in port. It occurred to me, and to most of the others, that someone had really goofed this time and put live bombs on those planes by mistake.

I saw a huge fireball and cloud of black smoke rise from the hangers on Ford Island and heard explosions. It did not occur to me that these were enemy planes. It was too incredible! "What a snafu," I moaned.

As I watched the explosions on Ford Island in amazement and disbelief, I felt the ship lurch. We didn't know it then, but we were being bombed and torpedoed by planes approaching from the opposite (port) side.

The bugler and boatswain's mate were on the fantail, ready to raise the colors at eight o'clock. In a matter of seconds, the bugler sounded "General Quarters."

I grabbed my first-aid bag and headed for my battle station amidship.

In Honolulu, Hugh Lytle, a reserve Army officer and the Associated Press correspondent for Honolulu, heard about the attack from a phone call. His duty officer called him when the bombs started to fall, ordering him to report to his Army outpost for immediate duty.

Lytle began his war service by disobeying—or, rather, delaying—the execution of the order. Before reporting for duty, he stopped in at his Associated Press office at the *Honolulu Star-Bulletin*, where he filed a brief account of the attack in progress. It was the first report of the war and the last one for several hours, as military censors prevented further dispatches for part of that day.

Spreading the News

Chester Burger, who was a page boy at CBS News New York, recalls:

> My job was to change the rolls of yellow paper on the Teletype machines that brought news from the Associated Press, United Press, and the now long-dead International News Service. If my memory is correct, there were some eleven Teletype printers clicking away at all hours. They were placed along two of the walls of the CBS newsroom, partly surrounding the editors and writers who prepared the radio news broadcasts.
>
> I shall always remember the sound of the ten bells ringing on the United Press machine to alert us to an incoming bulletin. There were a lot of bulletins in those days, and nobody paid particular attention to one more. I would tear off the bulletins and immediately bring them to the editors' desk. But this—in my memory, I can hear the bell ringing as I am speaking with you tonight—the bell kept ringing. It rang ten times signifying a "flash." I had never heard that before.
>
> Everyone jumped up and ran to the United Press teleprinter. It read: FLASH—WHITE HOUSE ANNOUNCES ATTACK ON PEARL HARBOR. 2:26 P.M. Only forty-six minutes after the news first reached President Roosevelt, he released the news to the nation. Everyone in the CBS news room was shocked. Astonished. Believing yet unbelieving. Suddenly, we were at war. Where was Pearl Harbor? Oh yes, Hawaii, of course. We were at war with Japan. It seemed incredible. I remember someone saying, "Let's wait a few minutes to confirm before we go with it."

In Red River County, Texas, Clarence Raultston remembers listening to the first broadcasts about Pearl Harbor in the mid-afternoon. He recalls:

> It was a cold, drizzling, foggy day in Red River County, and after hearing about Pearl Harbor, my spirits were very low. I

was one-and-a-half months past my twenty-first birthday and had a good notion about where I was headed. I had a brother just two years younger, and we both knew he was in the same boat. The whole nation was in a state of quiet panic.

The panic had been building for quite some time, but when the war broke out with the attack on Pearl Harbor, a large number of Americans were left scratching their heads as to where, exactly, Pearl Harbor was. Back then, the *World Almanac* listed Honolulu as a foreign city. In those days, Hawaii local time was five and a half hours behind Eastern Standard Time, so that the 6:30 A.M. Hawaii sunrise occurred at noon in Washington, D.C. The ninety-minute attack didn't finish until three o'clock in the afternoon, EST.

Raultston said:

> John Daly [who was soon to become the first television anchor for a television network that didn't even exist yet] was calling Oahu "Oh-ha-hu". Radio commentators such as Harry Von Zell, Fulton Lewis Jr., Walter Winchell, Elmer Davis, and Gabriel Heater were pronouncing Hawaii "Hi Wa Ya". They talked in shifts for almost twelve hours, and I don't remember any commercial breaks. President Roosevelt made a short statement urging people to remain calm and to listen to his address to Congress the next day.
>
> There would be no Jack Benny, or Fred Allen, or Fibber McGee and Molly that Sunday night.

In New York, news was getting out faster, but not by much. The president's own coordinator of information, "Wild Bill" Donovan, was at the Polo Grounds watching the NFL New York Giants host the Brooklyn Dodgers. More than fifty-five thousand fans packed the stadium for the 2:00 P.M. kickoff. It wasn't until deep in the first quarter that Donovan was paged by a public address announcement arranged by Captain James Roosevelt, the president's son.

At CBS News in New York, John Charles Daly was making final preparations for the regular 2:30 broadcast of the *World Today* when the United Press release came in from the White House. He broke immediately into the program the *Spirit of '41* to deliver a short bulletin, and then followed just minutes later with the *World Today* broadcast.

CBS had the only regularly scheduled news program on Sunday afternoons on any network, so it was in an enviable position. According to the broadcast standards of the day, interruptions of regular broadcasts had to be cleared with sponsors, but because CBS was broadcasting a news program anyway, it could devote almost half an hour of coverage to the crisis.

Daly introduced the *World Today* with a two-minute summary of the attack. The NBC Red Network, by contrast, had H.V. Kaltenborn on the air at 3:15 P.M., and the NBC Blue network and Mutual worked with bulletins until their regular news broadcasts in the evening.

During the half-hour broadcast, Daly brought in Albert Warner in Washington to speculate on President Roosevelt's next move. Bob Trout reported on the British reaction from London. Then, ten minutes into the broadcast, the Japanese struck Manila. CBS correspondent Ford Wilkins was there, but his broadcast was cut off by American military censors. Daly attempted to contact Honolulu, but the communications problems were too overwhelming. In fact, no live report from Honolulu was heard on any network until shortly after four o'clock, when NBC Red affiliate KGU made a report.

Washington Reacts

In Chicago, Clark Bane Hutchinson recalls: "I was listening to the radio, and we were having a house party for all these midshipmen, these ninety-day wonders and all."

The news broke in Chicago around 1:30 local time, or just as Donovan was being paged at the Polo Grounds. "Right in the middle of the [broadcast of the] symphony, they interrupted and talked about Pearl Harbor," Hutchinson said.

She immediately called Washington, D.C. Her father, Frank Bane, was secretary general of the Governor's Conference and a board member of the Office of Civilian Defense. Her parents were scheduled to be at the White House for a two o'clock luncheon, where the guests were beginning to arrive just as the attack started. They knew nothing and were told little else.

"And I started calling them at two o'clock, you know, just frantic," said Hutchinson. "And I, at last, got them at five o'clock because they kept waiting for President Roosevelt to come to lunch, and, at last, the butler came down and said, 'He will not be down for lunch because something is happening in the East.' And Daddy was thinking that it must be something in the Philippines."

The Philippines were almost as well known as Hawaii, at the time. Flamboyant former Army Chief of Staff Douglas MacArthur had been retained as head of the Philippine Army as the United States territory readied itself for its scheduled independence in 1946, amidst the brewing crises in the Far East. Hawaii was not well known, and no radio network had staff there. The story was flashed by the wire services, and details were sketchy because reporters were few and far between on a Sunday morning in Honolulu.

In Washington, the guests continued to mill around the White House, not sure what to do. Lunchtime became suppertime, and the while the President remained upstairs with his advisers, Eleanor Roosevelt was interviewed on the NBC Blue network at 6:45 P.M.

Invited to the White House that night were Edward R. Murrow and his wife, Janet. Upon hearing the news of the attack, they contacted the White House, but, to their surprise, the dinner was not cancelled. Frank Bane saw the Murrows arrive, but upon their arrival, they were escorted upstairs to the family dining room.

The president was meeting with congressional and military leaders, explained Mrs. Roosevelt, and would not be able to join them for supper. The president, in fact, was contemplating his next moves and drafting the short address he would make to Congress that the radio networks would carry.

After the dinner, Janet Murrow departed for their hotel, but Murrow was asked to stay. He joined the president and Bill Donovan, who made it in from New York for a midnight meeting with sandwiches and cold beer. There is no official record of the meeting, but Donovan later remarked that it concerned the public's reaction to the disaster.

Roosevelt was infuriated with the lack of preparation at Pearl Harbor. There had been considerable awareness of the possibility of hostilities, and yet Admiral Thomas Kimmel was caught completely by surprise.

"They caught our ships like lame ducks!" said Roosevelt. "Lame ducks, Bill. We told them at Pearl Harbor, and everywhere else, to have the lookouts manned. But they still took us by surprise."

The president asked Murrow and Donovan whether they thought the attack would unite Americans behind a declaration of war against the Axis powers. Donovan and Murrow said yes. Roosevelt then read a message he received from North Whitehead, a British Foreign Office official: "The dictator powers have presented us with a united America."

Roosevelt asked if Whitehead was right. Again he asked if America would support a declaration of war. Again, the two men said yes.

Murrow's Influence

Donovan's presence in the midnight meeting was no surprise. He was Roosevelt's point man for the government's gathering and distribution of information. But why was Murrow there?

It is surprising because in 1933, when Roosevelt was delivering his fireside chats to the American people, Murrow was just out of college and working for a national organization of student governments. By 1937, Murrow had yet to make a news broadcast. His network, CBS, did not even have a news staff. Instead, it relied on feeds from publicity men and rewrites of wire service stories, which were limited by agreement to no more than five minutes and never aired between 9:00 A.M. and 9:00 P.M.

What had happened between 1937 and 1941 is not only the story of Edward R. Murrow, but of the role of the American broadcast anchor. Far more than their print journalist colleagues, the leading anchors of the day—although they were not described as such until the 1950s—were considered to have an understanding of the American public. Their hold on its imagination far surpassed anything that previously had been seen in journalism.

Radio was not only immediate, it was personal, and its best practitioners had rapidly mastered the art of broadcasting. Roosevelt knew that the vast majority of Americans learned of Pearl Harbor by radio, and they were to hear him the next day on radio asking for a declaration of war against Japan.

The disaster at Pearl Harbor was not only a turning point in American broadcasting that required the radio journalists to think faster and improvise better than they ever had done before. It confirmed their ascendancy. The era of the broadcast anchors was truly upon us.

How anchors have dealt with the challenges of their times

and the challenges of their role is the major story of this book. It is also the major story of network news over the past sixty years—first in radio, but essentially in television. Each anchor has sought to establish a rapport with the American audience, to build a level of trust, and to find an audience and sustain it.

There are now more networks and more news broadcasts than ever. There may even be more news. Essential aspects of the anchor role are personality and judgment. Learning those skills and using them is the challenge that unites all the anchors across all the decades, and all the broadcasts and all the news.

Please now meet and get to know the legendary television news anchors. Their stories will inspire you as they guide you through the history of the last several decades. The anchors not only had a front row seat for history, but, in many ways, they played a part in it. These men and women are few in number, and you'll discover, as I did, that the status they achieved during their careers may never be achieved again. This is truly the end of an era.

Part One

The Pioneers

Chapter ONE
Edward R. Murrow

Courtesy of CBS

Murrow is one of those names, like Edison, Birdseye, Smucker, or Ford, that began as the last name of a self-made man, but today has become a byword for quality—a national brand. Not one person in a thousand could identify Smucker in a police line-up, but millions know, "With a name like Smucker, it has to be good."

So it was, and is, with Edward R. Murrow. People who never saw one of his broadcasts say, with confidence, that "he personified a spirit of excellence and set an unequalled standard for the broadcast news profession." Or so go the pale phrases used to describe him at the annual Edward R. Murrow award dinners of the Radio and Television News Directors Association.

But there was nothing pale about Edward R. Murrow, except perhaps his complexion, which perpetually was ashen from overwork and cigarettes. There was nothing mild about what he said or did, or how he said or did it. He was the Hemingway of the airwaves. He took big risks; he covered big stories with a lean, spare prose so unusual for the florid times in which he lived that it became a style unto itself and a standard for his industry.

It is impossible to deconstruct from this distance the hold he achieved over the public imagination. When the right man arrives at the right moment in history, it is an unanswerable question whether the man created the moment, or the moment created the man.

There is no doubt that Murrow created the voice. He worked at it. It was his instrument; people were transfixed by it. "Across the radio, across the Atlantic," Dan Rather recalls, "and across half the United States, his voice came, the deep rumble and the dramatic pause just when he said, 'This . . . is London.' I never got that out of my head. It was like a piece of music that has never stopped playing for me."

The voice was a deep, rich bass-baritone acquired in northwestern Washington, where Murrow was raised in the 1910s and 1920s. It was an era when the state's progressive politics, and a radicalism born of isolation, led Postmaster General Jim Farley to quip, "There are forty-seven states in the Union and the Soviet of Washington." Murrow always carried the stamp of that splendid isolation and resultant idealism.

The West was in his voice, with the long silences and spare phrasings of the northwestern farmer, the cadences of the chanting timber-cutting teams, the crystalline coast accent that cut through radio static and the background noise of war like a hot knife through butter, and the practical, plainspoken idealism of a town dominated by Jeffersonian small landowners, lumbermen, and the Methodist Church. He worked as a compass man for timber cruisers during high school and college vacations. Little did he know that he would be pointing the way for journalists in decades to come.

He was driven. A two-finger typist, he never banged the keys on a hunt-and-peck basis; it was seek and destroy. "Even now," Murrow wrote in 1961, "I'm probably more proficient with an axe than I am with a typewriter."

"He was a fast driver. Elmer Davis said in London, "I had heard of the horrors of war, but I didn't know they included Ed Murrow's driving."

He liked target sports. He was a golfer, a dart-thrower, and a shooter.

He had one foot in the forest and one foot in the ballrooms of the Eastern Establishment. He sang old logging songs and belonged to the Century Club of New York.

The pause was his signature. Ida Lou Anderson gave it to him, and Murrow never forgot it, or her. A diminutive woman crippled by polio, she nevertheless completed fifteen years as a speech professor at Washington State University and gave after-hours instruction to her prize students, Murrow chief among them. When illness forced her to retire in 1939, she continued to write weekly critiques of Murrow's broadcasts, and she suggested the dramatic pause to heighten the effect of his introductions from London during the Blitz. "*This* . . . is London" became his trademark, and we hear a faint echo of it today in, "*This* . . . is CBS".

Murrow recalled: "She taught me to love good books, good music, gave me the only sense of values I have. . . . The part of me that is decent, wants to do something, be something, is the part she created. She taught me to speak."

The pause injected drama into even the most straightforward

of broadcasts. Layered over the crackle of distance and the sounds of war, it became an additional actor in his broadcasts.

In later years, the public was transfixed by the face, for Murrow seemed to look exactly like a newscaster should look. He was handsome. The deep furrows in his brow suggested care and experience. The dark, flashing eyes suggested intelligence and conveyed astonishment, disbelief, humor, and, when called for, the sincerity of a crusader and patriot.

People trusted the face and the voice. When asked, the public associated him with the same bold, plainspoken quality they saw in Harry Truman; it was a quality the public thought of as particularly American. He had that unerring sense of what to say and how to say it—how to get the message across. Roosevelt recognized it on the night of December 7, 1941. As the president faced the task of turning American outrage over Pearl Harbor into a cohesive entry into World War II, he struggled to find the eloquence to rouse and direct the nation and used Murrow as a sounding board into the small hours of the night.

Roosevelt, and just about everyone else, saw in Murrow the common sense and straight talk of the frontiersman. People tuned in to his broadcasts like settlers listening to Kit Carson and Jedediah Smith on the Oregon Trail. His broadcasts were often stark, challenging, and uncomfortable. He was as suited to the dramatic 1930s and 1940s as he proved unsuited to the glacial pace of the late 1950s.

A Brass Set

Dan Rather put it plainly: "What separated Ed Murrow from the pack was courage."

Like all pioneers, Murrow had more than moxie; he was an innovator. Like all his contemporaries, he lived in a period

Associated Press

when the new media of radio and television required almost daily improvisation and invention. But his legacy was not in his improvisations. It was not even in the voice, or the pause, or the face, for these, no matter how dramatic, fade quickly into the background static of the airwaves.

What mattered in the end was how he organized the system of news reporting and set down the original standards for anchors with a startling completeness. Murrow never sat at the anchor desk on any national, televised, nightly news broadcast—not even once. But in every sense, he is revered as the author of the role. He personified the anchors, inspired them, and, in many cases, picked them—first hiring Howard K. Smith, Douglas Edwards, and, later, Walter Cronkite. John Daly, Harry Reasoner, and Dan Rather worked at his CBS early in their careers.

He developed the anchor role in radio fourteen years before it was referred to as "anchoring". Before Murrow, there were commentators, coordinators, crackpots, characters, mystics, loudmouths, analysts, hosts, and moderators. After him came the true anchors: equal parts journalist, celebrity, arranger, composer, and keeper of the public trust. It is his system, his ideal.

But it is not correct to say that it was his plan, for he began his career as a broadcaster by an accident of history in 1938. It was a bleak winter in the United States, and the country began to slide again into recession. Spring arrived with warmth, but without cheer. The year began with crises in Eastern Europe and finished with the dismemberment of Czechoslovakia under the Treaty of Munich. In between, there was the Anschluss, or forced union, of Austria and Germany into a terrifying national instrument of Nazi policy and Hitler's ambition.

In that hour, when people were, as commentator Bernard Devoto memorably put it, "hanging over their radios to hear the news from Europe," Murrow was a man with a problem far less threatening than the conquest of Europe. His was more immediate and personal. He was based in London to coordinate CBS European coverage. He was sent over in 1937 to line up cultural broadcasts and talks, but, instead, he stood on the precipice of history. As he went about his daily task of transmitting the voices of politics and culture from Europe to America, he rapidly realized that his role was changing to what Reuven Frank later summed up as the essential mission of network news, "transmitting experience."

But, for that moment, his role was coordination. CBS policy of the time avoided taking editorial positions, even to the point of forbidding staff members to make broadcasts. Nevertheless, Murrow hired Bill Shirer in Berlin to help him with the workload. The two fretted about their inactivity on the airwaves as they lined up politicians, composers, and writers, and they were forced to use newspaper reporters for hosts.

They appealed to New York to be allowed to broadcast as the events of 1937 unfolded, including the Italian-Ethiopian crisis and the general darkening of the prospects for peace. They consistently were turned down, but with the spring of 1938, the focus of European events moved from Rome and Berlin to Vienna as agitation for union of Germany and Austria heated up.

NBC had Max Jordan in Vienna, a veteran journalist with a knack for dramatic on-the-scene reporting. Murrow transferred Shirer to Vienna, and they pleaded again to be allowed to make broadcasts. In New York, CBS Chairman Bill Paley and CBS Radio head Ed Klauber stood firm. The head of CBS News in New York, Paul White, was supportive, but knew, as did Murrow and Shirer, that the Austrian broadcasting service, RAVAG, had an exclusive with NBC. On-the-spot reporting in the Jordan style was difficult, if not impossible.

Then, in March 1938, the Anschluss crisis exploded just as

Jordan temporarily left the country. Shirer was the only American radio staffer in the Austrian capital. How Murrow and CBS responded changed the face of broadcasting forever.

Anschluss . . . Get There!

Historians continue to argue about the origins of the Anschluss, some pointing to 1919 and the Treaty of Versailles, some back to 1866 and Prussia's famous victory over the Austrians at Sadowa, some even back to Napoleon or the Thirty Years' War.

But historians do not have to make broadcasts, and, for Murrow, the Anschluss crisis began with a phone call on March 11, 1938. It was from Bill Shirer in Vienna, who tracked him down in Warsaw, where Murrow was coordinating a children's broadcast for the *School of the Air* program.

"The opposing team has crossed the goal line," Shirer said.

"Are you sure?" Murrow asked.

"I'm paid to be sure," Shirer replied.

With Jordan out of the country, CBS had a singular opportunity to break a major story. Murrow agreed that Shirer should fly to London and make the broadcast. Owing to the circumstances, Paley and Klauber agreed, and Shirer broadcast the Anschluss story from London on Saturday, March 12. It was the first staff broadcast ever made at CBS; it remains one of the finest.

Murrow himself flew to Berlin, chartered a twenty-seven–seat Lufthansa transport for one thousand dollars, and flew to Vienna. He caught a streetcar into the city just as the troops arrived.

In New York, the effect of Shirer's broadcast was electric. But Max Jordan scrambled back to Vienna and began a series of on-the-spot reports throughout the morning of March 13.

Murrow was unable, initially, to secure a broadcasting facility, and CBS was silent from Vienna.

Throughout the day on March 13, as the Nazis streamed into the Austrian capital, NBC scooped CBS time after time. By late Sunday morning, New York time, it was clear to CBS executives that unless they changed the rules of the game, they would not be able to counter the effect of NBC's programming.

Hurried conversations proceeded between Paley, Klauber, and Paul White. Immediately, they realized that, although NBC had the edge in Vienna, CBS had a broader opportunity with unique, coordinated, global coverage using their American resources, as well as Murrow and Shirer in Europe.

Paley called it a "round-up," but even as Paul White scrambled to assemble a group report on the crisis, the CBS engineers announced that the broadcast could not be achieved. There was no news broadcast facility at CBS in New York, no precedent for switching between America and Europe in the way Paley wanted.

Throughout the day, Murrow and Shirer prepared their material in Europe, White scrambled to put together the facilities and team, and Klauber worked with the engineers to find technical solutions. By 8:00 P.M. on Sunday, March 13, they were ready. Robert Trout introduced the "round-up" from New York. There were interviews in Washington, Berlin, and Paris, as well as Shirer in London and Murrow in Vienna. Paul White later recalled how "we would flip from capital to capital via short-wave."

The effect of the static-laden, whistling short wave radio report was incredible. The focus was Murrow's balanced, authoritative reports from Vienna, which were enhanced by Shirer's reports of the reaction from London and broadened by the reports from the major American and European cities.

CBS knew it had a winner. The round-up was a success. A

second broadcast was scheduled for March 15, and the format was continued for ten days as the crisis unfolded. CBS completely outclassed NBC on breadth of coverage, overall coordination, and the incisive broadcasts from Vienna and London by Murrow and Shirer. Both men became overnight stars.

But more than that, Murrow's advocacy of a news organization with broadcasts from CBS staff correspondents on the scene was vindicated. For all the fame he gained in later years, this was perhaps his key contribution to broadcasting.

Further, he established an absolute standard, through his example, that news anchors should have well-established reputations as on-the-scene news reporters. Today, we think nothing of seeing Brokaw, Jennings, or Rather broadcasting directly from Moscow or Riyadh.

It was not inevitably the case. The famed BBC anchors, for instance, are newsreaders, not correspondents, and are chosen more on voice than experience. Australia's longest-serving anchor-newsreader, Brian Henderson, was a transplant from *Australian Bandstand*.

But after Murrow, American anchors were chosen from the pool of correspondents.

The Murrow Boys Go to War

Following the Anschluss, Paley made the decision not only to continue the round-up, but also to expand it. He authorized Murrow to recruit a small staff of European correspondents.

Murrow's team continues to be regarded today as the finest ever assembled. In addition to Murrow and Shirer, there were Eric Sevareid, Charles Collingwood, Howard K. Smith, Bill Downs, Larry LeSeuer, Richard Hottelet, Winston Burdett, Cecil Brown, Thomas Grandin, and Mary Marvin Breckinridge. All had fine careers; many, like Sevareid and Smith, went on to

Courtesy of CBS

become celebrities in their own right. They became known as "Murrow's Boys." One writer observed, "In the forties and fifties, the Murrow Boys were not only number one, [they] were in a class by themselves."

Murrow's role was to hire, inspire, and report from London, where American attention increasingly rested as the war approached. Murrow later described the philosophy with which he approached the gathering and reporting of news:

> New programs are broadcast solely for the purpose of enabling the listeners to know facts—so far as they are ascertainable— and so to elucidate, illuminate, and explain facts and situations as fairly as possible will enable the listener to weigh and judge for himself. We will endeavor to assist the listener in weighing

and judging developments throughout the world, but will refrain—particularly with respect to all controversial, political, social, and economic questions—from trying to make up the listener's mind for him.

We shall do our best to identify sources and to resist the temptation to use this microphone as a privileged platform from which to advocate action. It is not, I think, humanly possible for any reporter to be completely objective, for we are all, to some degree, prisoners of our own education, travel, reading, the sum total of our experience. And we shall try to remember that the mechanics of radio, which make it possible for an individual voice to be heard throughout the entire land, do not confer great wisdom or infallibility on that individual.

It is unwise to predict what will happen on a news program because that will be determined by the nature of the news. Being human, we will probably make mistakes, and the only thing that can be said about that in advance is that we shall do our utmost to be the first to correct them.

So it was that CBS arrived at the commencement of World War II not only with a news department, but an outlook, a standard, and a system of reporting. With that, based from a London studio connected to the New York broadcasting hub, Murrow and his cohort took on the coverage of the origins of a war that dwarfed any previous conflict in its scale, scope, velocity, and in its marriage of science and cruelty.

Murrow had his hands full at first explaining British policy and preparations. It was difficult to trace the contours of the one or to find much evidence of the other. Traditional British foreign policy in Europe has two tenets. The first is to prevent a major power from dominating Belgium. The second is to prevent one nation from becoming a dominant power in Europe. It was in defense of the former that Great Britain entered World War I. It was in defense of the latter that they entered World War II. But the policy was based on the assumption that

Britain would act before the other power reached its zenith. In this case, England's leadership not only watched the German rearmament, but did much to encourage it on the presumption that it would be used against the Soviet Union.

The British government of the day, headed by Neville Chamberlain, believed that the European tension flowed from legitimate German complaints that could be appeased. Observers such as Bill Shirer knew better, but, for some time, there seemed to be no end to the list of countries Chamberlain was prepared to sacrifice in order to prevent a general war.

But during 1938 and 1939, Chamberlain continued to pursue appeasement of Hitler, and the result was a see-saw cycle of Nazi provocation followed by European crisis, followed by French or British capitulation. The drama swung from country to country, capital to capital, and the CBS team of correspondents was perfectly situated to capture and report on what Churchill later termed "the gathering storm".

Chamberlain's appeasement policy ultimately failed. War broke out in 1939, and Chamberlain himself was ousted by a revolt amongst his own party in Parliament. In a famous debate, his long-time colleague Leo Amery cried, "In the name of God, go!" But in 1938, he was the most popular leader in Europe, even though Hillaire Belloc brilliantly satirized Chamberlain's Czech policy:

> Dear Czecho-Slovakia,
> I don't think they'll attack yer,
> But I'm not going to back yer.

The crisis was well suited to the resources of CBS, but, more than that, it was suited to the capabilities and immediacy of radio, and American radio especially. The CBS round-up brought reaction from Rome, Paris, London, and Berlin in the course of a half-hour, and listeners of the time felt the sting of approaching war more keenly than readers of print felt it a generation before when the Kaiser mobilized against Russia.

A Rising Star

The general tension society felt during that time provided the backdrop for Orson Welles's famed *War of the Worlds* broadcast. In October, 1938, it mimicked the style of network news radio broadcasting to describe a Martian invasion of Earth. It proved so compelling that an estimated four million listeners were convinced that Martians had landed in downstate New Jersey and were melting the local population with death rays.

If Welles was a rising star in fiction and drama, Murrow was the rising star of the real thing. Although the news broadcasts were controlled from New York, and though CBS's chief news commentator was the widely admired H.V. Kaltenborn, eyes began to focus on Murrow and his cadre of correspondents, Murrow's Boys. They covered the Czech crisis, the final dismemberment of Czechoslovakia in the spring of 1939, and the shocking Nazi-Soviet nonaggression pact signed in the summer.

Why Murrow, instead of, say, Shirer?

First, there was the voice. Then there was the fact that Murrow was a favorite of Paley. Murrow also was based in London, had easier access to the microphone, and was Shirer's boss.

But it was more than that. Murrow had a quality that was hard to replicate or explain. He had more than charisma; he had a laconic directness and a barely concealed idealism of a type that audiences later associated with Humphrey Bogart in *Casablanca*.

In August, 1939, with the Soviets neutralized, the German Army invaded Poland and demonstrated the efficacy of another new system, *blitzkrieg*. It was a highly mechanized and mobilized offensive based on fast-moving armor and air power.

Blitzkrieg was "the doctrine of overwhelming force" mounted on a rocket engine. It tore through defense lines, paralyzed communications, and practiced frightfulness as a military tactic. It shattered the Polish Army within days.

Only radio brought home to the United States the full terror of blitzkrieg, with the Stuka dive-bombers screaming down loaded with high explosives. Sound effects heightened the terror for listeners. To hear blitzkrieg was to understand immediately how people could be cowed so quickly into hopelessness and surrender. Print was no match for radio in transmitting the experience of this new kind of war.

Moreover, the pace of war increased so much that print hardly kept up. Although World War I was marked by stagnation and attrition, World War II opened with maneuvers and massive encirclements which trapped whole armies and army groups into liquidation and surrender. Germany smashed a million-strong Polish army and conquered the third-largest nation in Europe in less time than it took for the British to advance three miles at the Somme in 1916.

The increased pace of the war led to a significant change in radio programming. Regular news broadcasts were instituted for the first time to add to the commentary and special bulletins that were the source of news in the past. Murrow's boys, representing the neutral United States, had a unique vantage point, with correspondents in all the major capitals: Berlin, Rome, London, and Paris. They gave the first years of the war its most immediate and comprehensive coverage. American envoy Harry Hopkins later remarked: "Murrow is the man of our country who is doing the greatest job of all, of interpretation, representation, and understanding, of morale-building in England and the U.S."

A Radio Blitz

After the fall of Poland, an eerie silence descended over Europe, described in Berlin as "*sitzkrieg*" and in London as "the Phony War." In the spring of 1940, the Phony War ended, and the terror of blitzkrieg then descended on the citizens of Holland and Belgium. This included a horrific saturation bombing of Rotterdam that appalled the Allied and neutral nations alike. The German armor poured through the Ardennes and split the Allied forces, making the fall of France inevitable and trapping more than two hundred fifty thousand British troops in a liquidation pocket at Dunkirk. The Chamberlain government fell in the midst of the crisis, and Winston Churchill was named prime minister. Churchill observed, "I feared it would be my task to announce the largest surrender in British history." A fleet of navy regulars, merchantmen, and small boaters managed to rescue the British Expeditionary Force in a heroic evacuation, however.

The British were grateful to be spared, but "wars are not won by evacuations," Churchill warned. He warned Britain on the radio. Churchill himself focused the attention of Americans and the English on their radios, for he used the medium masterfully in a series of broadcasts through the summer of 1940 as the Battle of France ended and the Battle of Britain began.

With the coming of the war to England, Murrow found himself on the front lines, and with Churchill's eyes desperately fixed on America for help—and possibly for an alliance—Murrow became a vitally important figure in the war effort. His contacts improved, his access was assured. He used it masterfully himself.

Murrow's staff was able to obtain permission for a live,

remote broadcast on the night of August 24, 1940. Six days prior, the first bombs fell on London. The blitz began.

For the broadcast, CBS decided on the round-up approach used with so much success across Europe. In this case, however, it situated the correspondents around London: LeSeuer, Sevareid, Vincent Sheean, and J.B. Priestley. The style was a CBS trademark, but it had the added appeal of preventing the Luftwaffe from using a single radio beam as a "homing" beacon for their planes. The round-up would confuse them by broadcasting from multiple points around the city.

Murrow himself stood beside the Church of St. Martin-in-the-Fields, just a few hundred yards east of Parliament along Whitehall on the southeast corner of Trafalgar Square. The program was *London After Dark*, and the raids began in earnest before Murrow and his team went on air.

"*This* . . . is Trafalgar Square," Murrow began at 6:30 P.M. New York time. The American audience heard the war for the first time: the shuffle of Londoners to the air-raid shelters, the wail of the sirens, the anti-aircraft guns, and the normal street noises of the city. At one point, Murrow had to move aside so that people could get past him and into the shelters. At another, he leaned down to catch the sounds of their footsteps.

It was dangerous, it was new, and, to listeners, it was utterly unforgettable. As Peter Arnett of CNN later experienced in 1991 when he reported the bombing of Baghdad during the Gulf War, there is nothing more compelling to listeners than reports delivered by journalists actually in the line of fire at the time.

Journalists also discovered the dramatic effect that radio had when it was broadcast from a country on the defensive. For, on the defensive, a host country has a material interest in displaying its suffering to rouse international opinion against an aggressor. A journalist covering an army or nation on the defensive has far more access to staff, fronts, information, and insight. The correspondents found it much more difficult to cover offensive operations later in World War II because aggressors naturally traffic in secrecy and disinformation.

Murrow took his *London After Dark* program to a new level on September 21, when he received permission for a live broadcast from the rooftop of Broadcasting House. His goal was to capture the blitz on the radio as the bombs fell.

"I'm standing on a rooftop looking out over London," he reported. "Off to my left, far away in the distance, I can just see that faint, red, angry snap of antiaircraft bursts against the steel-blue sky . . . now you'll hear explosions—there they are!"

Broadcasting House was itself bombed on October 15, when a five hundred–pound unexploded bomb crashing through a seventh-story window. It exploded just as a bomb squad reached it, killing several and injuring many with glass and shrapnel. Murrow, who was in the sub-basement, escaped unharmed.

Hemingway defined courage as "grace under pressure," and Murrow was the calmest of the war correspondents, legendary for his low-key demeanor even as the bombs went off. Although the private Murrow was far more prone to outbursts of anger and feelings of genuine devastation at the effects of the war he witnessed, his personality on the radio was one of total calm and command.

From that point forward, the radio coverage of the war changed. The dry commentaries of the pre-war period were outdated; high-level political reporting remained. In fact, on the night of October 15, as Broadcasting House was bombed, Murrow focused on the possibility of Romania joining the Axis. But it was the live reporting that captured the sound and fury of war and, with it, the public imagination. The public's favorite broadcasts were often from the slower news nights when Murrow was forced to improvise, providing highly detailed portraits of the city streets and the effect of the blitz on ordinary life.

The blitz continued into the winter of 1940–41, but, in the spring, the war shifted to the Balkans, where the Germans were bailing Italy out in their offensive against the Greeks. Again, the CBS round-up coverage, anchored in New York and London, proved to be outstanding in conveying the drama and scope of the expanding war.

By the spring of 1941, Murrow's impact on reporting became evident when CBS sent along Elmer Davis to join Murrow in London. A brilliant scholar and print journalist, Davis's flat, midwestern delivery style was unpopular with CBS brass before the war, but Murrow's trademark understated style of plain-spoken intensity helped elevate Davis to a senior commentator's post. Davis was in London when the incendiary raids began on May 10. He and Murrow covered the first of the firestorms.

But with the Nazi invasion of Russia in June, 1941, the main theater of the war shifted beyond the scope of Western media. By the late summer, Murrow was increasingly far from the action, and he knew it. Although he was the most celebrated name in journalism with a book collection of his radio pieces scheduled for fall publication, he was ready to leave.

But leave where? Back to New York and CBS or to become a pro-war activist and help persuade Americans to enter the war? As Murrow tussled with the question, Bill Paley arranged a dinner in his honor in New York. One thousand guests honored him at the glittering November, 1941 dinner at the Waldorf-Astoria. Paley called him "a man fitted to his time and to his task; a student, a philosopher, at heart a poet of mankind and, therefore, a great reporter".

Archibald Macleish said: "Because you told them the truth, and because you destroyed the superstition of distance and of time which makes the truth turn false, you have earned the admiration of your countrymen."

The attack on Pearl Harbor settled the issue of what to do next for Murrow. Although he was pressured to take a role with the Office of War Information, he declined and returned to Europe as a war correspondent. Throughout 1942, he covered the war from London. He broke with the Roosevelt Administration only once, incurring strong criticism from Washington when he criticized a deal with Vichy Admiral Jean Darlan that brought the Nazi collaborator into a senior role with the allied invasion of North Africa.

Murrow moved his base to North Africa in the spring of 1943 and reported from Tunisia. In late 1943, he received, and eventually declined, the extraordinary offer as editor-in-chief of the BBC.

Africa, taken as a whole, was a blot on the record of news organizations during the war. The battles took place over a massive stretch of largely uninhabited desert, and where Murrow had entrenched correspondents in the European capitals, in North Africa, there were only makeshift press facilities, news handouts, briefings by the high command, and the difficulties of covering an offensive operation.

The news organizations in North Africa fell back on a staple of World War I coverage—the profiling, and often lionizing, of the leadership. Americans and British alike thus grew to know more about Field Marshal Montgomery and Field Marshal Rommel than perhaps any two other leaders of the war. It was popular, politic, well received by many in the military, but not great journalism.

Back in New York, changes came at CBS headquarters. Murrow's boss and chief supporter, Ed Klauber, resigned under pressure. Paul Kesten was moved into his job, with Frank Stanton as his deputy. The move presaged a change of emphasis from innovation to a more careful, calculated management style.

Murrow himself focused on broadcasts and personnel. He continued to raid the newspapers and wire services for talent. In 1943, he made his first attempt to hire Walter Cronkite, but was declined. Murrow represented the radio correspondents in the coordination committees for the Normandy invasions and led the coordination of the first pooled broadcast. He had the honor of making the first radio report of the invasion of France. Covering the second wave of the invasion was Murrow's Boy Larry LeSeuer. The final transmission of the day was from George Hicks of the fledgling ABC, a recorded broadcast from three miles offshore describing the first wave of the invasions.

One of Murrow's most famous broadcasts of the war was one he regarded as a failure. It was the Sunday broadcast he made on April 15, 1945, concerning the concentration camp Buchenwald. He arrived with a pool of correspondents on a Thursday. All the correspondents were overwhelmed by the ghastly scenes. Murrow had first heard rumors of mass murder through the French resistance in 1943, while he was deeply involved in covering the North African campaign. When he arrived at Buchenwald in 1945, there were still three hundred bodies. Piled near them were hundreds of shoes. His reaction was typical of the man who built his system of journalism not on scoops or "gotcha" exclusives, but on the understated, plainspoken, and therefore all the more dramatic description of the detail that illuminates the whole. But he felt powerless to describe Buchenwald.

"I could have described three pairs of those shoes . . . but hundreds of them! I just couldn't. The tragedy of it just overwhelmed me."

Yet Murrow never lost his ability to know what to say and

how to say it. Although his broadcast was neither the first, nor the most devastating, Murrow's received the most coverage and is the best remembered. It received front-page coverage in major newspapers and was replayed on the BBC. His coda in that broadcast was one of his most characteristic and most compelling. Plainspoken and earnest, he spoke to his audience with the intimacy of a personal conversation: "I pray for you to believe what I have said about Buchenwald. I have reported what I saw and heard, but only part of it. . . . If I've offended you by the rather mild account of Buchenwald—I'm not in the least sorry."

He went from Buchenwald to Paris, where he was able to reunite with most of the Murrow Boys at an impromptu celebration at the Hotel Scribe.

"We've seen what radio can do for the nation in war," cried the enthusiastic Murrow. "Now, let's go back to show what we can do in peace!"

From a Uniform to a Suit

After the end of the war and the birth of Murrow's son Casey, in November, 1945, Bill Paley offered Murrow a job in New York as vice president of the news division. Murrow initially was appalled that the offer wasn't made to Paul White. But Murrow realized that with the end of the war, it was natural that the importance of news would change, and there already was pressure on news budgets and news coverage. It was clear that White lacked the support from Paley, Kesten, and Stanton to "carry the can" for Murrow's vision of the news. So he accepted the job.

When he arrived in New York to take on his new job, he reported to Frank Stanton, the newly appointed network president, and then directly to Paley. His role, as he saw it, was to defend and expand the news programs and thereby enhance the prestige of the network. During his eighteen months as vice president, he introduced more than a dozen news features, including a nightly news round-up with Bob Trout at the anchor. A documentary unit produced occasional one-hour, commercial-free broadcasts that were widely and lavishly praised and were well received by listeners. CBS won two Peabody awards for its news coverage. The wartime staff, and CBS's wartime image as the premier news network, remained almost completely intact.

However, those were the go-go years of radio and the early years of television. After five years of war, the nation craved distraction. After five years of news, they wanted entertainment. After five years of savings bonds, they wanted conspicuous consumption. General Eisenhower was out, General Electric was in, and no single war correspondent—no matter how highly regarded—could change that.

In late 1946, too, came the Red-baiting and the House Un-American Activities Committee (HUAC). The hard-hitting, incisive documentaries that Murrow wanted were out of step with the strong anti-Communist movement in the country that branded any criticism of the American way of life unpatriotic. Meanwhile, there was an ongoing battle between the network and the FCC over the definition of a fairness doctrine for radio news. Finally, there was the ongoing battle with sponsors over the selection of program anchors. Murrow narrowly avoided being drafted by Campbell's Soup to host the nightly news program in place of Bob Trout. Quincy Howe was dropped from a nightly news program in favor of Eric Sevareid based on a sponsor request.

Murrow saw this eighteen-month period as an imprisonment. It finally came to an end when Bill Shirer left the network in the spring of 1947. The triggering event was the decision of Shirer's sponsor, a soap maker, to cancel its sponsorship and move toward sponsorship of more entertainment programming. Given the times, it was not an unusual decision.

Murrow and Paley required Shirer to move to another, far less visible, time slot. Shirer blamed Murrow and Paley for caving into sponsor pressure, which was a result of Shirer's independence and anti-Greek government broadcasts during the postwar crisis between the royalist and Communist forces. The dispute escalated in the press as a "feud" between Murrow and Shirer. There was talk about Murrow's "jealousy" over Shirer's unique position as an independently famous broadcaster and a proven print journalist. There was also talk that Murrow regarded Shirer as slacking on the job.

CBS insiders saw a different angle. Murrow, as famous as he became delivering the bad news to the American public in 1940, was uncomfortable delivering bad news one on one. Shirer received the news third-hand from the sponsor's agency and went ballistic.

Murrow himself denied jealousy and denied pressure from the sponsor. He didn't see it as a bad mark on his leadership, either. For Murrow's outlook was simple: the network chose the team and the sponsor decided which team member fit the broadcast it wanted. Then he got pressure from the conservative HUAC to hire the "correct" people and pressure from liberals to keep controversial broadcasters in prime time-slots, no matter what the sponsor might think.

What is clear is that Shirer left, both men were extremely troubled by the public manner in which it was handled, neither ever got over the personal experience of it, and Murrow himself resigned as vice president in July. The controversy convinced him that the proper place for an anchor is in the studio—not the executive suite. He went with Campbell's Soup after all, and a nightly news program. It was known as *Edward R. Murrow with the News*, and it debuted in 1947.

"Hear It Now," "See It Now"

The Murrow production of the news was a modern news broadcast in miniature. It lasted twelve minutes. There was a lead story backed by live and taped field reports from the CBS correspondents. There was commentary. Backed by Campbell's, it had a much larger budget than unsponsored or "sustaining" news broadcasts. For budget, for impact, for freedom, for access to Murrow, and for an extra fifty dollars from the sponsor for every story, it was the place for correspondents to be.

They covered the Greek crisis of 1947 and the takeover of Czechoslovakia in 1948, as well as the subjection of Poland and Hungary, the Truman Doctrine, the 1948 election season, the rise of Richard Nixon and the House Un-American Activities Committee, the Berlin airlift, the partition of Germany, the attempted assassination of Truman by Puerto Rican nationalists, the trial of Alger Hiss, and the fall of Nationalist China. They were seasons filled with news.

Murrow devoted his career to fair coverage, but fair coverage often meant unpopular coverage. His stature was never higher and his image was pro-American, but even thoughtful Americans were appalled by the actions of the Soviets after Yalta and the nation was nervous. Murrow was no radical, but his outlook was internationalist, and the country was turning rightward and isolationist. Outraged citizens arranged boycotts, and the boycotts rarely were directed at the broadcaster or the journalist. They were directed at the sponsor. They were directed at soup.

Campbell's looked at the mail and panicked. For not only did it sponsor the Murrow broadcast, as was customary in those days, it had Murrow's support in a series of personal appearances around the country. It had visions of Murrow driving away the crowds at chamber of commerce events and county fairs. It began to apply direct pressure on Murrow to adjust the tone of his broadcasts to fit the national mood.

Relations with Campbell's reached their zenith in late 1950 when, after a broadcast criticizing Senator Joe McCarthy, the sponsor was overwhelmed with letters threatening a boycott over Murrow's remarks. After two years of to-and-fro, the company finally decided to pull the plug.

Murrow's reaction was characteristic. He immediately prepared for a new show, but it was to be a new *type* of show, where his kind of journalism was welcome. His journalism would be produced with the latest production, something so innovative and compelling that the public could not resist the radio dial—or the channel changer, for Murrow finally decided that with this concept, he had to take on television.

Murrow sampled television in 1948 when he covered the Democratic and Republican conventions. He saw it grow massively in popularity in CBS after the war. He knew that it had been a long time coming, for the BBC had a limited television service even before the war. He was convinced that it ultimately would succeed radio.

Also in the late 1940s, Murrow developed a professional relationship with Fred Friendly, and they coproduced the best-selling LP *I Can Hear It Now, 1933–1945*. It was unlike any talking record that preceded it. It juxtaposed major political events with sporting moments, humorous on-air bloopers, and revealed the temper of the times just as accurately as it chronicled the events.

The formula was repeated in two follow-up LPs, and, in 1951, it became the basis of the new show. It was a round–up–style radio broadcast called *Hear It Now*. There was in-depth story focus; there were correspondents such as Red Barber and Abe Burrows commenting on sports and entertainment; there was Murrow himself. It was a singular success, and, after six months on the radio, Murrow moved to television in November, 1951, with *See It Now*.

For the first time, viewers saw Murrow live and, seemingly, unrehearsed—for he brought his trademark cool and composure to the broadcasts. Murrow dangled a cigarette from his lips with the care and precision of an artist. He could extract more drama from a cigarette than Winston Churchill could get out of a cigar. He held it like jazz singer about to snap his fingers, and he brought it to his lips like it was a source of oxygen, dragging enough smoke into his lungs to fill up a weather balloon.

When viewers first saw him, it looked as if the camera had stumbled into the control room at Studio 41 as Murrow was at work preparing a show. There was the buzz of pre-show noise: chatter on the cue channel ostensibly setting up a link with San Francisco. Behind Murrow was a set, but like no set any viewer had ever seen. Instead of hiding all the television equipment, on the suggestion of a young Don Hewitt, he used a control room as a set. Cameras, controls, and monitors presaged an entire era of newsroom-based broadcasts from the likes of CNN. Two monitors played simultaneous sweeps of the Pacific and Atlantic coasts.

The theme was immediacy and global reach. Viewers were entranced by the sense that they were catching Murrow as if by surprise, with the casual immediacy first pioneered by Franklin Roosevelt with his 1933 fireside chats taken to their logical end with newsroom-based sets at CNN in the 1980s.

It was a triumphant expansion of the original concept of the round-up achieved at a dizzying pace and presented in both sound and pictures. Howard K. Smith and Eric Sevareid contributed reports: Winston Churchill and Robert A. Taft appeared in reports. The most stunning report was from Robert Pierpoint. It was low-key, which made it all the more devastating. It was about a company of Army infantry holding an obscure part of the line in Korea. It featured the daily grind of life on the line—the life of the soldier from mail call to meal call.

Always, there was Murrow. Murrow had courage, but he also had the sort of understated charisma that pulled in viewers. He made his viewers feel as close to the events as possible, whether it was holding the microphone to the ground in 1940 London to catch the sound of fleeing footsteps or staging a show from the control room to suggest immediacy.

The visual elements of New York and San Francisco caught the public imagination. That was twelve years before the launch of the first telecommunications satellites, and the microwave relay used to link the live coast footage was new. No one ever saw it live before.

The show was a sensation. The only drawbacks were that its scale and imagination considerably exceeded the technology of the times, and the result was an overwhelming workload for Murrow, Friendly, Hewitt, and the staff. Murrow's worn face became even more gaunt under the strain, and he increased an already-volcanic level of cigarette consumption.

But the show, launched without a sponsor on a "sustaining" basis, was backed by Alcoa almost immediately. It went on to enjoy a substantial prime-time run. It was, in every sense of the word, from its director Don Hewitt to its mix of investigative journalism, profiles, humor, first-class writing, and dramatic presentation, the forerunner of *60 Minutes*.

Murrow's next major foray into television was *Person-to-Person*, which debuted in the fall of 1953. It featured Murrow interviewing celebrities in their homes and was a top ten hit immediately. It was a mainstay of CBS programming until 1959. He took a lot of criticism for *Person-to-Person* because its light approach was thought to be too "soft" for his image. By most accounts, he enjoyed the show and took pride in its substantial ratings, as well as the clout it enjoyed at an increasingly ratings-conscious network.

Taking on McCarthy

In March, 1954, Murrow was at the height of his game. He had *Edward R. Murrow with the News, Person-to-Person,* and *See It Now*—all smash successes either in ratings or prestige. He was the acknowledged giant of American broadcast journalism and was one of the leading stars of all television. He was on the board of directors of CBS. He put it all on the line with a thirty-minute *See It Now* installment entirely dedicated to McCarthyism titled, *A Report on Senator Joseph P. McCarthy.*

March 9, 1954 was the anniversary of the battle between the *Monitor* and the *Merrimac* at Hampton Roads, Virginia, in the first year of the Civil War. A battle without an obvious result between two sworn enemies representing utterly different political constellations, it nevertheless changed all naval history going forward. The night in 1954 was no different.

Preparations for the broadcast were normal in most respects. The routine of the 7:45 news broadcast was followed, and the makeup and studio preparations were followed as usual. There was unusual activity during the week to promote viewership, however, because CBS had determined to let the program air as quietly as possible, which prompted Murrow and Friendly to take out their own ad in the *New York Times.*

The journalists knew they had something special in the script and in the plan, but for the execution, all depended on Murrow. Long gone were the days of three or four broadcasts per night followed by debates until dawn with friends and colleagues. Murrow was gaunt, sick, and tired, but the subject invigorated him.

That March, Shakespeare was in the air courtesy of the Joseph L. Mankiewicz big-budget version of *Julius Caesar* that was nominated for several Academy Awards. The Oscar telecast itself was big news for the time because of its unusual bicoastal hook-up with simultaneous presentations in New York and Los Angeles televised on NBC. That week, the siege of Dien Bien Phu was undertaken by the Vietnamese. It resulted in the defeat of the French and the intervention of the Americans to prop up the toppling pro-Western government of South Vietnam. Westinghouse, Philco, RCA and others were readying the first color TVs for market. The NCAA basketball tournament was kicking off that night with the East Regionals.

Senator Joseph McCarthy was at the zenith of his influence by 1953, and as disquiet grew in the country over his methods of investigation, intimidation, and grandstanding, few authority figures dared to speak out in public.

McCarthy quoted from *Julius Caesar* in an attack on Secretary of the Army Robert Stevens over the promotion of an Army dentist later uncovered as a Communist. "Upon what meat does this our Caesar feed?" he thundered at the secretary.

"Upon which meat does Senator McCarthy feed?" asked Murrow in his broadcast. It was his triumph. Using his favored techniques of rapidly cutting between juxtaposed quotes and images, he showed McCarthy's contradictions, fabrications, lies, obfuscation, pettifoggery, self-pity, arrogance, and overweening pride.

Murrow was far from the first on the anti-McCarthy bandwagon. In fact, even among the Murrow Boys, he received criticism from Eric Sevareid for taking too long to come out against McCarthy. But he proved again that he knew what to say and how to say it, but also when to say it. He chose the right words, the right time, and the right tone, in what was technically a news broadcast, but is more properly thought of as a defense of everything that CBS News in general, and Ed Murrow in particular, held sacred.

It was no accident that McCarthy was a fallen star before the end of the year, censured by his own colleagues in the Senate, and discredited in the eyes of the "silent majority" of the nation.

Murrow threw his entire arsenal into the broadcast. Not just the excellent material prepared with his staff, but the performance, as well. He used just the right amount of earnestness to be deadly, just enough levity to be engaging, just enough eye contact, and just the right pace. Murrow's broadcast elicited more than one hundred thousand written responses from viewers, running 10:1 in favor.

Murrow included the American public in his indictment and quoted from *Julius Caesar* again. He said, "This is no time for men who oppose Senator McCarthy's methods to keep silent— or for those who approve. . . . Cassius was right. 'The fault, dear Brutus, is not in the stars, but in ourselves.'"

Murrow did not quote other words from that same speech by Cassius, but they applied to Murrow that night. Cassius said:

> Why, man, he doth bestride the narrow world
> Like a Colussus, and we petty men
> Walk under his huge legs and peep about
> To find ourselves dishonorable graves.

Hail Murrow

Courtesy of CBS

Following the McCarthy broadcast, Murrow was hailed as a public hero, but he characteristically lost the sponsor of *See It Now*. The show continued in a one-hour format on an occasional basis until the late 1950s. Out of its ashes rose the estimable CBS *Reports* and, later, *60 Minutes*. He was still much in the public eye owing to his successful run with *Person-to-Person*, but both his visibility on network programming and his health began a slow, steady decline.

By 1958, he was still a network star, but he resigned his CBS directorship, and *See It Now* appeared with less and less frequency. In the fall of 1958, he was invited to address the Radio-Television News Directors Association convention in Chicago.

For years, he had become increasingly concerned about the drift of network news into commercial chaos. His concerns were not new. The chairman of the FCC was on record as describing television as a "vast wasteland". But Murrow was among the first to speak out, and his remarks were delivered with typical forthrightness and courage. He began:

> This just might do nobody any good. At the end of this discourse, a few people may accuse this reporter of fouling his own comfortable nest, and your organization may be accused of having given hospitality to heretical and even dangerous thoughts. But the elaborate structure of networks, advertising agencies, and sponsors will not be shaken or altered. It is my desire, if not my duty, to try to talk to you journeymen with some candor about what is happening to radio and television.

His message was clear, uncompromising, uncomfortable, and unwelcome. But he hammered it home in any case:

> Several years ago, when we undertook to do a program on Egypt and Israel, well-meaning, experienced, and intelligent friends shook their heads and said, "This you cannot do—you will be handed your head. It is an emotion-packed controversy, and there is no room for reason in it." We did the program. Zionists, anti-Zionists, the friends of the Middle East, and Egyptian and Israeli officials said, with a faint tone of surprise, "It was a fair count. The information was there. We have no complaints."
>
> Our experience was similar with two half-hour programs dealing with cigarette smoking and lung cancer. Both the medical profession and the tobacco industry cooperated in a rather wary fashion. But, in the end of the day, they were both reasonably content. The subject of radioactive fall-out and the banning of nuclear tests were, and are, highly controversial. But, according to what little evidence there is, viewers were prepared to listen to both sides with reason and restraint. This is not said to claim any special or unusual

competence in the presentation of controversial subjects, but rather to indicate that timidity in these areas is not warranted by the evidence.

Murrow opened with strong words, but delivered examples of which the industry could be proud. But it was not his objective to flatter or to praise the industry, himself, or the governments in question. It was a feint, a tactic designed to distract his audience. Then he hit hard with the central theme of his jeremiad:

> Not so long ago, the president of the United States delivered a television address to the nation. He was discoursing on the possibility or probability of war between this nation and the Soviet Union and Communist China—a reasonably compelling subject. Two networks, CBS and NBC, delayed that broadcast for an hour and fifteen minutes. If this decision was dictated by anything other than financial reasons, the networks didn't deign to explain those reasons. That hour-and-fifteen-minute delay, by the way, is about twice the time required for an ICBM to travel from the Soviet Union to major targets in the United States. It is difficult to believe that this decision was made by men who love, respect, and understand news.

He showed the advance text of his speech to many in the industry and advised CBS of its contents. But, curiously, he did not go to any considerable effort to put the text in front of Bill Paley. Despite their close and long friendship, many understood the remarks to be an attack on Paley and the current state of affairs at CBS. Paley certainly thought so and remained bitter about the speech for years.

Murrow continued:

> We are currently wealthy, fat, comfortable, and complacent. We have currently a built-in allergy to unpleasant or disturbing information. Our mass media reflect this. But unless we get up off our fat surpluses and recognize that television, in the main, is being used to distract, delude, amuse, and insulate us, then

television and those who finance it—those who look at it and those who work at it— may see a totally different picture too late. . . .

I do not advocate that we turn television into a twenty-seven-inch wailing wall, where long-hairs constantly moan about the state of our culture and our defense. . . . This instrument can teach, it can illuminate; yes, and it can even inspire. But it can do so only to the extent that humans are determined to use it to those ends. Otherwise, it is merely wires and lights in a box.

When he finished, and when the inevitable headlines followed, it marked the end of Murrow's productive period at CBS. For he who sows a wind reaps a whirlwind. But it is a speech that is still remembered and still reverberates in his industry.

"As with many broadcast people of my generation," said Dan Rather in 1993, "that speech has crisscrossed over the back roads of my memory through a lifetime in this business."

But Murrow was finished in the business. He had launched a program called *Small World*, featuring major personalities from around the world hooked up into one broadcast a format that proved popular in the 1970s and 1980s as network access to satellite time increased. But there was considerable pressure from the top to lower Murrow's profile within the organization, and programs like *Small World* withered without support.

The Legacy

Murrow left for a yearlong sabbatical in 1959 and returned to find CBS not much changed from the organization he left. Desultory conversations proceeded about new shows. There was talk that he should take over the ailing *Face the Nation*. But, instead, he accepted a request to join the Kennedy Administration as head of the United States Information Agency

(USIA). He served admirably in the post until 1964, just after Kennedy's death.

By then, a lifelong addiction to overwork and cigarettes took its toll, and he fell ill with a serious form of lung cancer. He died on April 27, 1965.

His ghost lives today in the CBS hallways. There is the constant refrain, "Ed wouldn't do it that way," or "What would Ed think?"

But Murrow's legacy is not in the day-to-day news choices on which the broadcaster must focus. Nor is it in the specific remedies that he proposed from time to time to rescue this broadcast, or that program, or the entire industry. Not even in the voice, or the pause, or the face.

Though countless future broadcasters have doubtless stood at the mirror with an imaginary microphone and intoned, "*This* . . . is London," and dreamed of being one of Murrow's Boys, the specifics of his broadcasting style never have been duplicated and never will be.

But over the next fifty years, a succession of anchors faced many of the same choices, strains, opportunities, and temptations that Murrow faced. How they faced the challenges of their times is another story, but they will be measured against his standard.

Has there been another Murrow? Will there be?

It hardly matters, for as Socrates said to Glaucon in the late chapters of Plato's *Republic* when Glaucon complained that the ideal republic they were describing had no chance of ever being built:

> No, but it hovers in the skies, like a constellation,
> for those who have the imagination to see it;
> and when they see it, they will found a Republic in
> themselves.

Chapter TWO

Douglas Edwards, CBS

Courtesy of CBS

There have been only four nightly news anchors in the history of CBS News. Almost every news watcher can name Dan Rather, Walter Cronkite, and Connie Chung. But the fourth name causes people to scratch their heads and wonder who was on the air *before* Cronkite.

It is not surprising that so few people remember Douglas Edwards. For one thing, he left the anchor seat forty years ago. For another, there weren't all that many televisions around during his early years. And, then as now, fewer of them than desirable were tuned to the network news. It wasn't until two years after Edwards left the anchor seat that any single television program was watched by as many as twenty million households, and then the audience was for a January 6, 1964, broadcast of *The Beverly Hillbillies.* That was the episode in which Granny mistakes a boxing kangaroo for a giant jackrabbit. During that same week, Lyndon Johnson made his first State of the Union Address; Pope Paul became the first pope to leave Italy since 1809; Barry Goldwater announced his presidential candidacy; and two hundred ninety thousand people streamed through the Berlin Wall under a one-day Christmas holiday arrangement. Records of the network news ratings are not available, but, presumably, the news was a distant second.

But if Douglas Edwards is not widely remembered, he certainly should be—and with respect. He was the first to host a nightly television news broadcast, and he did so with distinction on CBS between 1948 and 1962. He was, in the narrow sense of the word, the dean of the television anchors. But it was not in his character to take an overly generous slice of personal credit for his role in the birth of television news. He cheerfully acknowledged that, as honored and respected as the position is today, he won the job in 1946 because, frankly, many of his competitors looked down on the new medium. Edward R. Murrow, for example, toasted the incoming New Year of 1950 with, "Here's hoping we don't have to make our living in television."

Napoleon once said, "I found the crown of France in the gutter and picked it up with my sword." It was much the same with Edwards. He took the job when television was lightly regarded even by those who respected its future. He shrugged off the earliest *opéra bouffe* aspects of network television news. He endured and became an institution among television viewers.

He won an audience that reached an estimated thirty-four million viewers at its peak. When the 1960s arrived and CBS executives determined that only a complete change in their news approach would allow them to compete with NBC's Chet Huntley and David Brinkley, Edwards gracefully relinquished the role in 1962 to Walter Cronkite.

"I knew him very well," Cronkite recalled. "I must say that when they decided that I should take over the broadcast, nobody was more gentlemanly toward the change than Doug Edwards. He was a great, very fair, very honest, decent guy."

The Right Stuff

Edwards was born in Ada, Oklahoma, in 1917. But it is inaccurate to say that he was a true Oklahoma Sooner. That well-known nickname is a throwback to 1889, when the western lands of the territory were opened to settlement. Sooners were pioneers who snuck across the border ahead of the official opening, many in the dead of night, to stake claims to the choicest parcels of land. Their brother pioneers, who waited for the sound of the official cannonfire, were known as Boomers.

The Sooners were mavericks, improvisers, rule-benders; Murrow and his boys were the Sooners of the broadcast news business. They arrived in radio just in time for the start of World War II and were, by and large, in Europe when the war broke out. They began their careers as journalists or, as in Murrow's case, as organizers of conferences and lectures. They ended the war as celebrities and came home triumphantly to America at the very peak of radio in 1945–46.

Edwards, like the generation of Boomers before him, arrived late on the scene. Although he was just nine years younger than Murrow, it was a crucial difference. Murrow and his generation had their formative experiences during the Roaring Twenties. Edwards's worldview was formed by the experience of growing up in rural Oklahoma during the 1930s. Those were the Dust Bowl years, when "Okie" was an insult and the state was a poster-child for everything wrong with American farming. His mother, a school principal, moved the family to rural Alabama in the mid-1930s, taking Edwards out of the time and place of *The Grapes of Wrath* and putting him smack dab in the middle of *To Kill a Mockingbird*.

Raised in the crushing poverty of the Depression that hit the rural South harder than almost anywhere else and amid the bigotry and limited horizons of a small town, it is no wonder that Edwards was so different from the sophisticated, polished Murrow Boys. Radio represented more to him than an outlet for his intellect; it had all the glamour and excitement that towns like Troy, Alabama, lacked. He had more in common with the career of Ronald Reagan, who also became a radio announcer in small towns in the 1930s, than he did with Murrow.

That world is gone, but it is important to remember it in order to understand the career of Douglas Edwards. It was a time when nothing was more respectable than a steady job at a great corporation. It was an era when Hoover gathered its door-to-door salesmen for weekly meetings, and the manager led the group in singing company songs. It was a time when you could say "our boys in Europe" or "gee whiz" or "he's a college man" without sounding hopelessly corny. And it was a time when New York City and Hollywood represented such faraway glamour that they might as well have been in Africa or on the dark side of the moon.

Small wonder, then, that he consistently followed a more conservative, company-man line than the groundbreaking Murrow Boys. Edwards volunteered for choice assignments, but accepted others when they were offered to him. He never left the network because he was overlooked. Those qualities made him a favorite of company executives, such as Paul White and Frank Stanton; in turn, the Murrow Boys found it hard to accept him as an equal, even when he joined them in Europe at the end of World War II.

There's a Radio Announcer Upstairs in the Bedroom

Douglas Edwards fixed his gaze early on radio. It was his ticket out of the South. A press release from CBS in 1943 described Douglas Edwards's very early days as a child reporter: "If you had visited the Edwards's home in Ada, Oklahoma, some thirteen years ago (1930) and heard odd sounds coming from the upstairs bedroom, you would have received the following explanation from Mrs. Edwards: 'Oh, that's just Doug. He thinks he's a radio announcer. I imagine it's just about time for his news broadcast now.'"

In turn, Edwards always credited his mother. When asked in 1943 to explain his success, he said: "My mother. I imagine I got on her nerves when I was a kid, with my continual chatter. She knew that I wanted to announce, and she helped me with my diction and dramatics. She was a principal in schools in Oklahoma and Alabama, and I think I inherited my voice from her."

Murrow was hired by CBS in 1935. The same year, Edwards graduated from high school and was lucky to pick up a part-time job at a station in Troy, Alabama. Edwards's job was to spin records, read the news, and occasionally to sing. His paycheck was $2.50 per week, but he was happy. Jobs were scarce, broadcasting jobs were even harder find, and if Troy, Alabama, was a minor market, at least it was a market, and it was radio. By day, he attended classes at the University of Alabama.

By the time Murrow and Shirer launched *World News*

Round-Up in 1938 during the Anschluss crisis, Edwards moved up as well. His progress was steady, if unspectacular. He was hired for a Dothan, Alabama, station as a senior announcer, and, in 1938, he moved to WXYZ radio in Detroit.

In 1940, Murrow and his team covered the London Blitz. Edwards became the assistant news director at WSB in Atlanta. Although it wasn't the network, it was a major market and it was news. The *Atlanta Journal* owned the station. There was no singing.

It was a fortunate assignment for Edwards. Atlanta was not only a major market, it was an interesting place at an interesting time. The regents of the University of Georgia founded the Peabody Awards that year, just down the road in Athens, Georgia. The passage of the Selective Service Act in 1940 brought a wave of draftees to reception centers, such as Fort McPherson and Fort Benning. *Gone with the Wind* was still on its record-breaking first run. Total radio sets in use in the United States passed fifty million for the first time. Edwards blossomed in Atlanta and was hired in 1942 at CBS.

His career soared immediately upon arrival in New York. He became an instant favorite with audiences and sponsors, and, in just a few weeks, he was asked to take over Mel Allen's daily four o'clock news period. When the demand for war correspondents swept John Daly to London in 1943, Paul White chose Edwards to take over for Daly as narrator of the weekly *Report to the Nation* and as the newscaster on the daily the *World Today*.

Joining the Murrow Gang . . . Sort Of

Edwards was considered, along with Bob Trout and John Daly, to be one of the "big three" of the New York broadcasters. He covered major events, such as the Casablanca conference of 1943 between Roosevelt and Churchill.

Meanwhile, Paul White, the New York–based news director, began the feud with Edward R. Murrow that ended with Murrow's departure from CBS in 1947. But in that period, White encouraged and advanced the careers of the New York broadcasters. Daly was sent to Europe in 1943. Trout was assigned as anchor of the nightly radio news program. Edwards, after much prodding, finally was given an overseas assignment in the winter of 1944–45.

It was a plum job: an eight thousand–mile roving assignment to inspect Army Air Corps Communications installations. Edwards traveled throughout Europe and the Middle East. By spring, he was in London, and he broadcast on V-E Day.

Edwards, thus, became one of Murrow's staff, but never became one of Murrow's Boys. Murrow did not hold Edwards in the same regard as he did Charles Collingwood, Eric Sevareid, Larry LeSeuer, and Howard K. Smith. Murrow preferred intellectuals, and his own wartime staff reflected that preference. In a sense, Edwards did not have the high marks for solid journalism that the others did, it seemed to Murrow. But Edwards received a fair shake and some major assignments from Murrow. And perhaps the tension over Edwards's acceptance had more to do with the long-simmering rivalry between Paul White and Murrow.

In the summer of 1945, a bureau chief job opened up in Paris, and White recommended Edwards. Murrow wanted Dave Schoenbrun; Edwards got the nod. He went to Paris in the summer of 1945 and reported on V-J Day for the network. He stayed in Paris until June 1946. After Murrow was elevated to vice president of the news division, Schoenbrun was assigned as Paris bureau chief.

Then, Edwards returned to New York as part of a general cutback of the number of European correspondents. He returned to a very different New York in June, 1946. First, there was peace. Second, Murrow was planning a number of innovative new programs. Third, Edwards had made a deep impression on sponsors and audiences alike. His voice and on-air presence received a great deal of attention. When Trout and several of the top correspondents were assigned to the big-budget new program, *Robert Trout with the News*, Edwards was named anchor of CBS Radio's *World News Round-Up*.

The Sweet Smell of Television News

By then, Edwards was considered at the top of the second echelon of CBS correspondents and one of the best pure newsreaders.

Courtesy of CBS

Murrow and his team continued to focus on radio, and so, when in 1946 the first opportunities in television came around, it was natural that the opportunities fell to Edwards.

At the same time, as an artistic medium, television was, for the most part, ripped apart by newspaper critics in an effort to stop the new threat to their advertising dollars. Television was live and low budget. It featured what were considered second- or third-rank talents, and always was cited for falling short of its potential.

In 1946, television was very much in its infancy. Although the technology was pioneered in the 1920s and NBC broadcast television in 1939, development was halted by the war effort. Only two hundred fifty thousand televisions were manufactured in 1947, versus eight million by 1955.

The studio sets in 1946 were small, cramped, and shared. Edwards shared a set with Dione Lucas, a top New York chef of the time, who had a cooking show on WCBS-TV. There was the smell of garlic or baked goods in the studio where Edwards read the news. He sat at an unassuming desk next to the cooking show set and delivered what many credit as the first actual television news broadcast. Edwards remembered in a 1988 *L.A. Herald Examiner* article, "It was rather difficult following the cooking school. Everybody's mouth watered. She always left food on the set. I was never hungry when I did the news."

The role of the television anchor in 1946 was no different from that of the radio anchor. But in the spring of 1947, television news briefly went to a new level when Gulf Oil, which had gas stations across the country, sponsored a thirteen-week Thursday night service called *Gulf News*. By then, Edwards's reputation as a broadcaster had grown to the point that he was requested by Gulf Oil's advertising agency to be the host. They

chose him over Larry LeSeuer, the former European correspondent and a close associate of Edward R. Murrow.

It seems incredible today to think that a choice as fundamental as the anchor role was left up to the sponsor. But in the
late 1940s, television executives had not yet learned how to
sell time. When commercials later became the primary means
of network revenue, they were fifteen, thirty, or sixty seconds
long. But initially, entire program units were sold to single
sponsors. Programs broadcast on that basis were considered
sponsored, and, by custom, the sponsor had the choice of anchor, although they could not control the list of available anchors that was prepared by the news division. Several
broadcasts were produced on a *continuing* basis, or without
sponsorships. However, big-budget news was not considered to
be compelling enough to produce without a sponsorship deal.
Television was expensive to produce, and the audiences were
small. It was risky for the networks without the sponsor.

By 1948, the audience figures for television soared, original
programming was needed, and the FCC pushed for more relevant programming than *Arthur Godfrey's Talent Scouts* or the
Texaco Star Theater with Milton Berle. So, in 1948, CBS made
the decision to put together an expanded coverage of the 1948
party conventions. Edwards was picked to host the convention
broadcasts and was paired with Murrow and several of the
other celebrity correspondents.

The networks had covered the conventions for years, and
they first televised convention reports as early as 1940. But for
this set of broadcasts, the networks brought in floor correspondents and mounted fixed cameras around the floor.

Murrow and the others found the effort daunting. Weighed
down with forty-pound remote sound packs as they combed
the crowded convention floors, they suffered in the soaring
summer Philadelphia temperatures. Even more, they suffered

the indignity of having to attract the attention of the camera-men, whose swiveling mounts made them look more like anti-aircraft gunners more than artists. The technology limited mobility and discouraged the free-flowing style that Murrow and his compatriots perfected on the streets of Europe during the war. The correspondents emerged from the work dripping with sweat—and it felt to them like flop sweat.

To critics, however, the convention coverage looked good. Despite the limitations of 1940s television, and despite a pair of conventions that were dull even by convention standards, the broadcasts were a success. Murrow was singled out for his commentary, and Edwards made a good impression, even though he was stuffed into a cramped, closet-like facility above the convention floor as the anchor of the broadcast.

The Birth of Network News

Courtesy of CBS

Following this success, Bill Paley agreed to Frank Stanton's proposal for a nightly televised news broadcast, *Douglas Edwards
and the News*, in parallel with *Edward R. Murrow and the News*.
The latter was the fifteen-minute radio broadcast that origi-
nally featured Bob Trout, but had been anchored by Murrow
since his return to full-time broadcasting in 1947. The broadcast combined headlines, field reports from the correspondents, and commentary from Murrow. It was the direction
Stanton wanted; CBS staffers knew, however, that the initial
product fell far short. CBS did not have enough cameras or
crews or even a means of transmitting live reports. Thus, it debuted without the correspondents—the very heart of the CBS
news organization. Accordingly, the commentators did their
best to stay away from it.

Edwards, meanwhile, had the experience and exposure of
Gulf News, plus he was not in a position to refuse easily and
lacked the star power of other correspondents. Stanton pressured Edwards to accept the anchor job, one that primarily
consisted of reading the headlines and introducing filmed segments from newsreel services like Movietone. Edwards, ever
the company man, agreed.

The first broadcast was made at 7:45 P.M., August 15, 1948,
live from New York to five stations. Edwards had a viewership
in the millions, a plain desk, a big microphone, three clocks,
and a calendar. The program was dreadful. It did not flame out
as spectacularly as the first night of radio's *Robert Trout with the
News*, when Paul White decided to combat preshow jitters with
alcohol and made a slurring introduction to the broadcast that
shocked the listeners and got White fired. But it did feature the
most mundane events imaginable, including beauty contests
and dog shows. In the early days of the broadcast, pictures
were mounted on easels, and there was no technology other
than film for saving images. CBS's star correspondents were

not amused. As late as 1950, Murrow wrote to a friend, "Here's hoping that in the coming year neither one of us will have to make a living on television."

The associate director of *Douglas Edwards and the News* was a young man named Don Hewitt, who later became known as the brains behind the news division and journalism's original super-show, *60 Minutes*. Hewitt remembers Edwards fondly, "Along with Dave Garroway and Ed Sullivan and Jack Webb and other pioneers, Edwards ushered in a television era. He was the first of that incredible array of CBS newsmen to make his leap from radio to television. Whatever is good and right about television news today, Edwards can claim a lion's share of the credit."

But the show, which eventually was transformed into the *CBS Evening News*, was born. It appeared four days a week, Thursday through Sunday. A month later, Edwards was introduced to the West Coast via a primitive and raw coast-to-coast hook-up. Then he opened his newscast with the line, "Good evening everyone from coast to coast." More stations were added by the month, and the true television networks were created.

By December, Murrow was so disappointed with the televised broadcast that he declined to include Edwards among the top broadcasters he brought in for his year-end round-up program. But Edwards had launched *Douglas Edwards and the News* and endured the initial disappointments with dignity and class. The broadcast, he knew, would get better.

By 1951, television became a fixture on the American landscape. Murrow was forced onto television with *See It Now*; ironically, he took on Don Hewitt as his director. By 1951, there were more than ten million households with televisions, and the number grew to almost fifty million by the end of the decade. NBC and ABC developed nightly news broadcasts of their own, with ABC featuring John Daly, whom Edwards had succeeded almost ten years prior back on CBS Radio.

In 1952, the season of political conventions returned, and although Edwards's nightly news program gained audience and respectability, the job of anchoring the convention broadcasts was given to Walter Cronkite. Murrow's cool attitude toward television cost him the opportunity, and Edwards was not considered to have the *gravitas* necessary for the major broadcast that the conventions had become. Edwards served as a floor correspondent for the Chicago-based telecasts.

Despite the setback, Edwards continued in his radio assignments and at the anchor desk of the *Douglas Edwards and the News* throughout the 1950s. He covered the Missouri River flooding Omaha in the early 1950s with news cameras on location, and he was the first to do so. He was the first to do an on-the-scene report from the chamber of the House of Representatives, when Puerto Rican nationalists shot five congressmen in March, 1954. And his was the first eyewitness television account of the sinking of the *Andrea Doria* in July, 1956.

The year 1956 was his high-water mark. By the time of the *Andrea Doria* disaster, his show reached thirty-four million viewers each week. That was an enormous audience for the time. He won the Peabody Award that year, beating out John Daly at ABC. Howard K. Smith, one of the Murrow crowd, added a commentary segment to the program during that period. Some of the highlights of the decade were the strong broadcasts and commentaries done on Edwards's show about the Little Rock desegregation crisis in 1957. Smith hailed from Louisiana and Edwards was raised in Alabama, yet no program was more unflinching in its coverage than *Douglas Edwards and the News.*

The program became known for being well thought out and

well written. Charles Kuralt noticed this immediately upon joining the staff in 1957 as a writer:

> Doug Edwards was an old-fashioned journalist of the best kind, always diligent and always fair, very accomplished as a writer and editor, and a calm presence before the camera. He was generous in giving credit to those who worked with him. He helped establish the credibility of news on the air. Viewers found him trustworthy; they were correct in their judgment of him. All of us who followed owe Douglas Edwards much gratitude for getting broadcast news off to such a good start.

The ultimate accolade, perhaps, was not in the ratings or in the Peabody Awards. Late in the decade, the broadcast had grown sufficiently in stature under Edwards's tutelage that CBS correspondents Charles Collingwood and Eric Sevareid individually approached management about taking over the broadcast. It is no surprise that CBS turned down Sevareid; his unease in front of the camera was legendary, and his strength, it was felt, was in short commentary rather than anchoring. He was an admirable commentator for two decades, but it rankled him that the anchor desk increasingly was seen as the top job.

It is more surprising that CBS turned down Collingwood. He had style, he was a noted journalist, and he was at ease in front of the camera. CBS was not always noted for its loyalty to its broadcasters—Smith and Murrow left during that period—but the network stuck by Edwards and rejected Collingwood's overture.

A Guiding Light Fades Out

However, in 1956, the seeds of Douglas Edwards's departure from the anchor desk were sown. Not from internal politicking, but from the dynamic combination of Chet Huntley and

David Brinkley at NBC. Their broadcasts from New York and Washington were electric, both in the substance of their coverage and even more in style, urbanity, and wit. Douglas Edwards could have matched one, or perhaps the other, but the combination overwhelmed him. Huntley and Brinkley took the nightly network news to an entirely different level, and CBS felt by 1961 that Edwards could not continue in the anchor chair if it ever hoped to beat NBC in the ratings.

The very qualities of solidity, fairness, and steady dedication to the improvement of the news that helped to elevate television news to respectability worked against Edwards. His broadcasts looked tame and old-fashioned, and although Edwards won a great measure of respect, he did not achieve the deep resonance with the American public that was required of the anchormen.

The decision was made to replace him in the spring of 1962. Ten years earlier, he was replaced by Cronkite at the conventions, and Cronkite ultimately succeeded him on the evening news. Edwards moved over to the anchor desk for the *Late News* on WCBS in New York. He continued to host *Newsbreak*, the televised, mid-morning CBS News update service, and, in 1966, he moved back into a radio anchor slot with the *World Tonight* and anchored several hourly news broadcasts.

By 1988, he had served almost fifty years with CBS News and had anchored a daily network news television news broadcast since 1948 without interruption—longer than any broadcast journalist. It is a longevity record perhaps only Peter Jennings will be able to rival, but not surpass, for Jennings was out of the anchor slot between 1968 and 1978.

Edwards retired in 1988 in a blaze of honors. Those accolades began in the mid-1960s when, with the continuing rise of the importance of the evening news broadcast, he became increasingly recognized for the pivotal role he played. He paved the way not only for Huntley and Brinkley, but also Cronkite and Rather, who succeeded him at CBS. Howard Stringer later paid tribute to Douglas Edwards: "The trail he blazed at the dawn of television is one that broadcast journalists can follow with great confidence and enormous admiration."

Edwards retired to Sarasota, where he died on October 14, 1990, of complications from cancer.

Chapter THREE

John Cameron Swayze, NBC

Courtesy of Globe Photo/NBC

When viewers turned on a television at 7:45 P.M. during the weekdays in the late 1940s or early 1950s and tuned in to NBC, they saw a smartly dressed man, possibly wearing a red carnation, delivering the news. Dapper fellow, they might have thought.

His voice had a flat, Kansas accent that drew no particular attention to itself. But in an era when a typical news broadcaster delivered reports in an earnest and sober *basso profundo* in imitation of Edward R. Murrow, this man's tone of voice was higher and noticeably more excited, more like a pitchman than a newsman.

The set was nothing special. There was a map, some in-out boxes, a phone, and a pen set. On his desk, however, there was an ashtray with a burning cigarette. Its smoke curled up and around the broadcaster throughout the fifteen-minute report. Swayze wasn't a smoker, though. He never inhaled the smoke. The cigarette was part of a sponsorship deal done for the money or, rather, done for the gig. Below the smoke and the ashtray was a sponsor's sign that read, *Camel News Caravan*. The camel in question was not a creature of the Sahara, it was a creature of the imaginations at the William Esty advertising agency in New York and R.J. Reynolds, maker of Camel cigarettes.

Next to the ashtray was a nameplate firmly stamped, John Cameron Swayze, as if there were the slightest possibility that viewers might otherwise forget exactly who the man was. He was unforgettable. And he never turned down a chance for a little promotion or a chance to ingratiate himself.

For one, he never took his eyes off the camera, except for the most occasional glance down at his notes. Today, in the era of the Teleprompter, we hardly give this a thought. But if you compare early Swayze broadcasts to the other networks, where respected broadcasters like Douglas Edwards bobbed their heads up and down between the camera and the script like Muhammad Ali ducking jabs from Joe Frazier, then the Swayze difference becomes apparent. He had a photographic memory and memorized the entire fifteen-minute news script before he went on the air.

Although Douglas Edwards launched the first nightly news broadcast, John Cameron Swayze passed him in the ratings with ease. The CBS producers and directors were stumped—*how do you compete with a guy who can memorize a fifteen-minute news broadcast?* Things got so desperate that CBS producer Don Hewitt actually, and apparently in all seriousness, suggested to

Douglas Edwards that he learn Braille so that he could read the news with his fingers. An interesting idea, but it represented a Rubicon in broadcast journalism that Edwards declined to cross. Meanwhile, Swayze kept his gaze right on the audience, notched up the ratings points, and introduced a level of eye contact that is, without question, the standard for anchors today.

When the day's broadcast was especially dull and there wasn't a strip of memorable film to run, Swayze brightly announced that it was time "to hopscotch the world for headlines." Then he read off a news report as if it were the most original, fascinating document in the world instead of a desperate ploy to fill up some time without having any images to run.

When it was time to close, he had a line for that too, and it was seemingly right out of Merrie Melodies. "Well, that's the story, folks! This is John Cameron Swayze, and I'm glad we could get together."

His style quickly became outdated, but between 1948 and 1955, John Cameron Swayze ruled the airwaves as NBC anchor. In that time, he set down an example of showmanship that later anchors would ignore at their peril. From Charles Osgood's bowties to Dan Rather's sweaters, there are traces of Swayze's influence on anchoring style to this day.

It would not be right to say that he was an American original, for, in fact, he represents a certain type of personality that we rarely see on the network news, but is in plentiful supply at Rotary Clubs and Chamber of Commerce mixers. In fact, at most business association meetings, there is at least one John Cameron Swayze by the door. He wears a flag or a carnation in his lapel. He shakes your hand heartily with a nervous excitement; he's mighty glad to see you even when you are a first-time visitor. He winks, he jokes, and he makes conversation with you. You like him. You like John Cameron Swayze. He's a character, a booster, an enthusiast, and a promoter. He gets you in the door, gets you started; you enjoy him and you are pleased.

Later on, perhaps, as you become more familiar in your surroundings, the carnation looks a little forced. Maybe the mannerisms begin to seem corny. Maybe you wish he weren't always so enthusiastic. Maybe he seems a tad commercial. He becomes "uncool". So, eventually, you move on make other friends, who are perhaps a little more wry or sophisticated, perhaps a little more polished, urbane, or straightforward. But you never lose the memory of the man at the door who was there for you on that first day. How easy he made it seem. That was John Cameron Swayze, the first anchor at NBC.

Growing Up on the Chisholm Trail

Swayze's roots were in the Kansas prairies and the Western pioneer experience. His family hailed from a town called Hope, Kansas, where a bundle of immigrants set forth in the years after the Civil War. The Swayzes arrived in 1871 and eventually had a livery business. The general store was owned by David Eisenhower, the father of the future president.

In this age of transportation dominated by airlines, Kansas has been sidestepped. But in pioneer days, and at the turn of the century, eastern Kansas was a primary crossroads of the country. Hope was ten miles from the Santa Fe Trail and located on the famed Chisholm Trail from Texas, where thousands of Longhorn cattle were driven to Abilene and the Kansas Pacific railhead.

Swayze's family eventually moved to Atchison, the former headquarters of the Pony Express, the Overland Stage and Mail Company, and the birthplace of Amelia Earhart. By the 1910s, when Swayze was growing up in Atchison, the town had long ceased to be a jumping-off point for western migration. However, it was a stop on the thirty-week Orpheum vaudeville circuit. Acts like the Marx Brothers and Jack Benny came through town in the 1910s and put stars in the eyes of teenagers like John Swayze.

In 1921, a local inventor named Fred Stein formed the Atchison Radio and Electric Company. Three years later, Stein developed the first no-battery radio, one that was plugged into a wall socket. It was one of the seminal moments in the development of radio, and it made Atchison, overnight, into a radio town. By 1927, Stein became Atchison's major employer, with more than one thousand employees. More than seven hundred radios were turned out per day.

Swayze graduated from Atchison High School in 1924 with a distinctive voice with which he won school oratory contests. After attending the University of Kansas, the star-struck Swayze left Kansas for New York, where he hoped to make it as an actor on Broadway. However, the stock market crash and the onset of the Depression foiled his plans, so he moved to Kansas City in 1930. There, he took a job with the *Kansas City Journal-Post*.

His interest was in radio. During the early 1930s, KMBC-AM kept a microphone in the *Journal-Post*'s newsroom, and Swayze provided news bulletins for the station. Later in the decade, he made a similar arrangement with WHB-AM, one of the top stations in the market. He also had a microphone and an office at the United Press Bureau in Kansas City, where Walter Cronkite worked just a few years later.

Chances and Camels

Courtesy of Globe Photo/NBC

In 1933, he made his first television appearance. Midland Radio and Television School (now the DeVry University) maintained experimental radio and television stations in Kansas City. He did a fifteen-minute news broadcast on the station three times each week until 1937. A viewer of the time, C.C. Jones, recalled the experience:

> We had an Echophone television set at our apartment. The receiver consisted of a glow lamp, a rotating disk with a spiral of pinhole-sized holes, a four-inch ground glass viewing screen. The impulses received from the station in the K.C. Power and Light Building at Fourteenth and Baltimore would cause the glow lamp to vary the light intensity, shine through the rotating pinholes, and show on the ground glass. With some imagination you could recognize the picture being broadcast.

In 1940, Swayze was hired full time as a newscaster at KMBC, and he stayed for four years, reporting the war from Kansas City while fellow United Press alums went over to Europe. Swayze made his own move in 1944, taking a job with NBC's Western News Division as a copy editor.

By the time Swayze reached network radio, he had fourteen years of journalism experience behind him, including four years on the radio. For a man who became legendary for his personality and voice and lacked the reporting credentials of his competitors, it is surprising to note that he was hired for a desk job. He made enough of an impact to be transferred to New York in 1947, where he became the voice of the morning network news broadcast from Rockefeller Center. Quickly, however, the show's audience waned, and his career as a newscaster was in jeopardy. Swayze was told he was finished at NBC radio in New York, but that a new television department was getting underway uptown on 106th Street in East Harlem.

At the time, NBC had experimented with television news for six years. In 1941, it simulcast the Lowell Thomas radio broadcasts on WNBT. During the war, it began a program called, *NBC Telenews*, a broadcast of a newsreel program produced by Hearst. In 1947, not long after Swayze's arrival in New York, Hearst signed a new contract with CBS, and *Telenews* moved over to the Tiffany Network, as CBS became known. However, the prospects for television picked up substantially. Set manufacturing, which had ceased during the war, resumed, and two hundred fifty thousand sets were sold in 1947.

The William Esty advertising company bought fifteen minutes of airtime at 7:45 P.M. EST for R.J. Reynolds and Camel cigarettes in February 1948, and they decided to sponsor the news. The footage was the problem. First of all, NBC had to secure rights to newsreel footage, for it was not even remotely possible at that time to produce in-house footage on the scale needed for a news broadcast. Film was difficult to get, slow to transport, and took time to develop. All of which made for old news. A crucial decision by NBC located the news film department uptown in the same building as the Pathé Laboratories so that the developed film could be used more quickly.

Meetings were held, a deal was struck with Fox Movietone to provide newsreel footage, and the *Camel Newsreel Theater* debuted in 1947. A Philadelphia-based NBC engineer of the time recalls: "There were three stations in the early NBC network:. New York, Philadelphia, and Washington, D.C. The phone company had an experimental relay system that tied New York to Washington, and we came in on a pass! Philco owned WPTZ. They also built microwave relays. So we tapped into the telephone company and joined the network."

After the first few shows, it was decided that a studio personality was needed to tie the stories together, a technique that also would permit some stories to be covered with words when pictures were not available. It also allowed use of crude maps and other visual devices.

NBC lavished far less care on the choice of the newsreader than the Fox deal or the selection of the department building. Swayze later recalled that the producers never asked him, or any of the other applicants, to speak. They sat them side-by-side, looked them over, and chose Swayze. So it was Swayze in the chair, and he fit it just fine. The public was enthusiastic about *Camel Newsreel Theater* and John Cameron Swayze. An observer of the time said:

> John had a high-pitched, exciting voice, a classic style for news reading and photographic memory. He could read a script, then look squarely into camera and deliver all those words flawlessly, from memory. Long before the Teleprompters came into being that would make this facility with words

available to every man, Swayze was there doing what came naturally.

Making Impressions

Reynolds was happy with the show, the budget was increased, and Swayze began to dominate the ratings. He became a highly paid star. The broadcast was renamed the *Camel News Caravan* and launched to a six-station network from Virginia to Massachusetts in February 1948.

It was not work for the faint-hearted. The studio cameras of the time, called iconoscopes, required so much light that the floor temperature in small studios could reach as high as 115 degrees. Only when NBC's parent, RCA, developed new light-sensitive cameras in 1947 was it possible to be comfortable in a studio.

Meanwhile, television grew at a meteoric rate, with the manufacture of sets quadrupling between 1947 and 1948. Unlike radio, which complemented the movie industry by promoting its many stars, television began to bite into movie revenues. Movie attendance had an all-time high in 1946, but began to plummet dramatically. The studios panicked, and one of their moves was to cut off supply of newsreel footage to the fledgling television networks. NBC and CBS went back to their radio staff to try to convince them to switch to television, but found few people wanting to switch. So they hired out and, for a time, NBC did a better job of recruiting top talent. Reuven Frank, who eventually paired Huntley and Brinkley together in 1956, said:

> The day I was hired, I said to the man in charge, "Why are you hiring me? All you know about me is I'm a friend of Gerry Green. NBC is an established, respected, worldwide news organization with top people." He told me no one in

radio who was any good would come to television. They weren't sure it would last.

NBC's original television news program was, by today's standards, crude and gimmicky. Throughout 1948, it was beset with classic broadcasting trainwrecks. During the 1948 Democratic Convention in Philadelphia, the Democrats opened the first session by releasing doves of peace in Convention Hall. An observer recalled, "The frightened birds did what frightened birds usually do, they defecated on the audience, and we were treated to some of the major names in the political world dodging the projectiles."

Yet the 1948 convention coverage, anchored by Swayze, was considered a success at the time. NBC coverage by its correspondents improved continually and reached a peak of quality during the Korean War. Then, Swayze was considerably ahead in the ratings. Reuven Frank recalled:

> The Korean War had just begun—on June 25. Our [NBC] staff cameraman in Tokyo, having shot newsreels for the entire Pacific War, was living fat and happy in Tokyo like many World War II correspondents. "Not all the money in New York" would get him to Korea, back to combat. Early in July, Charles and Eugene Jones, twins in their early twenties, walked into our Washington bureau. They wanted to film the war.
>
> They shot hours of film, much of it unusual. But they got in close. The GIs, who were of the same age, accepted them. Out of too much film, the few minutes the editors extracted brought the war home. There were nights when the *Camel News Caravan* had bigger audiences than Milton Berle, the first TV king. Vietnam was not the first living-room war, Korea was.
>
> But in 1950, less than half the country had TV stations, and where television was available, few people owned sets. Network feeds could not go west of Kansas City. We once interviewed an Arizona congressman who said things you

knew his constituents despised. I asked if he wasn't risking trouble. He said, "We don't have TV yet."

Yet, even with ratings success and excellent coverage of Korea, the Swayze program continued to attract more and more detractors. "It was so bad, it was a joke," former Caravan field reporter David Brinkley remembered to a reporter from the *Baltimore Sun*. Oscar Levant spoke of the NBC show as a series of catastrophes ended by a fashion show. What was the problem?

Some of the problem was Swayze and his gimmicky style. Some of it was the gimmicky nature of R.J. Reynolds. In fact, they were a bad combination of the sponsor who always asked for too much and the anchor who always accommodated.

Swayze, for instance, even offered to carry a pack of Camels with him on appearances even though he didn't smoke. So, there he sat with a lit cigarette in an ashtray on national television reading the news. At the end of each newscast, the camera zoomed in on that ashtray while an announcer bellowed, "This program has been produced for Camel Cigarettes by NBC News."

There were companion magazine ads featuring Swayze sitting at a news desk and a radio campaign. Afraid that Swayze would not attract enough women viewers, there were often stories on beauty contests, fashion shows, and other news the network felt would play more toward women.

The sponsorship contract with NBC called for the mandatory sponsor plugs and commercials, but also had three specific rules. There was never to be a live camel on the show (the sponsor thought camels were dirty and spat a lot), NBC would never show a No Smoking sign, and they were never allowed to show a cigar. Under these rules, NBC could not show Winston Churchill, who was almost never seen without his cigar. So the network went to Camel and, after much consideration, the sponsor granted special dispensation for Churchill and his cigar.

In her book, *The Evening Stars: The Making of the Network*

News Anchor (Ballantine Books), Barbara Matusow writes that Swayze had an obsessive concern about his appearance:

> The bold suits and gimmicks he would use would annoy his colleagues, and the crew would devil him endlessly about his toupee, sometime to the point of cruelty. They would sneak it out of his drawer and hide it, watching him erupt in anger as airtime drew near. Finally, with only fifteen or twenty seconds left, some relenting soul would toss him his hairpiece. The teasing got so bad that he had to keep it clamped on his head all the time.

By the time of the 1952 conventions, veteran journalist Bill Henry was handed the anchoring job, where he went up against Cronkite at CBS. However, Swayze's popularity with the public, while diminished, continued strong. Milton Bradley put out a board game based on his NBC news coverage. He was in demand as a host of other programs.

In fact, Swayze had become less and less of a journalist and more and more of a star. Both he and Douglas Edwards were well known for having increasingly little to do with the scripting of their broadcasts and focusing increasingly on performance.

Television audiences increased exponentially in the early 1950s. By 1951, there were 10.5 million television-owning households; by the 1954–55 season, there were thirty-one million. Entire sections of the population, including whole geographies that did not have access to network news in the 1940s, were tuning in. More and more, they chose CBS. The tenor of the times perhaps better suited Douglas Edwards's low-key style. Also, CBS's famed cadre of radio correspondents converted over to television at this time. In addition, NBC was scooped on the Army-McCarthy hearings of 1954, lacking the director coverage of ABC or the documentary reporting of *See It Now*.

Swayze's influence began to be felt to a lesser degree in the nightly news. The development of cue card systems at CBS helped Douglas Edwards eliminate the head bobbing and eliminated the advantage of Swayze's famous photographic memory. Meanwhile, his emphasis on show business elements and softer coverage was copied and greatly improved by Edward R. Murrow, who had the exciting-to-look-at *See It Now* and softer *Person-to-Person* running simultaneously. Plus, now that television was the main focus of the networks, NBC lost the advantage it held by devoting more resources to television when it was in its experimental phase. Reuven Frank wrote:

> When it came time to pick the anchor for 1956, I had progressed to where I would be heard among the others. The brass wanted Bill Henry again, but I disagreed. I had been working with Chet Huntley, newly arrived from California. I admired David Brinkley, who did Washington reports for the *Camel News Caravan*. I was unsure which would be the better convention anchor. . . . Although our bosses, all the way up to Pat Weaver, were not taken with our idea, without a better one they went along. . . . They succeeded so well the brass picked them to replace John Swayze.

And so Swayze's nine-year occupation of the anchor seat came to a close. He had one more shot at the anchor role in 1960 when, after the departure of John Daly, ABC teamed him with Bill Lawrence and Al Mann. Swayze came on at the beginning of each program, read the headlines, and reappeared at the end of the show with a feature report. His once-bright stardom began to flicker in this limited role at ABC. A Detroit newsman, Bill Sheehan, replaced Mann, and this began a revolving door of news anchors at ABC, which lasted for several years.

He Keeps on Ticking

Swayze continued in the public eye, but in a new role. The William Esty advertising agency had another client, Timex watches, and they hired Swayze as their pitchman. The commercials were a huge success. Timex became that for which he is best remembered. He put Timex watches to the test. The watches were strapped to turtles, beat up by Kung Fu fighters, even thrown out of airplanes: you name it. The slogan, "It takes a licking and keeps on ticking" is forever associated with Swayze.

In May of 1960, Swayze got a quick shot of re-energized stardom when three of his commercials aired in the *Frank Sinatra Timex Show — Welcome Back Elvis* that starred the Rat Pack (less Dean Martin) welcoming back Elvis from his stint in the army. Swayze stood by a dolphin named Nellie as she tested out some early models at Marine World in Florida.

Timex loved the advertising campaign and stuck with it for many years. It even captured the legal community's attention when Timex was sued over one of the spots. Julia Ptasznik wrote for *Visual Times*:

> In this humorous spot, a tall, dark, and lanky fellow is brought into a lab-type room by a couple of guys wearing white coats. He sits down next to a table and starts concentrating. The camera then pans to the table and everything on it, including a Timex watch, a fork, and a spoon, starts shaking. The fork, spoon, and watch bend; the entire table flips over . . . and here comes the famous newsman John Cameron Swayze's payoff line: "It takes a licking and keeps on ticking." Incidentally, the spot has won a Cleo.
>
> Uri Geller, an Israeli psychic known in the seventies and eighties for allegedly bending utensils with his mind, sued, claiming that the spot not only uses a look-alike, but that it also copies his "act". Mr. Raymond, representing the defendant, takes Mr. Geller's deposition, marking a fork as an exhibit and asking the plaintiff to bend it, which he refuses to do. In the end, Mr. Raymond's client won the suit on summary judgment.

The irony of a psychic suing a broadcaster for "copying his act" was obviously lost on Uri Geller, but there's something right about it. For it's a good way to remember John Cameron Swayze. He not only developed a successful act, but he showed the broadcast industry that peril befalls the anchor who doesn't have one too. Time has not been kind to Swayze's broadcasting style—for, like Milton Berle or Howdy Doody, his over-the-top style looks corny—but the lesson of having a shtick is one for the ages. The example of Camel's sponsorship is a cautionary tale for sponsors and networks alike. The lesson of looking into the camera is with us still. The benefits of dressing well are not lost on several of our brightest stars today. And Swayze's penchant for breezy enthusiasm still influences the tone of the morning shows.

Not bad for a guy from Atchison, Kansas, who grew up after all the stagecoaches went through, watching the vaudeville acts at the Orpheum, and dreaming of acting on Broadway. He was Atchison's last pioneer, and his legacy is at least the equal of fellow Atchisonian Amelia Earhart's, even if his personality is less suited to our times.

John Cameron Swayze died on August 15, 1995 at his home in Sarasota, Florida. Timex stopped producing watches in 1998. The anchor torch was passed at NBC only three times from 1956 to 2004.

Chapter FOUR

John Charles Daly, ABC

Courtesy of ABC

When we think of so many of our favorite news anchors, we think of their signature opening and closing lines. "*This* . . . is London," was Edward R. Murrow's. "That's the way it is," was Walter Cronkite's. "Courage!" was Dan Rather's. "Good night, Chet. Good night, David. And good night for NBC News," was

Huntley and Brinkley's. In fact, Huntley and Brinkley hated the line, and Brinkley, in particular, thought it was silly and asinine. Yet, even decades after Chet Huntley died, fans of the show greeted Brinkley on the street with, "Good night, David."

John Charles Daly had a closing line of his own at ABC News, where he was a distinguished anchor between 1953 and 1960. It was, "Good night, and a good tomorrow." But when viewers flagged down John Charles Daly in the street, it was never with that phrase. His trademark line, instead, was, "Will the next guest enter and sign in, please?" It was heard Sunday nights for seventeen years on the long-running monster hit, *What's My Line?*, which aired live at 10:30 P.M. on, of all networks, CBS. It served as an unbeatable lead-in for the CBS late evening news, which always trounced ABC late-evening news programming. Incredibly, during most of this period, Daly served as head of the ABC news division and was responsible for beating CBS and, by extension, beating *What's My Line?*

What's My Line? indeed. It was a question that plagued Daly all his career. Was he an erudite entertainer, game show host, and occasional guest star of *Superman* or *Father Knows Best?* Or was he the brilliant newscaster and author who covered national events with distinction for more than forty years? Daly's career shows that anchors can have one foot in the entertainment business and one foot in the news business without diminishing news standards. For example, during his long run with *What's My Line?*, he received not only an Emmy for his news commentary, but the 1955 Peabody Award. The honors speak volumes about his charm and poise, but even more about his legitimate news credentials.

But when people remember Daly, invariably they talk about his manner. He was a man for whom it seemed the adjective "urbane" was invented. It was an era when the public had a fascination with witty, erudite personalities such as Alexander Woollcott (*Talk of the Town*) and Oscar Levant (*Information Please*). Right at the head of the pack of such personalities was Daly.

He arrived at CBS News in the New York operation just after Edward R. Murrow left for Europe. The staff was incredibly small then. Just a handful of broadcasters such as Bob Trout, Ned Calmer, and Daly worked under Paul White. In November, 1941, Bill Paley brought Murrow back to the United States to a festive celebration of CBS News coverage of the war in Europe. To fill in for Murrow, CBS's lead New York anchor, Bob Trout, was sent to London. John Daly became the lead anchor in New York for the *World Today* and other news broadcasts.

"We Interrupt This Program . . ."

On the afternoon of December 7, 1941, John Daly was in the New York studio preparing for the broadcast of the *World Today* at 2:30 P.M. There is a myth that Daly interrupted the New York

Courtesy of ABC

75

Philharmonic broadcast that afternoon with the following bulletin: "We interrupt this program for a special announcement . . . the Japanese have attacked Pearl Harbor, Hawaii, by air!"

In fact, Daly did break into regular programming, but it was a program called the *Spirit of '41*. The Philharmonic was scheduled for three o'clock. While the events of December 7th are covered in more detail earlier in this book, it is important to note that the "we interrupt" announcement remembered by most people is partially faked by, of all people, Edward R. Murrow. The second part belongs to his actual broadcast on December 7th, but Fred Friendly and Murrow, when preparing their classic LP *I Can Hear It Now* after the war, lifted the phrase, "we interrupt this program," from Daly's 1945 announcement of the death of President Roosevelt.

Daly's role was crucial in the coverage. Five minutes after the first flash of the Pearl Harbor attack, his program went forward with the *World Today* news broadcast, but the broadcast was completely recast on the fly based on the updates from Pearl Harbor. Robert Trout had the reputation of being the best of the CBS staff for improvisation, but Daly's considerable skills were in evidence throughout the broadcast, as well as during the first half-hour of coverage and only minutes after the attack. The NBC Red Network, by contrast, had H.V. Kaltenborn on the air at 3:15 P.M., and the NBC Blue network (later ABC) and Mutual worked with bulletins until their regular news broadcasts in the evening. In fact, Daly began the first half-hour of full coverage on CBS two minutes before the NBC Blue network broke into programming with its first flash during a *Great Plays* radio drama, "The Inspector General."

During the half-hour broadcast, Daly brought in Albert Warner in Washington to speculate on President Roosevelt's next move. Trout reported on the British reaction from London. Then, ten minutes into the broadcast, the Japanese struck

Manila. CBS correspondent Ford Wilkins was there, but was cut off in mid-broadcast by American military censors, who simply pulled the plug. Daly attempted to contact Honolulu, but the communications problems were too overwhelming. In fact, no live report from Honolulu was heard on any network until shortly after four o'clock, when NBC Red affiliate KGU made a report.

By three o'clock in New York, it was evening time in London, too late for Trout to assemble a cohesive report based on reaction from Churchill. It was late at night in Moscow and Cairo. European reaction was not at hand until December 8th. Meanwhile, reports began to come in of Japanese attacks on Malaya and the Dutch East Indies. But ground reports were impossible to gather. The decision was made to report the news via short interruptions, and, at three o'clock, CBS switched to the New York Philharmonic broadcast.

Given today's twenty-four–hour news cycle and relentless crisis coverage, it may seem odd that anchor John Charles Daly closed the half-hour program with these words: "Columbia will bring you important bulletins during the broadcast of the New York Philharmonic Society, which follows this program." Trout himself criticized the decision years later:

> Now, if you're asking at this point why, in the midst of the greatest military crisis of the century, news would yield to the New York Philharmonic, you've asked a good question. The truth is, modern broadcast journalism might have been born on that afternoon, but it was not. Inconceivable as it may seem now, hardly a single network program was canceled that day or night for news.

Following Pearl Harbor, Daly continued as a key CBS broadcaster in New York for most of the war. He was one of the first to report, in March, 1942, of the growing concerns regarding the Nazi treatment of the Jews based on reports that were coming out of unoccupied Vichy, France.

He had several memorable opportunities to display his quick, dry wit and ability to improvise when anchoring Larry LeSeuer's attempts to transmit radio reports from the Russian Urals. The Soviet government and foreign diplomatic and press corps relocated to Kuibyshev when the battle for Moscow began. LeSeuer, who had to broadcast at 4:00 A.M. because of the time difference, routinely fought subzero temperatures only to discover that his broadcasts were not received in New York. "We are informed," Daly quipped one day on air, "that, after a good deal of trying, we may be able to get a direct report from Kuibyshev." Half a sentence into LeSeuer's broadcast, the airwaves went dead, and Daly had to improvise.

Hold on to Patton

In 1943, Daly himself was posted in Italy, where he covered George Patton, Omar Bradley, and the American advances through Sicily and Italy. Daly was deeply involved in one of the most famous incidents of the war, a furor that erupted when Patton slapped a soldier he believed to be a malingerer in a field hospital in front of the medical staff.

Daly was one of the leaders of the press contingent that went to Algiers to see Bedell Smith, Eisenhower's chief of staff, to recommend that Patton be relieved of his command. Eisenhower saw the seriousness of the situation and asked to meet and talk with Daly and the other correspondents. "Look," he said, "I can't stop you from filing your reports and from stating what happened, but I beg you, in the name of Allied unity, I need this man. I can't win the war without Patton. And if this thing becomes public, he's probably going to get relieved, and I may have to send him home. And I'd ask you, you know, as a gentleman's agreement, to keep this in confidence."

For a man who made his reputation as a conversationalist and reporter, it is surprising that Daly decided to sit on the sensational story. But he always had an interesting angle on reporting and conversation. He said: "The art of conversation lies not only in saying the right thing at the right time, but in leaving unsaid the wrong thing at the tempting moment." Apparently, it was a philosophy that no one managed to communicate to Drew Pearson, the famed *Washington Post* correspondent, who broke the story on the radio in November, 1943.

"Will the Next Guest Enter and Sign in, Please?"

Daly, like most of the war correspondents, returned to the United States right after the end of the war. His urbane manner, strong voice, and considerable poise had made a deep impression, and he was given a number of choice assignments at CBS during the late 1940s. For one, he was part of the celebrated team covering the 1948 conventions. Perhaps his best assignment was anchoring the program, *You Are There*, which took historic events and dramatized them with "live radio" coverage. The show began with "live" background coverage of the events unfolding. Then the sounds and characters involved took over. Often, participants were interviewed or the show cut to another reporter's evaluation of the event. Among the programs was a recreation of Lee and Grant at Appomattox, the *Monitor* versus the *Merrimac* at Hampton Roads, and July 4, 1776, at Independence Hall in Philadelphia for the birth of the *Declaration of Independence*.

Daly's forays into game shows began during his last years at CBS. In 1948, Bob Trout started a game show called, *Who Said That?* Walter Kiernan and Daly served as substitute hosts. The show was the first successful prime time quiz show on television, and it ushered in an entire generation of quiz shows. It is not surprising that Daly was pitched a show of his own. The concept was from Mark Goodson and Bill Tolman and ultimately developed into *What's My Line?* in 1950. *What's My Line?* became one of the storied successes among quiz shows of the 1950s. It was certainly the most witty and elegant, thanks to the tuxedo-clad Daly and regular panelists Arlene Francis, Dorothy Kilgallen, and Bennett Cerf. An observer of the time wrote:

> Not only does Mr. Daly exude charm, textbook manners, and an air of eruditeness not seen since the 1940s, but he is surrounded with two of television's snootiest panelists, Arlene Francis and Dorothy Kilgallen, who both speak the king's English with their noses held high in the air. Bennett Cerf, publisher of Random House, rounds out the panel. . . . But there simply [isn't anything like] listening to the bow-tied, tuxedo-clad Daly utter those immortal phrases, "Bennett, we'll begin the questioning with you," and my very favorite, "That's three down and seven to go."

By late 1950, *What's My Line?* was a hit and in the early stretches of a seventeen-year-long run on CBS. Daly began to host another quiz show, *It's News to Me*, which also appeared on CBS. It was another Goodson-Todman production.

The Politics of News

In 1952, Daly was again selected to be part of the convention coverage team. Unlike four years earlier, when radio coverage was the major focus and television was an afterthought, this time Walter Cronkite was in the anchor chair and television was the focus. It was Daly's last hurrah with CBS News, for, shortly after the conventions, he was lured over to ABC by

Leonard Goldenson, where new ownership was trying to effect a miracle of turning ABC into a real competitor in television.

It is difficult to convey just how far behind ABC was in those days. The network owed its existence to a ruling by the Federal Communications Commission (FCC) that NBC, which owned two radio networks at the time (NBC Blue and NBC Red), could not own two competing television networks. In 1941, the weaker Blue radio and television networks were sold to manufacturer Edward Noble for eight million dollars and renamed the American Broadcasting Company. While the radio network was successful, ABC's forays into television were underfunded and unspectacular.

Television news at ABC consisted of the fifteen-minute show, *News and Views*. It ran from August, 1948, until October, 1952. It never garnered much of an audience, and ABC finally gave up on it. *After the Deadlines* and *All-Star News* were the next two botched attempts by ABC to become a player in the television news business. During that time in the late 1940s, Noble, who invented Lifesavers Candy, was already trying to sell the network.

The movie studios valued television as an outlet for their back catalog of films, and both Paramount and Warner expressed an interest in buying the networks. However, the Justice Department was pressuring the companies to spin-off their production and theater-chain businesses. Paramount finally spun off both its theater chain and motion picture production divisions in order to buy ABC, which it did in 1951.

The result of all those motions was a revolving door among the top executives of the company and a lack of focus on the news division. The news experiments that ABC aired were financial disasters, and the new management was determined to do something about it.

Leonard Goldenson was a consummate deal-maker who

brought Daly over to the network during that period. He also outmaneuvered NBC and not only acquired the broadcast rights to *Disneyland*, which was the biggest-rated show on the network from 1954 to 1956, but acquired a 33 percent stake in the theme park at the same time for five hundred thousand dollars. (The fact that it was later sold for $7.5 million later paved the way for Disney's acquisition of ABC in the 1990s.)

Goldenson was determined to create something interesting for the news division, and, as a result, he and network president Robert Kintner announced a new program for 1953: *John Daly and the News*. At ABC, Daly was among a strong group of radio broadcasters such as Paul Harvey, Walter Winchell, and Drew Pearson. But they were fighting for resources to get the news on, and it seemed like every day a new set of problems cropped up with news feeds, lost film, wiring, etc. John Daly was a champ about it. His ability to ad lib during complete meltdowns made him a standout.

There were no fancy sets, and Daly stood at a podium delivering the news instead of a desk. ABC was far behind in newsgathering, and, many nights, it found itself with very little film to run. Daly did a commentary in each show, and its time allotment was varied based on the amount of dead time it had to fill. Despite his popularity, Daly was hard-pressed to knock off Douglas Edwards and John Cameron Swayze, who had been on the air for almost five years at that point.

Live—at What Cost?

But ABC was about to get noticed. Daly, besides being the anchor, was essentially in charge of the news department at that time. When Daly had heard that the Army/McCarthy hearing would not be carried by CBS and NBC, he went to Robert Kintner, the network president, and suggested that ABC carry the hearings live. Kintner played with the idea and decided to take a chance. The hearings lasted for almost a month. ABC aired them day after day, and it paid off. People talked about ABC news for perhaps the first time, Daly was seen off and on by nearly thirty million people, and the way McCarthy acted in those hearing was better than any soap opera.

Daly's success, and the small in-roads he made in the ratings, caused some concern at NBC; his success came primarily at the expense of John Cameron Swayze, who could not match Daly either for journalistic integrity or worldly charm. With Douglas Edwards gaining strength at CBS, NBC saw Swayze getting squeezed by both CBS and ABC. Following the 1956 conventions, NBC put the *Huntley-Brinkley Report* together in response.

Almost immediately, the Huntley and Brinkley combination overwhelmed Daly in the ratings. The same happened to Douglas Edwards, but Daly had less of an audience to begin with. So in late 1958, ABC tried to put Daly on at 10:30 at night in a new attempt to get news ratings for the network. But NBC had just made its historic (and for ABC, killing) switch, moving the evening news from 7:45 P.M. to 7:15 P.M., putting it head to head with CBS and ABC. ABC took a huge hit it could ill afford. The 10:30 gambit failed despite Daly's evident success at 10:30 P.M. on Sundays with the game show, so Daly went back to the early news. By 1960, ABC was still not making any headway in the news ratings race, and although Daly was a solid anchor, there was talk again that hosting game shows was diluting his journalistic integrity. Besides *What's My Line?*, Daly appeared as a dog catcher in an episode of *Superman*. He also hosted many cultural programs on ABC, including the *Voice of Firestone*, a weekly concert series featuring classical and semiclassical performances and artists.

ABC once again decided to experiment with multiple

anchors and a more flashy approach to news. For a network concerned about integrity, bringing in John Cameron Swayze directly from a Timex set might seem a tad opportunistic. But a more interesting angle to consider is the fact that the nominal vice president of news and public affairs was Daly himself. He continued in his executive role at the network, representing ABC in the three-network negotiations for the historic Kennedy-Nixon debates in 1960. He also supervised the documentary series, *Close-Up*. In a narrow and technical sense, Daly fired himself as anchor.

It was a flap over *Close-Up* that finally prodded Daly to leave ABC in 1961. When an outside production group was brought in to create four episodes of the program, Daly packed up his desk and headed for the door, saying good-bye to his years at the alphabet network.

He Did It All!

It is probable that he was looking for an exit. For Daly was, by then, one of the most well known and highly regarded people in the country. He married the daughter of Chief Justice Earl Warren, and he was still in the middle of his astonishing run on CBS with *What's My Line?*. He was in demand for cameos, and he appeared in a range of shows, from *Bye Bye Birdie* to an episode of *Green Acres*. He hosted the Miss Universe Pageant and the Emmys. He settled into a regimen of book writing throughout the 1960s and 1970s, and his output was astonishing.

He continued with *What's My Line?* until September, 1967, when at last, CBS ended the long run as it made another in a series of attempts to lower the age of its audiences. Daly immediately succeeded John Chancellor as the director of the *Voice of America*, where he stayed until the end of 1968, coordinating coverage of events from the controversial 1968

Olympic games in Mexico City to the assassinations of Robert Kennedy and Martin Luther King Jr.

Following his retirement from the *Voice of America*, the fifty-four-year-old Daly moved onto the lecture circuit and increased his output of writing, publishing sixty volumes in total. He chaired or moderated significant debates from time to time on public television and moderated panels of the American Enterprise Institute and other think tanks. He raised significant amounts of money for Tifton School in Connecticut, where he served as a director.

His final major broadcast was typical of the man. It was a retrospective of *What's My Line?* aired in 1975 on the twenty-fifth anniversary of the debut of the program. Daly was the host, and both Mark Goodson and Arlene Francis made appearances. The irony of it is that the special was taped at, of all networks, NBC, the one major network for which he never worked. It was aired on ABC. It may be the only time in broadcasting history that a show celebrating a long-running hit at one network was taped in the studios of a second and aired on a third.

John Charles Daly died at his home in Carmel, California, on February 24, 1991. He personified a tradition of broadcasters with one foot in the entertainment industry and one solid foot in journalism. His work during the war established his news credentials for all time, and he showed a good instinct as a news executive, especially in his proposal to carry the Army/McCarthy hearings. Since Daly, there have been numerous anchors who have carried on in his tradition of wit and entertainment. Peter Jennings has perhaps inherited his mantle as an anchor. But no one has emulated his style and panache, or matched the way he carried himself in a tuxedo.

Part Two

The Golden Years

Chapter FIVE

Chet Huntley and David Brinkley, NBC

Courtesy of Globe Photo/NBC

The *Huntley-Brinkley Report* remains, for many, the best news program ever broadcast on television. For some, Chet Huntley and David Brinkley were the 1927 Yankees or the 1972 Miami Dolphins—the summit, the untouchables. By any and every empirical measurement, it was the most successful broadcast news program ever in ratings and share. As a cultural and sales phenomenon, Huntley and Brinkley were like Elvis, and, like the king of rock 'n' roll, they arrived in 1956.

The *Huntley-Brinkley Report* commanded, at one memorable point, an astounding 84 audience share. Why were they big? It's not just that they were fresh and good. Fresh doesn't carry anyone for ten years at number one, and good doesn't explain why they surpassed Walter Cronkite in the early years then fell behind him at the end.

Chet Huntley and David Brinkley had an objective to put out a credible, fair, truthful, and timely broadcast. But to see the *Huntley-Brinkley Report* in terms of its impact, we have to look at it not from the point of view of a broadcast being pumped out, but also from the living room tuning in.

From Quiz Shows and Westerns

To see Chet Huntley and David Brinkley's appeal in 1956, look no further than old copies of *TV Guide*. Between 1955 and 1958, the formative years of the *Huntley-Brinkley Report*, there was an incredible rise in the number and popularity of shows in two entertainment genres: quiz shows and westerns. Beyond just three or four shows, these new forms of entertainment were phenomena against which the meteoric rise of today's reality programming cannot even compare.

The year 1956 was that of the quiz and game shows. They began to appear in the late 1940s in radio, but, by 1956, they seemed to be all over the dial. It was a time of clever contestants and witty, urbane hosts. It's not all that surprising that it became a time for the clever, witty, and urbane David Brinkley.

Westerns also came to television in 1956. It was a time of ruggedly handsome, plainspoken, fearless western men. It's no surprise that it also was a time for the ruggedly handsome, plainspoken, fearless Chet Huntley.

One could say that the *Huntley-Brinkley Report* was pure news and Huntley and Brinkley were pure journalists, but that the structure of the show was pure *Wagon Train*. *Wagon Train* and the *Huntley-Brinkley Report* were two of the biggest phenomena of the last half of the decade on television. What did they have in common? The anchors and correspondents (replacing the dashing frontier scouts) provided the recurring cast, and the news provided the perils and adventures. The structures provided anchor "characters" with a stable news team, a weekly guest star, and an ever-changing landscape of news events.

The *Huntley-Brinkley Report*'s undoing was the 1967 American Federation of Television and Radio Artists (AFTRA) strike. Brinkley famously refused to cross the picket line, but Huntley did. Brinkley surmised afterward that he was reviled for perceived greed, and Huntley was reviled for perceived insensitivity to the strikers. For several weeks, the unit was broken, right in front of the audience.

Within weeks, Huntley and Brinkley lost the ratings lead to Walter Cronkite and never recovered it. Huntley hung it up a few years later, in 1970. Although David Brinkley went on to, arguably, an equally distinguished solo career from 1970 to 1995, there never again was a show constructed just like the *Huntley-Brinkley Report*. Networks copied the format, but never the spirit. And never again has a network news program so captured the public imagination.

Huntley Gets "Train-ed"

Chet Huntley was born on December 10, 1911, in a Northern Pacific Railroad depot in Cardwell, Montana. Cardwell sits along the Jefferson River, just a few miles from Three Forks of the Missouri. The landscape was dominated by mountains, the Great Northern Railroad, cattle, and mining. Rich in minerals, the land was unfit for cultivation much beyond a tough prairie grass. In the 1800s, it was easy to get land for homesteading, and Huntley's family took several hundred acres.

His father worked for the railroads, and Huntley was fascinated by them all his life. Late in his life, he chose not to write a full memoir, and wrote instead a book called, *The Generous Years*. It concentrated on a boyhood spent on the last frontier, about Huntley's childhood and the four people who shaped his life.

Radio arrived in 1920. He remembered it with a poignancy that echoed how, in a later generation, people recalled the first sighting of *Sputnik*:

> It was perhaps that same winter, 1920, when Dad brought home one day a curious package of coils and knobs . . . I sat and watched as Dad and his friend connected the wires and the strange instruments, adjusted earphones on their heads, and gently moved a little handle. They smiled with satisfaction and nodded to each other. Although Dad worked in Morse code he could follow the gist of a conversation or transmission in International code. Finally, he clamped the phones over my ears, and I heard, for the first time, the strange beeps coming mysteriously out of the night. Dad said the transmission was from a ship somewhere off the West Coast . . . far out in the Pacific.

He remembered the coming of the first commercial radio stations, and his memoir of this experience is one of the few descriptions we have, from an anchor, of the birth of the broadcast medium:

> Dad became a genuine radio enthusiast. Several years later, after we had moved to southern Montana, we owned the first

radio receiver in town. That set boasted a loudspeaker, and on the cold, clear winter nights, KDKA, Pittsburgh, would come piping in, and we got to know the Night Hawks from Kansas City and Bill Hay from Hastings, Nebraska. Our living room was usually filled with neighbors and townspeople who dropped by to hear radio for the first time.

It was that humble upbringing that gave Chet Huntley a certain grounding that was apparent in virtually every word he spoke on television. In 1929, he left the Montana frontier and headed for Seattle, where he enrolled at the University of Washington.

Brinkley's Voice Change

David Brinkley grew up in Wilmington, North Carolina. In an article written for the *New Yorker* some years ago, he remembered himself to William Whitworth as a lonely boy. Like Huntley, Brinkley's father also was a railroad man, but he died when he was only eight years old. His mother was very religious. Brinkley told A&E's *Biography*, "The only thing she liked in life were dogs, babies, and flowers—that's all she cared about. She cared about nothing else including me."

Brinkley, along with his two brothers and two sisters, worked while in elementary school. Even during the summers, Brinkley took odd jobs near their beach home as a soda jerk or changing light bulbs at a local dance hall. He was quiet and developed a reading addiction by the time he was ten. In high school, he excelled in English and began to think of himself as a writer. It was an English teacher who approached Brinkley about his writing, according to the A&E interview. "My English teacher said to me, 'David, maybe you should be a journalist.' It was the first time it had crossed my mind."

He had another mentor in public librarian Emma Woodward,

who told him that he had promise, that he needed more than he received at the high school, and that she would tutor him. He enrolled in her class, and, for four years, he spent between two and four hours a day in her academy.

His entrance into journalism came when he took a part-time job at the Wilmington *Star-News*, where he quickly became a reporter. He wanted to get into broadcasting, but he knew he had to work on his voice. He had a southern accent, and he knew that wouldn't play on the radio. There were no accents on national radio at the time. He met a speech major from Emerson College in Boston, and she worked with him to change his voice.

Brinkley entered the service at the start of World War II, and soon after, he was given an honorable medical discharge. He believed he had an offer from CBS Radio in Washington, and he headed for the capital.

He showed up at the front door of CBS. He told *Biography*: "I went there . . . to see Paul White. I went to his office, and he said there was no job. I asked his secretary to send in a note from me saying, 'Go to hell.' I came out, walked over to Fourteenth and York where NBC was, I was hired in ten minutes, and stayed there for thirty-eight years."

He began as a writer, but didn't have any notoriety when he joined the broadcast team in 1943. He had to work hard for any recognition. His clear writing style was hard for some of the announcers to read. Brinkley wrote with feeling, and the announcers had a habit of just reading the words without looking at the punctuation marks. Sometimes, they totally missed the meaning Brinkley intended.

Eventually, he began to get some experience on the air. He was assigned to the White House at age twenty-three under President Roosevelt. Brinkley said:

He had two press conferences a week with twelve to fourteen reporters. He didn't like us. He thought we were too thinly educated. He complained all the time that we weren't good enough to tell the people what he was up to. That was the origin of the "fireside chats". It was to go over our heads. The press cooperated about his paralysis. There was a deference. Would we be better off if the press had not been willing to maintain that fiction? I don't know.

Brinkley recalled the extraordinary lengths that the White House went to conceal Roosevelt's infirmity. The Statler Hotel at Sixteenth Street and K was redesigned to accommodate an entire car being driven into the conference theater. The car was driven through the door and backstage, and then the Secret Service rolled him onto the stage while out of the sight of the public.

"Now?" Brinkley asks. "It's not as polite a time. There is less and less deference, less a degree of respect. Then, the cameramen put their cameras down when Roosevelt came out, without being asked."

By the time Truman became president, Brinkley noticed that the gloves were already coming off, and a rougher age of journalism was dawning.

The next step in his career was, of course, television. He read a ten-minute newscast for the network. When he read his own words, it became clear that he had some talent. He realized that with pictures, you often had to stop and let the video run so the viewers have a few seconds to absorb it. This was a revelation in those days, and it became common practice in the years to come.

He later spoke about the problems of the big names in radio as they attempted the transition to television. "Elmer Davis. Kaltenborn. Lowell Thomas. Their job consisted of sitting at the mike in shirtsleeves reading a script. One by one all these grand old men faded away. They couldn't make the transition, they were too set in their ways. Younger people came along."

NBC made him a reporter for the *Camel News Caravan* with John Cameron Swayze. Brinkley covered Washington. He sat at a desk in Washington with cigarette smoke wafting in front of him on camera and said, "Now back to the *Camel News* headquarters in New York."

Huntley and Who?: Conventional Wisdom

Meanwhile, Huntley was working his way through college in Seattle as a pre-med student when, in his senior year, he landed a job at KPCB radio, which eventually became KIRO, the powerful CBS affiliate. He was not only a writer and announcer, but also a salesman. It was a one hundred–watt station, which was common for the time, but the listeners were numbered in the hundred of thousands, not the tens of thousands. With a salary of just ten dollars per month, Huntley was bitten by the radio bug. But he moved on to stations in Spokane and Portland, gathering experience. In 1937, he made what was then the transition to the big time by signing on with KFI Los Angeles. Then, in 1939, he took a job with CBS News.

He joined CBS during the earliest years of the Murrow Boys, but unlike Walter Cronkite, Howard K. Smith, and others during this era, Huntley was not made a war correspondent. Instead, his rich basso-baritone became a regular feature on Los Angeles radio news, and he stayed at CBS until 1951, when he switched over to ABC. He stayed four years at ABC, then in television.

"In those days," said David Brinkley, "all the networks wanted a Murrow. We all envied CBS." Brinkley recalled that NBC combed the country looking for the next Murrow. It sent teams to scour the countryside and check into cities without calling the local affiliate in advance so that they could check out the broadcasters. That was, according to Brinkley, how NBC discovered Huntley. He had a great voice, good looks, great Murrow-esque presence. Like Murrow, he candidly criticized Senator Joseph McCarthy's outrageous allegations of Communist sympathy among government officials and members of Hollywood's film industry.

NBC hired him in 1955, brought him to New York, and then couldn't figure out what to do with him. Then along came the 1956 conventions and what Reuven Frank called "a miracle of casting."

The conventions were still the Olympics of the news calendar, and NBC was determined to pull even with CBS, which ran away with critical acclaim and the ratings in 1952. Brinkley remembered how the NBC anchors narrated the conventions:

> Some forgotten senator finished an easily forgettable speech, folded his script, put it in his pocket, and walked back down to his seat. Henry, the radio veteran, talked over the television picture as he walked, saying, "The senator finishes his speech . . . folds his script . . . and puts it in his pocket . . . and returns to his seat." That was narration for radio, not television.

Brinkley himself thought the conventions were all boring and were only given four days of coverage because the networks were falling all over themselves to please powerful interests in Washington—the same folk who controlled, for one thing, broadcast licenses. Brinkley thought they could do a lot better.

The producer of NBC convention coverage was the legendary Reuven Frank, the closest thing at NBC to a Don Hewitt. He wanted Brinkley. Others wanted Huntley. Some pushed for a third or a fourth choice as the anchor. Frank later recalled how it almost accidentally occurred to them that they could have two anchors: "It was like a light bulb going on over some-one's head in the comics." Four days of coverage, with the see-saw of events, and ballots, and the action on multiple fronts simultaneously, was a demanding job. Cronkite pulled it off for CBS in 1952, but at NBC in 1956, the concept of two anchors gave them a sense that they would have good coverage and enough ad libbing and occasional insight to carry the broadcast.

There was universal agreement that Huntley should be one of the two, but Huntley and who? The producers disagreed, and the decision was referred to David Sarnoff, the chairman of RCA, who chose Brinkley. Thus the partnership was born.

The two had never met, but the partnership worked. Hunt-ley brought a steady, Murrow-like voice and the ability to edi-torialize with his eyebrows. Brinkley brought wit, coolness, unbeatable connections, and an insight born of thirteen years of covering Washington. Brinkley was thirty-six, and Huntley was forty-four.

It was almost like a football game, with Huntley doing the play-by-play and Brinkley doing the color commentary. Brink-ley found little tidbits of information to liven up each broadcast with real behind-the-scenes material:

> HUNTLEY: David, you have some remarks to make, so come in with your observations, if you will.
>
> BRINKLEY: Well, we're off to a flying start in many ways, Chet. I was staggered to see this convention start on time, and so were the delegates because they weren't here.

Because CBS was so matter-of-fact with its coverage, NBC got real viewer attention, but it wasn't only the viewers who no-ticed. *New York Times* television columnist Jack Gould wrote under the headline, BRINKLEY LIVENS UP NBC CONVENTION COVER-AGE: "A quiet southerner with a dry wit and a heaven-sent ap-preciation of brevity has stolen the television limelight . . .

Mr. Brinkley quite possibly could be the forerunner of a new school of television commentator."

Reviews like that one popped up in newspapers across the country. The ratings were solid—they didn't match Cronkite's, but they more than held their own. But the combination of ratings and critical acclaim made NBC executives, who were increasingly aware of the ratings slide of John Cameron Swayze, ready to make a change. With the teleprompter coming, his days were numbered. His 7:45 P.M. slot was not generating the kind of viewership that NBC could build on for prime time, and the Camel and Plymouth sponsorships were not enough for NBC.

Pumped Up by Texaco

NBC decided to make the change. Reuven Frank was named producer. The program was titled the *Huntley-Brinkley Report*, and it went to air on October 29, 1956.

Just minutes before the first program was to air, Huntley and Brinkley both asked how they should close the show. Reuven Frank, in haste and not knowing what to do about this pretty trivial matter just said, "Say goodnight to each other." Brinkley remembers, "I didn't like it, Huntley didn't either. He thought it sounded kind of sissified, two men saying good night to each other. It was kind of silly saying good night to each other instead of the audience." So they went on the air and did their first broadcast, which ended:

> HUNTLEY: Goodnight, David.
>
> BRINKLEY: Goodnight, Chet.
>
> HUNTLEY: Goodnight for the staff of NBC News.

As we know, the close became a fixture in American television and is now in just about every famous quotation book.

The program did not improve ratings in its first months. In fact, ratings slid mightily, and advertisers fell away. During the summer of 1957, the entire broadcast was on a sustaining (earning zero sponsorship dollars) basis for thirteen consecutive weeks.

What was the problem? Brinkley recalled that things got so bad that there was talk of replacing Huntley—talk credible enough that Huntley bought farmland and readied himself to get out of the news business. But it wasn't Huntley and Brinkley. There was more than that going on.

In the early 1950s, television news was much later in the programming schedule. Only the little-watched ABC news came on at 7:15. CBS aired the news at 7:30, and NBC waited until 7:45. Presumably, the news made a good lead-in for the prime time entertainment programming, which started at eight o'clock. During the days of John Cameron Swayze and the early 1950s, NBC, the peacock station, ruled at eight o'clock. All of its eight o'clock shows were top-fifteen rated programs.

By 1957, all three network news shows fell out of the top fifteen or off the air. Meanwhile, CBS and ABC debuted their own top-fifteen programs, not only in the eight o'clock slot, but also at 7:30. The key was that ABC and CBS competed against other news shows or local programming. NBC didn't compete against one broadcast—it competed against one every night.

In 1956, very few families had a second television—how many of us recall the generation-gap battle over what to watch (or later, what show would play on the color set)? To watch Douglas Edwards, you had to skip local programming from NBC and John Daly on ABC. To watch *Huntley-Brinkley* that season required explaining to the family why there would be no *Robin Hood*, *Disneyland*, *Lone Ranger*, *Rin Tin Tin*, or *My Friend Flicka*. One can almost hear the plaintive wailing of the young children echo across the decades, condemning NBC to singles and empty-nesters.

During the 1957–58 season, after the endless sustaining summer, the broadcast was moved out of prime time and into the early evening position it holds today. Ratings began to climb immediately, and Texaco signed on as exclusive sponsor. There was a corresponding increase in the news budget, and *Huntley-Brinkley* was on its way. It caught up with Douglas Edwards in 1958 and held the lead unchallenged from 1960 to 1967.

Huntley and Brinkley were celebrated for a rapport that, in many ways, was an artifice of television. Brinkley was in Washington, and Huntley was in New York. They were friends, but not intimates. They visited each other and were joined at broadcast time via monitors in the studio, but the seamless world of "Chet" and "David" was something the viewer experienced like a special effect. In fact, even using each other's names when switching back and forth was an artifice. It let the control people in New York know when to switch the signal to Washington, and when to switch it back.

Brinkley had never met anyone quite like Chet Huntley. He often tells a story about Huntley seeing the local Washington weathergirl in the background of Brinkley's monitor and asking, "Who's that?" Brinkley explained that it was the weathergirl. "Is she married?" Huntley asked. Within a month, Huntley was down in Washington to court her. In two months, they were married.

By 1960, the *Huntley-Brinkley Report* was firmly established on the broadcast landscape, and with the conventions coming up, it was CBS that was shuffling to try to make an impact. Despite Cronkite's impressive record of success, there was talk of pairing him with Murrow. That said more that was positive about the impact of Huntley and Brinkley than a negative on

Cronkite. CBS did pair Cronkite with Murrow, the coverage was not the success that Cronkite had enjoyed as sole anchor, and Huntley and Brinkley had their biggest success to date.

The Kennedy Years

In 1962, Cronkite was given the anchor job at CBS, and the networks prepared to do battle. Chet Huntley was solid through the Cuban Missile Crisis, and Brinkley, while busy getting the latest information from the Washington bureau, had a questioning tone in his voice. Walter Cronkite had just taken over for Douglas Edwards at CBS, and there were now two horses in the evening news race. Those days in October, 1962, were critical ones for both networks. People sampled Cronkite as an alternative to the steadfast NBC news programming. ABC rotated anchor people and tinkered with a late-night news broadcast. There was no question that the *Huntley-Brinkley Report* had clout.

In 1962, President Kennedy was angered by a report aired on the *Report*, which included a "long speech by somebody who took the president apart". Kennedy called in Chairman of the Federal Communications Commission (FCC) Newton Minow, who remembered the conversation this way:

> JFK: Did you see that goddamn thing on *Huntley-Brinkley*?
> MINOW: Yes.
>
> JFK: I thought they were supposed to be our friends. I want you to do something about that. You do something about that.

The popular interpretation of the event was that Kennedy tried to get Huntley and Brinkley taken off the air, which Minow denies. But it is an important marker in the continuing story of the influence of the anchors.

JFK wasn't only struggling with Labor and Castro, but also

with what was going on in Vietnam. A memorable broadcast on NBC was the night that Huntley and Brinkley interviewed Kennedy about our role there:

HUNTLEY: Are we likely to reduce our aid to South Vietnam now?

JFK: I don't think we think that would be helpful at this time. If you reduce your aid, it is possible you could have some effect upon the government structure there. On the other hand, you might have a situation which could bring about a collapse. Strongly in our mind is what happened in the case of China at the end of World War II, where China was lost a weak government became increasingly unable to control events. We don't want that.

BRINKLEY: Mr. President, have you had any reason to doubt this so-called "domino theory" that if South Vietnam falls, the rest of Southeast Asia will go behind it?

JFK: No, I believe it. I believe it. I think that the struggle is close enough. China is so large, looms so high just beyond the frontiers, that if South Vietnam went, it would not only give them an improved geographic position for a guerrilla assault on Malaya, but would also give the impression that the wave of the future in Southeast Asia was China and the Communists. So I believe it.

The news broadcasts made their historic leap to thirty minutes in 1963, with CBS leading and NBC immediately matching. The increased time doubled sponsorship revenue and more than doubled the impact of the news on the country. The anchors had more prominence than ever, and their news choices were lauded by most. There was a backlash by conservatives, however, who resented the New York–Washington nexus on principle, as well as what they regarded as undue bias toward liberal viewpoints and causes.

Before that debate was fully engaged, the nation was rocked by the Kennedy assassination. The nation turned to Cronkite and *Huntley-Brinkley* on the network news in greater numbers than ever before. Immediately after the shooting, Robert Mac-Neil, the NBC reporter in Dallas, was frantic to find a phone to report what had happened. There is a story that MacNeil ran into Lee Harvey Oswald, who was just leaving the Book Depository, and asked where the nearest phone was. Oswald actually escorted MacNeil to a phone before heading back to his rooming house, according to police reports.

What happened next is also incredible. MacNeil reached New York and shouted, "This is MacNeil in Dallas!" The person who answered the phone told him to wait a minute, put down the phone, and never came back. Huntley and Brinkley were quickly on the air, but Dan Rather, the CBS bureau chief in Dallas, did not have MacNeil's problems, and CBS had the advantage in immediate coverage. It is Cronkite we remember announcing the president's death.

Two nights later, NBC was the only network that aired the transfer of Lee Harvey Oswald from the city jail to Dallas County jail. CBS and ABC decided to send only film crews. Jack Ruby stepped out of the crowd, shot Oswald, and the story was carried live on NBC.

Brinkley was more involved in the aftermath of the assassination than most people know. He wrote that a few days after the assassination of JFK, Robert and Ted Kennedy, along with their wives, visited Brinkley at his Chevy Chase home. They were "drained and tired and in need of a little company outside the family," Brinkley writes. It was "the first time any of them had been out since the funeral."

The nation turned to television that winter of 1963–64, with a crippling news strike in New York coupled with the bleakness of the season and the gloom of the assassination hanging over everyone. Four of the fifty top-rated television programs of all time came from that long winter, a record only exceeded in 1977 and 1983, when the mini-series *Roots* and the *Thorn Birds* were aired, respectively.

A Ratings War: Who Crosses the Line?

Seven months after the Kennedy assassination, it was time for the 1964 Republican convention at the Cow Palace in San Francisco. Brinkley remembers it as an orgy of excitement over Barry Goldwater and an orgy of loathing directed at the news media—David Brinkley and Chet Huntley most prominent among them. Former President Eisenhower gave a speech in which he criticized the influence of the television news anchors, and his mild, if critical, remarks led to thunderous ovations, demonstrations on the floor, and daily threats of violence against the television anchors.

Huntley and Brinkley had arrived. In eight short years, they rose from obscurity to that—the punching bag for a rallying conservative moment. Part of it was residual anti-communism of the 1950s style, part was the new activities of the ultra–right-wing John Birch Society, and part was due to the unrest that the Civil Rights movement was uncovering in many sections of the country.

Part also was due simply to the overwhelming influence of the network news and the awesome responsibility of the anchors as the managing editors of their programs. The preeminence of the anchors reached the point where President Lyndon Johnson once tracked Brinkley down at a Sunday picnic and sent a helicopter to spirit him away to Camp David for dinner and a movie. Reason? To quiz him about why Washington intellectuals disliked him so much.

The convention coverage pitted Cronkite against *Huntley-Brinkley*, but NBC had the added advantage of an experienced and charismatic group of correspondents: Sander Vanocur,

John Chancellor, and Frank McGee. Both CBS and NBC offered substance, but NBC was perceived by everyone as the style leader, and the anchors were singled out for their entertaining coverage of a difficult convention.

The convention was conducted against a backdrop of the Civil Rights movement, the state's rights resistance, the growing war in Vietnam, the nerve-wracking nuclear stalemate in the Cold War, the still-unsettled Cuban situation, and Lyndon Johnson's plans to launch a series of government programs that came to be known as the "Great Society".

The Republicans were hostile. Not only to the anchors, which could be understood, and the Democrats, which was traditional, but to their own. New York Governor Nelson Rockefeller was described by Teddy White in *The Making of the President 1964*: "This was the man who called them kooks and now, like kooks, they responded to prove his point . . . as he taunted them, they raged. Nor did they, apparently, know what they were raging at: the East, or New York, or Communists, or liberals."

It was public, it was ugly, it was nearly violent, and it was stunning television. The *Columbia Journalism Review* reported: "So potent was the *Huntley-Brinkley* synergy that after the 1964 Republican convention in San Francisco, CBS, in a panic, ejected Walter Cronkite from his anchor seat and replaced him with their own dynamic duo (Robert Trout and Roger Mudd), a team that fared even worse in the ratings war against the surging NBC News." During the Democratic conclave in Atlantic City that year, the *Huntley-Brinkley* coverage, at one point, earned an astonishing 84 percent of the tuned-in audience, perhaps the highest share in television history.

Brinkley continue to regard the conventions as boring. "The sad truth," he said, "is that people who don't live here [in Washington] don't give a darn."

About his success, he was aware of the ratings, but remained self-effacing about the success he and Huntley had. "The one function that TV news performs very well is that when there is no news, we give it to you with the same emphasis as if it were," he wrote. But he was proud of their success because he believed that it validated their concept of an accurate, truthful, straightforward newscast.

By 1965, their audience grew to more than twenty million viewers, and, according to a published report, Huntley and Brinkley were more recognizable to American adults than such famous stars as Cary Grant, James Stewart, or the Beatles.

The anchors settled into a nightly routine of news and commentary. They received approximately two hundred thousand dollars a year, which, in those days, was a significant salary for news anchors. Over at CBS, Cronkite plugged away and slowly gained ground in the ratings.

The undoing of the *Huntley-Brinkley Report* began during, of all things, a labor stoppage at NBC in 1967. The American Federation of Television and Radio Artists (AFTRA), to which both Brinkley and Huntley were required to belong, called a strike. Neither was particularly well informed as to what exactly the strike was about. It ultimately came down to a dispute over royalties that had nothing to do with the news. Nevertheless, the union was striking, they were in the union, and people wanted to know what they would do about it.

For once, the pair couldn't get it together. Brinkley, although he opposed the strike, respected the picket line. Huntley disregarded the strike, the union, and Brinkley, and went on the air. The headline on the first page of the *New York Daily News* read: CHET TALKS, DAVE WALKS. Mail ran heavily against them. Brinkley was in hot water for perceived greed, Huntley for perceived insensitivity. Since they had disagreed publicly, they couldn't even defend the other's position.

"I'm Not Going to Get Into the Gutter . . ."

By the end of 1967, the long-running dominance of *Huntley-Brinkley* was over, and they were neck-and-neck with Cronkite in the ratings. The loss of John Chancellor to the *Voice of America* hadn't helped: the up-and-comers were now the second echelon at CBS, reporters like Harry Reasoner and Dan Rather.

Huntley and Brinkley also seemed to have difficulties meshing on the coverage of Vietnam. Huntley was the hawk. Brinkley was more circumspect. Privately, he asked President Johnson why he kept the war going when he had no reason to do so and got such terrible coverage from the press. Johnson told him that he would not be the first president to lose a war. Simple as that.

With Nixon's election in 1968, the premium on trust began to reach epic proportions. Nixon ran his press relations like siege warfare. The Nixon Administration eventually collapsed under the weight of the Watergate scandals. But his presidency outlasted the *Huntley-Brinkley Report* and, in fact, Chet Huntley.

The Nixon years began on a high note with a notable Inaugural Address aimed at conciliation, rather than inflammation. But by November, the Nixon Administration saw the television "establishment" as a legitimate target for their attacks and a rallying point for the conservative movement. What was remarkable about a November 13, 1969, speech by Vice President Agnew was neither the polemic tone nor some of the issues raised. What was remarkable was the fact that he made the speech so far outside of the political "season" and that it contrasted with the perspective offered by Nixon in the campaign. Politicians campaign with rhetoric and move to the pragmatic center in government. But now what had been perceived in 1964 as campaign rhetoric was now being pursued as administration policy. Agnew's words reverberate even today in the debates over network news bias long after the journalists cited are gone:

> We cannot measure this power and influence by traditional democratic standards. They can make or break—by their coverage and commentary—a moratorium on the war. They can elevate men from local obscurity to national prominence within a week. They can reward some politicians with national exposure and ignore others. For millions of Americans, the network reporter who covers a continuing issue, like ABM or civil rights, becomes, in effect, the presiding judge in a national trial by jury.
>
> We do know that, to a man, these commentators and producers live and work in the geographic and political confines of Washington, D.C. or New York City—the latter of which James Reston terms the "most unrepresentative community in the entire United States." Both communities bask in their own provincialism, their own parochialism. We can deduce that these men thus read the same newspapers and draw their political and social views from the same sources. Worse, they talk constantly to one another, thereby providing artificial reinforcement of their own viewpoints.
>
> Less than a week before the 1968 election, [ABC's Frank Reynolds] charged that President Nixon's campaign commitments were no more durable than campaign balloons. He claimed, were it not for fear of a hostile reaction, Richard Nixon would be giving into, and I quote the commentator, "his natural instinct to smash the enemy with a club or go after him with a meat-axe." Had this slander been made by one political candidate about another, it would have been dismissed by most commentators as a partisan assault. But this attack emanated from the privileged sanctuary of a network studio and therefore had the apparent dignity of an objective statement.
>
> We have heard demands that senators and congressmen and judges make known their financial connections—so that the public will know who and what influences their decisions or votes. Strong arguments can be made for that view. But

when a single commentator or producer, night after night, determines for millions of people how much of each side of a great issue they are going to see and hear, should he not first disclose his personal views on the issue as well?

[The networks should] turn their critical powers on themselves. They are challenged to direct their energy, talent, and conviction toward improving the quality and objectivity of news presentation. . . . And the people of America are challenged too. . . . This is one case where the people must defend themselves, where the citizen—not the government—must be the reformer, where the consumer can be the most effective crusader.

We would never trust such powers I've described over public opinion in the hands of an elected government. It is time we questioned it in the hands of a small and unelected elite. The great networks have dominated America's airwaves for decades. The people are entitled to a full accounting of their stewardship.

I'm not asking for government censorship. . . . I'm asking whether a form of censorship already exists when the news that forty million Americans receive each night is determined by a handful of men responsible only to their corporate employers.

The speech was well received by supporters of the administration, but it polarized the nation. Huntley simply and famously responded: "I'm not going to get into the gutter with that guy." And he packed up, resigned, and left the network within eight months. Declining ratings, a difficult social environment, and the attacks of the administration took their toll.

Brinkley responded with irrefutable logic: "If I were objective or if you were objective or if anyone was, he would have to be put away somewhere in an institution because he'd be some sort of vegetable."

Huntley came back to the subject again. "Journalists were never intended to be the cheerleaders of a society, the conductors of applause, the sycophants. Tragically, that is their assigned role in authoritarian societies, but not here—not yet. [I used to believe] the government was the answer to all our problems. But the . . . government, I've concluded, is now an insufferable jungle of self-serving bureaucrats."

Goodnight David, Goodnight Chet

Courtesy of Globe Photo/NBC

The infamous "goodnight" closing was last heard on NBC on July 31, 1970. But instead of the traditional closing, Huntley left his audience with one final plea: "Be patient and have courage—there will be better and happier news some day, if we work at it."

NBC gave Huntley a horse, and back to Montana he went. There, he developed a resort called Big Sky, but fell ill with stomach cancer and died in March, 1974.

The administration continued to step up its campaign, commissioning a private poll comparing Brinkley to Cronkite, intending to circulate the results if it painted Brinkley in a bad light. It urged NBC advertisers to complain to the network. Undaunted, David Brinkley saw Nixon as just another politician with an attitude.

David Brinkley stayed on the air, and NBC began playing musical anchor chairs, using Frank McGee and John Chancellor seven nights a week under the title, *NBC Nightly News*. The experiment confused viewers more than entertained them, as if NBC had learned little from Huntley and Brinkley of the vital importance of continuity.

When in 1971 John Chancellor became the lone anchor, David Brinkley continued to work at NBC doing one award-winning documentary after another. He was back on the broadcast between 1976 and 1979 when Chancellor's ratings sagged, but the partnership did not work as expected. Although ratings were solid, they were not spectacular. Brinkley came off, and in a few years, Chancellor left too, leaving the chair to Tom Brokaw.

Brokaw credits Huntley and Brinkley as a major influence on his own career:

> I grew up with Huntley and Brinkley and their wonderfully contrasting styles. I watched them carefully. Not so much on the night-to-night basis as much as I did on election coverage or special coverage. I was particularly taken by David's ability to always develop a narrative and form and shape his information into a sort of anecdotal style. He had a wonderful way of punctuating each word and his pieces of information before he handed off to another correspondent. And there was a little telling story at the very end or some other piece of information that you were led into. He was a real craftsman. He was a wonderful writer, and I think he wrote beautifully.

In 1981, Roone Arledge asked Brinkley to join ABC as a Washington insider, and he took to the air on the alphabet network with *This Week with David Brinkley*. The show was developed by Arledge as part of his major expansion of ABC News—even to the point of giving the show the temporary name, *This Week with ——.* The *Wagon Train* approach was back in place, courtesy of Arledge, who learned so much in such a short time at ABC News. There was the regular newscast, the ever-changing story, and big weekly guest star. Each member of the cast was chosen for distinction as a journalist or commentator, but also they mixed together beautifully: Sam Donaldson for the tough question; George Will for the thought-provoking commentary; Cokie Roberts for an encyclopedic knowledge of issues, facts, and personalities; and Brinkley for his wit and ironic detachment, as well as his considerable skill at managing a roundtable. *This Week with David Brinkley* became known for thoughtfulness, grace, gentility, and excellence. In many ways, it is a legacy that is the equal of *Huntley-Brinkley's.* It also was a considerable success in terms of ratings, proving once again that it is possible to have journalistic and commercial success.

Brinkley became one of the few journalists to receive the Medal of Freedom, all the more remarkable given that he was a Washington-based correspondent. The others were New York journalists who could take a more detached view of Washington than Brinkley. He wrote two bestsellers and hosted a number of documentaries before announcing his retirement.

He spoke only occasionally about Huntley, but always with warmth and praise. "A successful man is one who can lay a firm foundation with the bricks that others throw at him," he said. They were hit with bricks from the industry when they were new and unproven, hit with bricks from politicians when they were at their peak. According to Brinkley's formula, they had enough bricks to build a very firm foundation indeed.

Their beneficiaries are all of us who were in the living room during the years they were on the air. In the future, people will see in their teamwork, structure, and poise an elegant example of how to win and hold an audience while delivering the news and nothing but the news.

Walter Cronkite, CBS

K*ronkiter* is a Swedish word that appeared in the language approximately forty years ago. It means "to anchor a news broadcast." No one since has thought such a succinct way to say it as the Swedes: Walter Cronkite remains, to many observers, the one true king, the quintessential anchor. Moreover, he was like everyone's favorite uncle, thus he was known in some circles as "Uncle Walter".

The term *anchor* was developed, in fact, to describe him. Don Hewitt recalls that it came from the 1952 conventions. Cronkite was appointed as the key member of the coverage team. In planning the broadcast, the producers compared the broadcast to a track relay; Cronkite was the key man, or "the anchor".

From the first, then, Walter Cronkite was billed as anchor, but, in those days, it was a technical term devoid of real loyalty. He did have, even as early as 1952, a certain air of authority when it came to news broadcasts. In fact, a key strength throughout his career was the smooth, calm, dignified manner with which he handled the most complex of events. It was an authority that was greatly aided by his appearance. For he was pleasant looking, but no matinee idol. Despite his long years in New York, he retained an appearance of midwestern solidity. Rin Powell wrote, "Walter Cronkite looked less like an Eastern intellectual than a Tulsa general practitioner."

His news-reporting style was crisp and fact-focused, honed by years of service with the deadline-oriented wire services. Those years taught him well how to cope with the heavy and insistent flow of world news and how to cut through events with a broad, simple storyline to which facts clung. He was a "front page editor" of the first rank.

When viewers came to know Cronkite better in the 1950s, the admiration for his editing skills was complemented by an appreciation of his considerable talent for improvisation. It came out at the conventions, where storylines changed instantaneously, and moments of genuine drama were often joined by periods of sudden dead time which needed filling.

For his entire career, he retained a reporter's instinct for fact and storyline and an aversion to overt commentary or emotionalism. But because of his absolute commitment to "just the facts," viewers became aware, without anyone telling them, of his evident distaste for lying and prevarication. It often showed through his reporter's mask; he became indelibly associated with the truth. Because viewers discovered it long before anyone rolled it up into a promotional line, they always felt like they had a relationship with Walter Cronkite. He wasn't fed to them as a hollow image by marketing geniuses. He was a pause in their day that was welcome, trusted, and delightful.

A *New York Times* editorial stated, "People know that newspapers can make mistakes. But they are convinced that Walter Cronkite has never lied to them." By 1966, an Oliver Quayle survey identified him as the most trusted figure in America. People liked the fact that the man who visited them in their living rooms every evening had no axe to grind, was not an issues-monger, or even much of a commentator. Biographer Doug James wrote, "His approach was not so much a cold and disembodied television network news reader as a caring and concerned Victorian father who gathered his family around him in the parlor after dinner to read the newspaper aloud and explain the days' events."

James's comments are written with real insight, for everything about Cronkite's delivery style suggested storytelling in a parlor room. It began with the deep, steady *basso profundo* of a father's voice—not the shrillness of the speaking platform, the tense syllables of debate, the rapid fluctuation in tone of humor or stress, or the drawled half-sentences of ordinary communications in the home. His tone was rich, well-modulated, and came from deep in the larynx and diaphragm like the voices of all the great singers.

There was a cadence to his words, with much of it (including his famous tag line, "and that's the way it is") written in that most flexible and hypnotic of meters, the iambic trimeter of Sophocles and Aeschylus. It was a rhythm that predated not only the Teleprompter, but the English language itself. It was developed in the theaters of the classical era, when the great tragedies were passed along through telling, not reading.

His posture would pass muster at any Toastmasters gathering, with no clenching of script or tightening of facial muscles to convey tension or nerves. No hunching of shoulders, no darting of eyes. Steady as a good ship.

The longer he stayed in people's living rooms, the more they saw that he was driven by values more than issues. The values shone through even when he took no direct position on the issues before the country.

A True Trailblazer

Walter Cronkite was born in St. Joseph, Missouri, on November 4, 1916, in the town that was the starting point of the Oregon and California Trails. His family relocated to Kansas City when he was one year old, and to Texas when he was eleven. Of the three locations, Kansas City was his town.

His first newspaper jobs were on the San Jacinto High School newspaper and the *Daily Texan* at the University of Texas in Austin. He covered sports for the latter, but he dropped out of college in 1935, when he hooked on as a reporter with the *Houston Press*. His assignments were mundane, covering the firehouse to the pulpit.

Walter Cronkite was a legendary stickler for accuracy, and he learned his lessons at the *Press*. In his memoir, *A Reporter's Life*, he wrote:

> "Cronkite!"
>
> The barely innocent-until-proven-guilty hastened to the dock.
>
> "The *Chronicle* spells this guy's name S-m-y-t-h. We've got it S-m-i-t-h. Which is it?" Or, "The Chronicle says it was at 1412, we say 1414 Westheimer. Who's right?"
>
> He was a stickler for accuracy, but most editors were in those days. They understood a fundamental truth about newspapers and how the public perceived them. One mistake—"y" or "i," "1412" or "1414"—standing alone didn't make that much difference perhaps. But for each such mistake,

there was a given number of readers who recognized the errors and whose trust in the paper was diminished thereby. And each of them probably told their friends, and the circle of doubt grew thereby.

Cronkite tired of the mundane assignments and low pay, and, in 1936, he took a job as news and sports reporter at KCMO, a one hundred–watt station in Kansas City. In those days, KCMO could not afford remote football broadcasts, and so Cronkite re-created the game based on wire-service teletype copy. It was a technique used also by a young Ronald Reagan at WHO in Des Moines, Iowa.

Over the next three years, Cronkite took a series of jobs: United Press in 1937, WKY Oklahoma City in the fall of 1937 as the football announcer, a publicity job with Braniff, then back to United Press in Kansas City in 1939 as a night editor.

Kansas City was a key stop—perhaps *the* key stop—in Cronkite's career. "I don't think there's a tougher job than that," he recalled with Doug James. "I didn't just work in the newsroom. I was the newsroom. In effect, I was making up the front pages of the small dailies."

Cronkite's job was to edit stories from the East and West Coasts and relay them to UP newspapers and subscribers. The teletype circuits of the day all terminated in Kansas City, so it was the critical relay station in the network, connecting the eastern and western news feeds, as well as the regional, state, and local wires. "Banks of teletype machines clattered twenty-four–hours a day," Cronkite recalled in *A Reporter's Life*. "An insatiable maw demanding sixty words of copy every minute."

"The night wire from New York opened at three o'clock," recalled Cronkite's colleague, Margaret Richards. "The wires which Kansas City relayed opened at five o'clock. The New York circuit was a double trunk—two wires. So when your wire opened, you already had an accumulation of four hours of copy staring you in the face."

The essence of the United Press operation was the creation of a "front page" of the news under immense time pressure. This daily grind was doubled with an emphasis on accuracy and speed because of the intense competition with the Associated Press. Cronkite operated a similar service in Kansas City to the one he later ran in his years at CBS, creating a national "front page" service for the evening news broadcast.

"It was a blistering, relentless battle," he recalled. "It was said that somewhere in the United States or among our worldwide clients, there was a paper going to press every minute. It meant that we faced a deadline every minute. I haven't the slightest doubt that at least a period of press service apprenticeship should be mandatory for anyone who pretends to a career in journalism."

When the war broke out, Cronkite was assigned to New York and then London. Overseas, he became part of an elite group of writers that became known as the Writing 69th. He also landed with invading troops in North Africa, went on B-17 raids over Germany, watched the airborne land in Holland, and was there for the Normandy landing. After the war, he spoke with *Look* magazine about his war service:

> People take a look at my record, and it sounds great. I'm embarrassed when I'm introduced for speeches and somebody takes a CBS handout and reads it because it makes me sound like some sort of hero: the battle of the North Atlantic, the landing in Africa, the beachhead on D-day, dropping with the 101st Airborne, the Battle of the Bulge. I was scared to death all the time. I did everything possible to avoid getting into combat. Except the ultimate thing of not doing it. I did it. But the truth is that I did everything only once. It didn't take any great courage to do it once. If you go back and do it a second time, knowing how bad it is, that's courage.

Cronkite went on to cover the Nuremberg trials of Göring, Hess, and other top Nazis. From 1946 to 1948, he was chief correspondent for United Press in Moscow. It was a prestigious assignment, but not a productive one, owing to the stringent censorship that existed at the time, mangling most manuscripts except regurgitated Soviet press releases.

Cronkite remembered: "It was psychologically difficult for any reporter from the Western countries. Two years in Russia was two years under arrest, practically. Not behind bars, but no freedom of movement whatsoever. To get a car, you had to hire a driver because the whole purpose of this was to keep track of foreigners. All these people worked for the secret police. And that's how they kept track of you."

Setting a (President) or Two

When he returned to the States in 1948, he was unsure what step to take next in his career. He opted to strike out on his

own, serving as Washington correspondent for a syndicate of ten midwestern radio stations. In 1950, he joined CBS News and moved into television, initially serving as news anchor for the CBS's WTOP in Washington.

It was primitive, featuring overly bright and hot studio lights with fuzzy reception in many homes. Plus, he was at the local D.C. television station. Cronkite was initially disappointed, not only because of this questionable assignment, but because the original plan called for him to serve as a CBS correspondent in Korea. Cronkite put his head down, plugged away, made his mark, and, in 1951, he was given a job as moderator of *Man of the Week*, a competitor of *Meet the Press*.

In 1952, he got his breakthrough opportunity when he was invited to anchor the CBS convention coverage. Cronkite was not the network's first choice, but Murrow and Charles Collingwood declined the opportunity. Sig Mickelson, the CBS news director, surprised many by pushing for Cronkite over other CBS figures, such as Robert Trout and Douglas Edwards. Everyone at CBS knew of Cronkite's credentials as a solid journalist and the fine job he had done at WTOP, but what Mickelson saw was an ability to improvise dialogue in a way that complemented the television picture rather than overwhelmed it. He saw Cronkite talking to the monitor. No one else had done that. Cronkite, with less radio experience than any other major CBS figure, had picked up on a critical difference between television and radio journalism: the talkative, descriptive, "hot" style of radio was not needed. The medium demanded a "cool" style.

The year 1952 was crucial to CBS News because the two coasts were hooked up for the first time, and Mickelson figured that the conventions would represent a turning point in network coverage. First, they were always big news in that era. Second, with Truman retiring, both parties were choosing new candidates, and it promised to be a particularly exciting season.

On July 7, 1952, the Republican convention got under way in Chicago, and, by the end of the day, news had changed. Radio was swept aside, and a new star was born. The loud, gaudy, long-winded, smoke-filled political conventions that hardly changed their formats in thirty years transformed themselves within weeks of being covered on national television for the first time. President Harry Truman followed the first two days of the Democratic convention via television, watching it "in flight" on his presidential plane, *Independence.* Much of the American public watched it as well, and, in 1952, the conventions began the long march from smoke-filled room to balloon-filled political commercial.

Cronkite brought all the skills he honed working the overnight wire in Kansas City, as well as an unmatched ability to work solo on multiple stories and angles at the same time, to the convention coverage. He worked off ten television monitors (six brought him floor pictures, four broke down the balloting by geographic region), two independent earphones with chatter coming simultaneously, and had a writer who passed him notes up through the desk. With thirteen independent sources of information, he was able to maintain a focus on the camera, a cool demeanor, and an ability to improvise dialogue to fill any combination of events, pictures, or to fill a lull. Mickelson and director Don Hewitt provided him with a horn-of-plenty of information, and he handled it with the aplomb of a true son of United Press.

When the convention season was over, Cronkite was quickly reassigned to the prominent national programs, *Twentieth Century, Eyewitness to History,* and, a personal favorite of his, *You Are There.* The latter was a program John Charles Daly had hosted before moving to ABC. It recreated famous moments in history.

Cronkite also was selected to anchor the election night coverage in November, when CBS became the first to "call" the election, with an indication at 8:30 P.M. that Eisenhower would win by a landslide. The forecast was provided by Univac, a computer, marking the first time one that one was used on a newscast. Univac's initial prediction of 488 electoral votes for Eisenhower caused a sensation in the CBS newsroom, and the CBS news team did not announce the forecast. Two more forecasts were made, and still CBS was the first to call the election for Eisenhower. The Univac was within four electoral votes of Eisenhower's actual total of 442, and the result helped CBS further burnish its growing reputation for election night coverage.

Walter Cronkite became the first anchorman to cover presidents one-on-one. He covered Truman and Eisenhower as a journalist and taped one-on-one interviews with Kennedy, Johnson, Nixon, and Carter as an anchor.

He was critical of the flash judgments pronounced on Truman and Eisenhower by the press corps. "I'd known of Harry Truman quite well living in Kansas City. My father was in the same battalion with him in the war, and my uncle knew him quite well from his haberdashery right across from my uncle's office. I thought of him as a member of the Pendergast machine and just another kind of county seat politician."

But Truman's performance changed his mind. "I think he'll go down in history as one of the greats because of his conscience, his determination to stick with what he knew was right."

About Eisenhower, Cronkite recalled:

> . . . The common wisdom among the press corps in Washington was that he operated the White House on a staff basis and probably wasn't very familiar with a lot of the things his

underlings were doing. The old image of him playing golf in the Oval Office was the image that a lot of us had until I started traveling and spending some time with him. This was after his presidency, when we made the D-day trip; we spent a week together, revisiting the principal sites of the Normandy invasion. . . . I was amazed—overwhelmed—by his intimate knowledge of what had gone on. I sat there with a lap full of notes, he had none, and there wasn't a single question that I brought up that he wasn't entirely conversant with and quite [at ease] about discussing. So I decided that our flash judgments in Washington were wrong.

The Murrow-to-Cronkite Transition

It was during the mid-1950s that a serious professional rift began to develop between Murrow and Cronkite. Today, Cronkite is generous in his comments about Murrow, particularly for his radio commentary and his performance during the McCarthy period.

Cronkite said, "There are very few occasions where even a powerful broadcaster like Murrow can actually change the direction of history by a broadcast. It could be said that Murrow did so with his McCarthy broadcast. I don't think there's any doubt that that broadcast is an example of the exception when a broadcast could change the course of history."

But in the mid-1950s, Cronkite and Murrow represented two different species of journalist. Both were skilled news presenters with a solid grasp of how to dramatize news. Both shared an extremely high standard, a belief in the importance of independent news organizations, and the need for a vibrant "Fourth Estate." But they were from different universes when it came to basic journalism—Cronkite was essentially a "front page" editor, and Murrow was an "op-ed page" editor. Murrow saw the anchorman not only as a trusted news source, but also as an informed commentator who could, would, and should take positions on major issues of the day. Cronkite was not comfortable with that. He was not the type of anchor who did broadcasts of the type that Murrow's McCarthy broadcast epitomized.

The role of an anchor evolved to be more in the Cronkite style: *Dragnet*-like, "just the facts, ma'am," with the occasional arched eyebrow or hint of a smile as a reaction to a news item. Classic Murrow anchoring—part reporter, part public defender—eventually evolved into a separate and lesser commentator role. There are fewer commentators now, but they were considered integral to CBS broadcasts of the 1960s and 1970s. Howard K. Smith, Harry Reasoner, and, eventually, John Chancellor fell into the category of great commentators and fine anchors who, forced to choose, had difficulty finding their proper specialization.

When Murrow's star began to wane in the late 1950s, it was natural to assume that Cronkite's star would rise more rapidly. But Cronkite had a reputation as a hard-nosed reporter, and because he took on a number of "soft" projects, his star dimmed. In 1954, CBS launched a morning show to compete with NBC's *Today* called, memorably, *Morning Show*. Cronkite, in this case, was not given the newscasting responsibility. It was assigned to Charles Collingwood. Instead, Cronkite was given the job as host. He was given two puppets, Charlemagne the Lion and Humphrey the Hound-Dog, as sidekicks.

Further, Cronkite's reputation was hurt when he sought to host a game show in the 1950s, which prompted the network to issue a policy banning news personnel from hosting entertainment programming. It is ironic that CBS did this because their own Sunday night hit game show, *What's My Line?*, was hosted by the ABC news anchor John Daly. Nevertheless, the policy was implemented and still stands.

Cronkite continued as a noted correspondent. He hosted the 1956 conventions again to general acclaim, but his thunder that year was stolen by NBC, which had paired Huntley and Brinkley together in a format so popular that they were awarded the network news soon after. Their broadcast rapidly became the most popular in the country, outpacing Douglas Edwards of CBS.

By 1962, Cronkite's reputation was fully rehabilitated following a successful 1960 season of political coverage and because of his work as chief correspondent for the CBS public affairs show, *Eyewitness*. Meanwhile, it seemed that Douglas Edwards, with the *Evening News*, fell permanently behind *Huntley-Brinkley*. Bill Paley asked for a change of anchor on the CBS *Evening News* and got it. Cronkite was appointed in 1962.

The transition went smoothly on the surface. Edwards was extremely gracious in the transition, surprising Cronkite. Don Hewitt was retained as director. However, when Cronkite debuted, the ratings on CBS actually fell. There were negative commentaries written in local newspapers and thousands of angry calls to the network.

CBS decided to give the news division a boost and the viewers fifteen more minutes of news in September of 1963. The inaugural broadcast was an exclusive interview with President Kennedy. Cronkite remembered that night: "It was very special getting that interview with Kennedy. It was promised to us with the president up at Hyannisport at his home." But the day before the interview, Cronkite was upset that the Associated Press reported that the president was going to make an important statement about Vietnam during his interview. Cronkite said, "I went to Pierre Salinger, the president's press secretary, and said if you planted this thing with the AP, I want you to know something—just because you did, I'm *not* going to ask anything about Vietnam." Cronkite admits he learned a lesson when the president brought up Vietnam on his own. "What I was, of course, to naïve to realize, was that I didn't control the interview, the interviewee controls the interview. If the interviewee wants to pop up with something, it doesn't matter whether you ask him a question or not."

Thirteen Days of Hell

In October, the Cuban Missile crisis riveted the nation to the news for thirteen days. Nuclear missiles were deployed in Cuba, and there was a real possibility that the United States would end up at war with the Soviet Union, which would target American cities. At age ten, I had a hard time grasping what was actually going on until my father sat me down in front of the TV and made me watch the news. And there was Cronkite, with his glasses in his hand, explaining to the nation what was going on. I suddenly got very quiet and was scared to death.

"We were all scared to death," Cronkite remembers. "We just didn't know whether this was going to evolve into a nuclear exchange or not. If you remember, through days of the crisis we were telling kids how to seek shelter under their desks at school and where to listen for air raid sirens and how to get into the basement which may be a little bit safer place in most buildings. It was not at all comfortable for me or anyone, and the whole nation was in a state of alarm."

There was a sudden and uncompromised level of cooperation between the government and the news media. During the Cuban Missile Crisis, coverage attained a new degree of sophistication. The technology of war took a leap forward during the Eisenhower Administration, and it progressed further during Kennedy's administration because of Defense Secretary Robert McNamara's emphasis on electronic surveillance. American audiences saw, perhaps for the first time, surveillance pictures taken from spy planes, live government briefings, and on-air analysis. The coverage made the country alert, informed, terrified, and yet riveted to broadcasters like Cronkite. Perhaps as well as anyone, Cronkite gauged the popular mood, as Murrow had in his own time.

The United States, faced with the choice of permitting the nuclear missiles or invading Cuba to remove them, had the happy inspiration of ordering a blockade of Cuba. It was technically an act of war, but in the television era, it looked close enough to peace because it effectively cut off the island from the outside world. Days later, President Kennedy addressed the nation to say that Khrushchev had decided to dismantle the missiles aimed at the United States.

"And That's the Way It Is"

Shortly after the missile crisis, CBS management gave the go-ahead for the expansion of the news broadcast from fifteen to thirty minutes. Although affiliates were unhappy about the potential for erosion of their profits, the network finally decided that nothing less than one half hour would give CBS and Cronkite a chance to overtake NBC in the ratings. With the expansion in time, there was a corresponding increase in revenue and budget. A new, modern set was built. The old reliance on film flown in from on-the-scene locations diminished with the advent of satellites and videotape. New news bureaus opened in Atlanta, Los Angeles, and Dallas.

With the introduction of the thirty-minute broadcast, Cronkite introduced the tagline that became his trademark: "And that's the way it is." He said:

> That came from me. Again I was somewhat naïve. I thought moving from fifteen minutes to thirty minutes—I believed that I would have enough time to end the broadcast with the

kind of stories I used to love going on the United Press about the quirks in the news which were just little one to three paragraphs that could be tragic or humorous or exceedingly odd anything that could have lightened the news, the news day, or brought people up to date with a new little aspect of human nature.

So, I thought that would be kind of fun to do at the end of the broadcast, but I realized that if I did, I really had to sign off in some way letting people know that this was not a story of great seriousness that they could expect a lot more information on. I had to sign it off, and in thinking about how I would do it, I realized that I was going to be able to use these stories, and it gave me an opportunity with, "That's the way it is"—to either end with a chuckle or a little tear (not actually), but obviously a little sadness about the story with that kind of a sign-off.

I used it the first night, and Dick Salant, the president of CBS News, who was a stickler for form and straight news reporting, called me into his office and said, "What the devil was that close you got there? I don't like that!" I said, "What don't you like about it?" He said, "You're telling people that's the way it is, and how do you know that's the way it is?" Maybe we made a mistake with the broadcast, and I agreed that that was a problem, but it turned out that almost overnight the sign-off caught on, and by the end of the week, I was still using it. Salant said, "Go ahead and keep it, it's not as bad as I thought it was."

"Three Shots Were Fired"

It was lunchtime on a November day in 1963. Just about everyone was out of the newsroom except Cronkite, who usually ate at his desk. A news editor ran into the room with a piece of wire copy, yelling that the president had just been shot. Cronkite grabbed it and said something to the effect of, "Don't worry about writing it, just get me on the air." Moments later, at 1:40, CBS interrupted *As the World Turns*. Cronkite announced: "In Dallas, Texas, three shots were fired at President Kennedy's motorcade in downtown Dallas. The first reports say that President Kennedy has been seriously wounded by this shooting."

Thomas Doherty, writing for the TV Museum, remembers what happened next:

> Eddie Barker, news director for CBS's Dallas affiliate KRLD-TV, reports live from the Trade Mart, where the president was to have attended a luncheon. As a stationary camera pans the ballroom, closing in on a black waiter who wipes tears from his face, Barker relates rumors "that the president is dead." Back in New York, a voice off camera tells Cronkite the same news, which the anchorman stresses is "totally unconfirmed." Switching back to Dallas, Barker again reports, "The word we have is that the president is dead." Though he cautions, "This we do not know for a fact," the visual image at the Trade Mart is ominous—workman can be seen removing the presidential seal from a podium on the dais.
>
> Behind the scenes, at KRLD's newsroom, CBS's Dallas bureau chief Dan Rather scrambles for information. He learns from two sources at Parkland Hospital that the president has died, a report that goes out prematurely over CBS Radio. Citing Rather, Cronkite reports the president's death, but notes the lack of any official conformation. At 2:37 P.M., CBS news editor Ed Bliss Jr. hands Cronkite an AP wire report. Cronkite takes a long second to read it to himself before intoning: "From Dallas, Texas, the flash, apparently official. President Kennedy died at 1:00 P.M. Central Standard Time, two o'clock Eastern Standard Time," he pauses and looks at the studio clock, "some thirty-eight minutes ago . . ." Momentarily losing his composure, Cronkite winces, removes his eyeglasses, and clears his throat before resuming with the observation that Vice President Lyndon Johnson will presumably take the oath of office to become the thirty-sixth president of the United States.

Of all the actions of the newsmen that day, none is so well remembered as Cronkite removing his glasses and pausing to compose himself. Cronkite emphasizes in his recollections of the event the way in which he stuck to his primary vision of the news anchor as a fact-getter, fact-relater, and fact-explainer. Yet it was neither the first nor the last time we saw Walter Cronkite's humanity.

Of Ratings and Hurt Feelings

The dawn of the Johnson Administration found the nation in mourning. Cronkite was in second place in the ratings and about to face his greatest crisis in his CBS career. He finished out the Johnson Administration as the undisputed anchor of the top-rated evening news. He was also the most trusted man in America and in such a position of perceived power that the incoming vice president, Spiro Agnew, singled out the network news for left-wing bias and blasted them in a number of celebrated attacks.

What happened? The story between 1964 and 1969 is essentially a contrast between Walter Cronkite and President Lyndon Johnson. The facile way to put is that Cronkite, in the 1964 conventions, talked too much, and Johnson, starting in 1965, talked too little. Cronkite's poor performance in the 1964 Republican Convention, when he was roundly criticized for over-talking the coverage, led to his replacement for the Democratic Convention He was offended at being replaced because he felt that he was made a scapegoat for the poor performance of the entire CBS team. He considered resigning from the network. The situation indicated that Cronkite was at his best when there were the fewest hands available and drama was at its highest.

Cronkite was replaced by Roger Mudd and Robert Trout. They

fared even more poorly in the ratings. The *Huntley-Brinkley Report* just killed everyone that season, and so Cronkite promptly was brought back. Beginning in 1965, Cronkite's ratings for the nightly newscast climbed rapidly. At first, he began to close the gap with *Huntley-Brinkley*, and, by 1967, he passed them, then never lost the lead. In 1966, the first survey appeared naming him "the most trusted man in America".

There were two sets of developments. First, the Johnson Administration lost its momentum. As the nation turned from the end of segregation to the war on poverty and the war in Vietnam, support gave way to suspicion. For both efforts, the resources required for victory seemed to grow exponentially with each passing month, and the promised results never seemed to be achieved.

Second, in 1965 and 1966, the United States entered the most active phase of its manned space program. Between 1961 and 1964, six men were launched into space. With the two-man Gemini program, twenty astronauts and ten missions would take place in under two years. The duration of the flights increased dramatically as well, from fifty-four mission hours in Project Mercury to 897 hours in Project Gemini.

While all the network news anchors shared in a general shift of public trust from government to journalists between 1965 and 1975, Cronkite had the added benefit of being the anchor of the CBS space coverage. He benefited from the positive feelings and face time that came with the anchoring of the broadcasts.

"Go, Baby, Go!"

The space program fascinated the public, even if many questioned the enormous cost, and it fascinated Cronkite. Viewers spent hours watching intricate scientific explanations from experts about trajectories, rendezvous, re-entries, docking, and a host of small technical issues that today are greeted with a yawn or, worse, no television coverage at all. But, at the time, it was new, there was the time pressure of the stated goal of landing on the moon before the decade ended, and each team of astronauts was treated not only like the heroes they were, but as celebrities.

Walter Cronkite showed the enthusiastic, almost boyish, side of his personality in his coverage of launches and missions. "Go, baby, go!" he cried at the launch of the Apollo 11 moon landing mission. "Hot diggety dog!" he cried when the lunar lander lifted off again from the moon's surface. The drama was personal to him. He later recalled, "Rocketry was so uncertain then. We had been watching failure after failure— rockets blowing up on the pad, tumbling from the air a few hundred feet up. And now, suddenly, a man was going to sit on top of all that fireworks. I just didn't know whether or not I was going to be able to watch, I was so caught up in it."

Cronkite went through his own intense training for each mission, mastering the subject of rocketry and manned space flight like no correspondent before or since. He visited manufacturers, tracking stations, and assembly buildings. He also spent time with the astronauts and in a number of simulators, from a moon gravity simulator that he rode on camera to an unfilmed ride in the NASA's famed "vomit comet"—a parabolic flight that allowed him to experience weightlessness.

He became known as the "fourth astronaut" during the Apollo missions, renowned for his detailed yet vivid descriptions of the launch and famed for his narrative during the mission itself. The *New York Times* gave kudos for Apollo 11 coverage to CBS: "In alertness, diversity, and know-how, CBS was ahead by a wide margin."

From Apollo 11 forward, Cronkite was paired with Wally

Schirra, a veteran of three flights himself, in what was promoted as, "Walter-to-Walter coverage." It was his most successful pairing. The two got along famously both on camera and off, and those who had written off Cronkite as an "air hog" were forced to reconsider their opinions.

It is fair to speculate that Cronkite's added exposure via the space coverage and the manner in which he used it were the greatest factors in propelling him to a lead in the network news ratings. They also led to his reputation for trust and unshakeable commitment to truth that he maintained for the rest of his career. At the same time, the United States government, increasingly mired in Vietnam and then Watergate, turned away from the Great Society as Johnson envisioned it, toward a "closed society" which Cronkite and CBS did as much as anyone to combat.

A War and a Scandal

Vietnam became even more of a persistent visitor to American living rooms than the space program by 1966. Troop deployments rose tenfold, and the draft began to bite deeply, provoking widespread opposition to the war from young Americans. CBS had numerous correspondents in the field, and reports from faraway Saigon were part of the daily news diet.

Increasingly in 1966 and especially in 1967–68, CBS's coverage offered a different portrait of the war than was offered by the Johnson Administration and General Westmoreland, the ground commander in Vietnam. Correspondents like Morley Safer offered portraits of a total war, including the burning of entire Vietnamese villages. Such a perspective contrasted markedly with the official portrait of a country that gained the upper hand against an illegitimate and unpopular communist insurgency.

Cronkite's famous criticism of the administration's characterization of the state of the war came after the North Vietnamese's Tet Offensive in February, 1968. The problem was that the public had been led to believe that such an offensive was impossible and that victory in Vietnam was just around the corner. Tet was a failure as an offensive, and it became clear that the administration was completely out of touch with the capabilities of the North Vietnamese, their support in the south, and the real prospects for peace. The Tet Offensive was a factor in Johnson's stunning defeat in the 1968 New Hampshire primary to anti-war Senator Eugene McCarthy and Johnson's hurried exit from the presidential race.

But Richard Nixon's election brought neither immediate peace in Vietnam nor an improvement in relations between CBS and the administration. As a matter of fact, the network was the subject of a series of blistering attacks by Vice President Agnew against "media elites" with a "liberal bias". Such a charge was heard during the disastrous 1964 Republican Convention and echoes today in books such as the acclaimed, *Bias: A CBS Insider Exposes How the Media Distorts the News*, by Bernard Goldberg.

Between November 1969 and January 1970, Agnew made a number of celebrated speeches on the topic. Of those surveyed, 49 percent of the country agreed with him that there was liberal bias at the networks, that there was a "tiny, enclosed fraternity of privileged men elected by no one and enjoying a monopoly sanctioned and license". He decried the pursuit of "more action, more excitement, more drama" by the television networks and insisted that they needed to become "more responsive to the views of the nation and more responsive to the people they serve."

Agnew and the Nixon Administration were out of office and in disgrace before these charges were explored fully in national debate. But it is a fair conclusion to draw today that the explosion in television stations and networks radically reduced the influence of the "dozen anchormen, commentators, and executives" cited by Agnew.

However, the proliferation of news sources has not made the charges of bias go away. In fact, the charges have grown more insistent, and the critics within and outside of the news industry have pointed increasingly to a progressive lowering of news standards. So, was Agnew right?

Cronkite didn't think so. He pointed not to a liberal bias, but to the demise of the two-newspaper town as a systematic contributor to the lowering of news standards. The evil, he thought, was not bias—it was monopoly. Yet since 1980, there has been a dramatic increase in the volume of television news. Is the reporting more accurate? Is there less action, less excitement, less drama? In fact, charges of superficial reporting are on the rise. Cronkite's analysis of the news problem was accurate in the 1970s and 1980s, but perhaps more forces are at work today.

While the debate about media bias was revisited but not resolved during the Nixon years, Nixon's fate was resolved by Watergate. By 1973, the problems of his administration were aggressively taken up by the Judiciary Committees in the House and Senate. On October 27–28, 1972, the *CBS Evening News* broadcast two long stories about the Watergate break-in and the entire range of unsavory activities by the 1972 Nixon campaign. CBS was a reporter of the great drama in those years.

The ongoing investigations and the growing scandal dominated CBS coverage in 1973–74, with only the Yom Kippur War and the resultant Arab oil embargo that October giving the administration much relief from its own bad news. President Nixon lashed out at Cronkite and CBS in a November press conference.

By then, however, the scandal had reached feeding-frenzy proportions in Washington, and with a Democratic-controlled House and Senate, the networks could simply report the facts as a startling series of revelations came from Nixon staffers and, ultimately, from the White House tapes.

How Dare the CIA!

After Nixon's resignation in August, 1974, the credibility of the press stood, perhaps, at its all-time high water mark. With the government in complete disarray, the military discredited by Vietnam, and business leaders undermined by a sharp recession and the incursions of foreign exporters, there weren't too many folk to look up to.

Therefore, it came as an incredibly unwelcome development when, in 1976, it was revealed that a list of journalists who had allegedly spied for the CIA existed. Cronkite's name was on the list. It also was revealed that former CBS news president Richard Salant gave the CIA outtakes of CBS news film years before.

Cronkite angrily demanded that CIA Director George Bush give him the names of any reporters who were CIA agents or aiding the CIA. Bush refused the request, but a week later, Cronkite was able to report on the *Evening News* that two correspondents for CBS had indeed secretly worked for the CIA.

Also in the late 1970s, there was a singular incident that portrayed the almost statesmanlike aura that the leading anchormen enjoyed in the aftermath of Watergate—Cronkite in particular. He always declined credit for bringing together Egyptian President Anwar Sadat and Israeli Prime Minister Menachem Begin. But as he reported the story in his memoir, *A Reporter's Life*, there isn't another conclusion that can be drawn readily.

Sadat indicated a possible willingness to visit Israel in a November, 1977, interview with Cronkite. At the time, Sadat said he would go "just as soon as there is peace". On November 14, 1977, Cronkite interviewed Sadat via satellite.

"I asked if he had any plans to go to Jerusalem," Cronkite recalled in his memoirs. "He would like to go very much, he said, and I asked what I knew would be the definitive question: what are your conditions for going? Whereupon he went into the usual litany of Egyptian demands on Israel—withdrawal from the Sinai and the Golan Heights, and on and on."

Cronkite was able to get Prime Minister Begin via satellite, who said, "Tell him he's got an invitation . . . I will come back home next Friday after my visit to London and Geneva, and then he may come the other Monday . . . but anyhow, anytime, any day he's prepared to come, I will receive him cordially at the airport, go together with him to Jerusalem, also present him to the Knesset and let him make his speech to our Parliament."

The invitation tied a ribbon around the story, but in many ways, it tied a ribbon around Cronkite's career. Like Murrow, he became a quasi-statesmen, the intimate of world leaders. There was no laurel, it seemed, left to earn, and so he turned to the subject of his retirement.

He Reports, You Decide

Cronkite's colleague, Harry Reasoner, once said, "Walter is not a commentator. He feels as strongly about being objective as I do. I suppose if you watched him regularly over the years—from out in the country somewhere—you would have the feeling that he hates bullies. He hates liars. He hates pretension, and he hates phonies."

Cronkite said, "Our job is to hold up the mirror—to tell and show the public what has happened, and then it is the job of the people to decide whether they have faith in their leaders or governments." In Cronkite's mirror, we saw events, we saw ourselves and our society, and, as often as not, we saw Walter Cronkite. He was one of us, he was on our side, and we shared common reactions.

When Kennedy was shot, he wept. Millions wept with him. Not one in a million could quote to you exactly what he said—it was a simple human gesture for which he will be remembered always.

When man went into space, the excitement could be heard in his voice. It was America's excitement too—the romance of the adventure, the gee whiz of technology, the can-do spirit of NASA—which reminded us so much of what we believe about ourselves, our culture, and what remains in us from the pioneer experience.

When America went into Vietnam, Cronkite followed. He never specifically spoke out against the Vietnam War—or against war in general or anticommunist wars in particular—but in February, 1968, he spoke with truth and candor when, after the Tet Offensive, he said that the war appeared to be headed for a stalemate.

The Johnson Administration was shocked. President Johnson said, "If I've lost Cronkite, I've lost Middle America." That was his shrewd and correct read of the political landscape. Johnson didn't even discuss pulling out of the race with some of his closest advisers. He went back on the television from which the bad news had come and announced directly and clearly that he was out. And that's the way it was.

After Tet, Johnson wrapped up Middle America with big, blue Republican ribbon and handed it to, of all people, Richard Milhous Nixon. Nixon wrapped it back up again with Watergate, and then it was Jimmy Carter's turn. President Carter said he would never lie, and he never did—except to say that things would get better under his presidency.

For both Nixon and Carter, Cronkite's no-nonsense, tell-it-like-it-is reporting was devastating to their administrations, which traded in secrecy perfect for Cold War *realpolitik*, but which did not impress Americans. John Chancellor once memorably observed that television news was not a creator of opinion, but rather it intensified opinions and divisions already existing in the country. But Middle America elects its presidential leadership on the basis of character and temperament as much positions on the issues.

As Lloyd George said to Neville Chamberlain in 1940 on the eve of the blitz, "The nation is prepared for every sacrifice so long as the governments show clearly what they are aiming at, and so long as the nation is confident that those who are leading it are doing their best." That was Cronkite's ground: the accurate, dispassionate, sometimes sympathetic, but always watchful measurement of performance against declared goals. President Carter announced that he would make the return of the hostages his central focus, and, in turn, Cronkite closed each broadcast with a count of days of their captivity. President Nixon announced in early 1973 that he would root out the corruption in his administration by the appointment of a special prosecutor, and Cronkite and CBS traced the administration's progress toward its self-declared target.

The Nixon Administration, in particular, took exception to CBS coverage and rankled at Cronkite's influence. That influence grew with every fresh scandal and revelation that fell out of the West Wing. By 1974, our political leaders trapped the country in Watergate and Vietnam, our industrial leaders trapped themselves in stagflation and the Rust Belt, and our moral leadership was tangled in a seemingly unending battle over what exactly constituted social justice and faith. It is not difficult to see why the country turned to Cronkite.

They saw in him a skepticism that was classic Missouri "don't tell me, show me," mixed with an unabashed though undeclared patriotism, and tempered by occasional flights of enthusiasm on subjects like the moon shots. To colleagues, he showed a different side—a fierce competitor of the highest standard with little patience for sermons from the news desk or shoddy preparation of the news. To a trusting public, he gave a consistency that flowed as deep and steady as the Missouri River by which he was born.

And That's the Way It Will Be

The final broadcast of the *CBS Evening News with Walter Cronkite* was on March 6, 1981; he stepped down at age sixty-five in accordance with CBS policy of the time. Looking back, he says:

> I've enjoyed most of the news coverage that we've had to do. . . . And we have all kinds of stories that we cover, and they each have their own satisfaction in them. There are the breaking stories that you don't expect, like the assassinations or a natural disaster, there are the stories where you actually work on them and plan them and plot them to get potentially exclusive coverage. . . . There are the stories that you can prepare for that are of historical nature, like the moon landing, which was a great news story, but you had that time to prepare it. There are election nights and that kind of thing, where you've got a lot of notes to work with and some advance film, perhaps. All those things create a different kind of story. Each of those has its own sense of accomplishment and thrill if you do it right.

Following his departure, he hosted several acclaimed CBS documentary programs, including the Emmy-winning *Children of Apartheid* and the CBS News science magazine series, *Walter*

Cronkite's Universe. In 1985, he was inducted into the Academy of Television Arts and Sciences Hall of Fame. He remains a special correspondent for CBS and continues to host many public affairs and cultural programs for PBS and syndication. Walter Cronkite has won just about every award that's ever been created for his years of outstanding service.

To this day, he is the only journalist to be voted one of the top ten "most influential decision-makers in America" in surveys conducted by *U.S. News and World Report.* He also was named the "most influential person" in broadcasting. And, in a nationwide viewer opinion survey conducted in 1995—more than a decade after leaving the CBS anchor desk—he again was voted "Most Trusted Man in Television News."

Times are very different today than when he sat down in that anchor chair in 1962. With the advent of cable news and the Internet, television networks are feeling increased pressure to turn a profit. News is expensive to produce, and there is new pressure on journalists to be a profit center for their companies. Cronkite reflected on the changes:

> Of course there are things wrong, with probably the most obvious manifestation being the tabloidization of too much of our work. Mainline journalism seems to have accepted the standards of what once was known as the penny press. It is to worry. And, of course, the bottom line of our discomfort is the bottom line itself. With almost total unanimity, our big, corporate owners, infected with the greed that marks the end of the twentieth century, stretch constantly for ever-increasing profit, condemning quality to take the hindmost. If there is any solution to this problem, it might be found in educating the shareholding public to their responsibility in owning this business which is fundamental to the preservation of our democracy.
>
> If they understood the nature of this public service and treated their investment in it accordingly, we would be saved from compromising journalistic integrity in the mad scramble

for ratings and circulation. In other words, if they did not expect the constantly increasing, unconscionable profits now expected from most investments, but accepted a rational and steady return on their investment in this essential public service of newspapers and broadcast news.

You might give some thought to this organization promoting this idea. Utopian? Oh, I suppose so. But besides serving democracy, it has its practical side of direct benefit to you. By making this case, you'll get the monkey off your backs and direct the public's dissatisfaction with our broadcasts and press where it belongs.

But we all know what is wrong—and as professionals, we all know how to fix it if given the mandate from our bosses, or if we can wrest control from the bottom-liners. Let our battle cry be: editors, not auditors.

Despite all the changes in the world today, the new politics of the era, and corporate owners and business models constantly attempting to tamper with the purity of journalism, Cronkite remains proud:

> I'm mighty proud of our profession. I'm proud of the physical courage shown by many—in war and civil insurrection and in dozens of less spectacular ways. I'm proud of those who expose the culpable even at the risk of their freedom, or even their lives.
>
> I'm proud of those who have the courage to reject the favors of the newsmakers; those who do not become part of the establishment, who preserve access to the inner circle without becoming members of it.
>
> I'm proud of those with courage to withstand the wrath of their neighbors and face social ostracism in pursuit of the truth. I'm proud of those who have the courage to reject conformity with their colleagues and hold on to their vision of the truth while others around them seem blind and scornful.
>
> I'm proud, too, of all those who work in the backrooms of our media—on rewrite, copy desks, assignment desks, editing film and tape—professionals all. Their devotion to this

business may be greater than all those media stars they make look so good. There are bad apples in our barrel, of course, but as a class, there is a purity of intent and purpose in journalism that is unique.

Thomas Jefferson said, and Cronkite was known to quote, "A nation that expects to be ignorant and free expects what never can and never will be." Perhaps no one did more, by riveting our attention to a nightly broadcast like no one before or since, to keep the public educated during the years of the American ascendancy. He is proud of the legacy he has in the news business, but there is a certain amount of pride also that this statesman among anchors should have for the positive influence he had on the country during some of its darkest hours.

Where would we be without Cronkite? The answer is pure speculation and well outside the boundaries of journalism, but it is a fair speculation that we would be by far the poorer without his influence and his presence in our living rooms through all those years.

Chapter SEVEN

Frank Reynolds, ABC

Courtesy of ABC

Of the nineteen network news anchors profiled in this book, four were awarded the Presidential Medal of Freedom, the nation's highest civilian honor. The third to receive the award, posthumously in 1985, was Frank Reynolds. Like Peter Jennings, he took two turns at the anchor desk. Reynolds had his first tour in the late 1960s, and then he returned with the launch of *World News Tonight* to share the anchor desk with Peter Jennings and Max Robinson.

He characterized his career as "Lazarus-like" because he and Jennings were the first anchors ever to be dropped and then reinstated by the same network (John Cameron Swayze reappeared on ABC several years after being replaced at NBC). In 1979, one year after his return, he won the George Peabody Award for excellence in broadcast journalism. In his acceptance speech, he focused on the simplest, the most straightforward of themes. The role of the anchor is nothing more, he said, than "to help people understand what's going on". Reynolds was from the anchor school of getting the information to the people in a straightforward manner with little commentary attached. He knew the difference between news and commentary and did both well.

After the battles at ABC between Howard K. Smith, Harry Reasoner, and Barbara Walters over who should rightfully occupy the throne, Reynolds was a breath of fresh air. His conception of the job was a chair at a desk with a lens, and at the other end of the lens, an American public tuned in to his broadcast. His sole object was sorting the news of the day into a story and a semblance of order.

In the early 1980s, reporter and essayist Lewis H. Lapham wrote, "People come up against so many bits and pieces of information—in the papers, on the television networks, in newsletters, and market reports—that they cannot discern a coherent unity." In an industry transitioning from "scoop" to "get" with "gotcha" somewhere in between, Reynolds left the scoops, gets, and gotchas to others and concentrated on "understanding". There was no nonsense in the man as a broadcaster. He was known for it.

As a broadcaster, Reynolds was a perfect instrument for ABC News president Roone Arledge, who came to ABC News in 1977 with a mandate to improve the performance of the division. Arledge was to lead ABC, finally, out of the wilderness in which it had languished since its days as the NBC Blue network. Arledge began by spending some of the substantial proceeds of the successful entertainment division that rose from being perennially third to first on a news organization with a new level of substance. He looked for deeply experienced correspondents, rather than anchor personalities. That led him to

Reynolds, Jennings, Robinson, and Koppel. First, they established the undeniable credibility of ABC News, and, ultimately, by 1991, ABC pulled ahead of both NBC and CBS in the ratings.

Reynolds was the straight man, the conservative. He did not swear and had a distaste for those who did. He did not go out with the gang after a telecast. He was the father of five boys and spent most of his time away from the network at home. He wasn't much of a socialite and only went to parties and social gatherings at the prompting of his employer. He was known to ask that the soap opera in the newsroom be turned off because of the sexual content. Ironically, he became known as the first network news anchor to swear on camera, but that is getting ahead of the story.

An upright man, Reynolds had strong opinions and wasn't loathe to unload them—even on viewers from time to time. One letter, from a professor of communications, has Reynolds's reply on the reverse. It begins, "Are you serious? Is there really a school that employs someone as ignorant as you to teach broadcast journalism?" Another letter from a complaining viewer was apparently returned after having been opened. The last line of the letter to a Mr. Peptu reads, "Mr. Peptu, go to hell."

Reynolds's prose could be devastating on air, as well. In 1969, Vice President Agnew quoted him in his highly controversial speech regarding the influence of the network news anchors. Agnew said, "Less than a week before the 1968 election, he charged that President Nixon's campaign commitments were no more durable than campaign balloons. He claimed, were it not for fear of a hostile reaction, Richard Nixon would be giving into, and I quote the commentator, 'his natural instinct to smash the enemy with a club or go after him with a meat-axe.'"

Reynolds often was accused of seeing things only in black and white. He was opinionated, and his body language often revealed his feelings. He had a habit of tapping his fingers on the desk, sometimes loudly, when a story annoyed him.

As a broadcaster, his drive for clarity took him far beyond elucidation and into enunciation. The Association for the Deaf designated Reynolds as the anchor with the most readable lips. He was a stand-out on the *Captioned ABC News*, a nightly PBS rebroadcast of *World News Tonight* with open captions.

His straight-arrow style left him open to parody. Among broadcasters, Reynolds had the rare distinction of having two regulars on *Saturday Night Live*, Harry Shearer and Phil Hartman, do imitations of him. They imitated him during his second tour at the anchor desk. In his first run, he wasn't able to generate enough ratings to establish either a major presence in the national consciousness or to fulfill the expectations of the executives at ABC. His broadcasting style was similar in both tours, but he benefited the second time around from bigger budgets and better production values. Particularly important the second time was the fact that by 1982, he was competing with Tom Brokaw, John Chancellor, and Dan Rather instead of Walter Cronkite and the *Huntley-Brinkley Report*.

By the time of his death in 1983 at the young age of fifty-nine, he carved out a significant reputation for himself for fearlessness and a clarity that bordered on bluntness.

Early Values

Frank Reynolds was born in East Chicago, Indiana, in 1923, and he attended high school in Hammond. His father was a steel industry manager, who raised his family on strict values that remained with Reynolds all his life.

A history major at Wabash College, Reynolds joined the army in 1942. He served in the European theater, won the Purple Heart, and was discharged in 1945 as a staff sergeant.

After his military service, he returned to the Midwest, where he finished his degree at Wabash in 1946. The same year, he was hired at WJOB-A.M. in Hammond as a sports and news announcer. Then he moved to WBKB-TV, which later became the CBS affiliate WBBM, and covered local and national news there until 1960.

He became noted in the 1950s for a series of news specials he produced on his travels to the Middle East and other regions. A report on Egypt, Syria, Lebanon, Israel, and Algeria in the late 1950s won the World Understanding Award from the Chicago Council on Foreign Relations.

In 1963, he moved to the Chicago ABC affiliate, where he had his first anchoring experience with the highly regarded *Frank Reynolds and the News*. During that period, ABC went through anchors in a rapid succession, and the quality of Reynolds's broadcasts, although local, were not overlooked at ABC headquarters in New York. In 1964, he was assigned to cover the political conventions at the network level, and he covered the Midwest for the network during the primary and general election campaigns. He covered Barry Goldwater's stunning victory in the Illinois primary in April, where Goldwater won 65 percent of the vote and set Nelson Rockefeller's campaign on its ear. He also covered George Wallace's surprisingly strong showing in the Indiana primary in May. In March of 1965, he became the first Chicago television reporter to travel to and report from South Vietnam.

His political credentials fully established by his reporting throughout the turbulent Goldwater campaign of 1964, he was offered a job by ABC in 1965 as the White House correspondent for the network. Despite having to accept a 50 percent pay cut, Reynolds took the job.

In 1967, ABC News continued its news format experiments to capture audiences, but everything failed. The major problem was the length of the broadcast. At fifteen minutes, it still clung to the 1950s format. Besides, NBC and CBS offered thirty minutes. Peter Jennings was at the ABC anchor desk, but he lacked the experience he later obtained as a foreign correspondent and the substantial resources he later gained at *World News Tonight*. He was mired in a distant third in the ratings, so the decision was made to put Jennings back on the street as a reporter.

Reynolds was forty-four years old and a real television journalist. At one time, he anchored at one of the biggest local stations in the country. Everyone at ABC news agreed it was time for him to take his turn on the anchor desk. Everyone except Frank Reynolds, that is. He told journalist Barbara Matusow for her book *The Evening Stars*, "It was such a fascinating time at the White House, not always pleasant, but fascinating. There was Vietnam, the turmoil in the streets. I felt what I was doing was far more important and personally satisfying than anchoring would be. I felt that they could find someone else to sit there and read the news."

So, Bob Young was put on the evening news, and Reynolds stayed in Washington, D.C. It was January, 1968. Many of the affiliates did not even run the evening news program. There was great affiliate pressure to make ABC news competitive with CBS and NBC, so Young's anchoring career was short-lived. ABC needed Reynolds to change his mind. Howard K. Smith wrote that the network came to him, and he suggested that they go back to Reynolds and try again.

The executives at ABC exerted tremendous pressure on Reynolds, and he finally gave in. He debuted as ABC evening news anchor in May, 1968, just after the assassination of Martin Luther King Jr. and two months prior to the assassination of Robert F. Kennedy. The quadrennial conventions, the centerpiece of network coverage at the time, were less than three months away, with the Republicans in Miami Beach and the Democrats in Chicago.

In the process of putting Reynolds at the desk, ABC also made the decision to go permanently to a thirty-minute format. Reynolds had the task of learning on the job, marshaling the troops to deliver an extended broadcast. He competed against the established Huntley and Brinkley and a newly resurgent Walter Cronkite, who took the lead in the ratings the year before.

Conventional Wisdom

The Monday, August 5, 1968 broadcast demonstrated Reynolds's style. That night, the Republican convention got

Courtesy of ABC

underway in Miami Beach, and Reynolds anchored from Florida. His correspondents included Roger Grimsby and Sam Donaldson.

The broadcast began with a short introduction from Reynolds and a summary of the first session of the convention. California Governor Ronald Reagan put his hat in the race to try and stop Richard Nixon from winning on the first ballot. ABC gave delegate projections showing Nixon just sixty-six votes shy of a first-ballot victory. A note from Reynolds that the delegates were ignoring virtually everything said by the speakers segued into a floor report from the convention itself. The floor report featured Governor Romney, the Michigan Republican, who had been expected to come to Miami as a front-runner until his campaign collapsed after he suggested during the primary campaign that he had been subjected to brainwashing on the Vietnam issue. Reynolds reported on the battle over Maryland, where Governor Spiro Agnew, a favorite-son candidate, considered throwing his support to Nixon.

Following a commercial break, Reynolds returned with a story on the three candidates themselves, with Nixon yet to arrive. Rockefeller predicted that Nixon would not win a victory on the first ballot, and Reagan worked the floor.

Correspondent Sam Donaldson then interviewed Governor Reagan. Reagan stated his belief that there would be no winner on the first ballot, that it would become an open convention, and that he had no intention of accepting a vice presidential nomination.

Back to the studio, Reynolds reported that Nixon supporters were getting ready to welcome the candidate at the airport. At that point, Roger Grimsby contributed a report from New York on Nixon's departure, including a stop at the Immigration Building to act as a character witness for two members of his household staff in a citizenship petition. Nixon joked that he was there to nail down two votes for November.

After approximately nine minutes, Reynolds moved the broadcast over to a local report by correspondent Ralph Schoenstein on the feelings of local Miami residents about the candidates. Following a commercial break, Reynolds returned with a report on the short list for the vice presidential nomination, including Senators Hatfield of Oregon, Percy of Illinois, and

Baker of Tennessee. A "draft Lindsay" movement was discouraged by Lindsay himself.

Fourteen minutes into the broadcast, Reynolds moved to coverage of national and foreign news, with a studio report on the fighting in Vietnam and an update on tensions along the Jordan River between Israel and Jordan.

The broadcast then moved back to the convention for soft news of the convention delegates at large in Miami Beach. This was followed by a report from correspondent Jim Burnes on the wooing of delegates seen through the experiences of an Arkansas delegate.

From the studio, Reynolds then reported Barry Goldwater's arrival at the convention. James Kilpatrick then reported on the lingering affection for Goldwater and a movement toward Reagan on the floor. Reynolds then switched back to national coverage, with reports on steel prices and President Johnson's physical.

The final report was commentary from Reynolds, including an acerbic but witty portrayal of Ohio Governor James Rhodes. Reynolds commented that Nixon's staff said that Rhodes waited too long to help Rockefeller and that now Nixon didn't need him. Reynolds finished by predicting, "Rhodes will be remembered as man who outsmarted all, including himself."

It is a good, solid broadcast and a milestone for ABC because it covered all the angles that a thirty-minute broadcast should cover. Its structure was especially strong, with the initial high-level reports giving way to more in-depth features on the candidates, the delegates, and the vice presidential hopefuls. The correspondents did not make a brilliant mark, and the short commentary lacked an incisive edge, but it marked the first convention for which ABC could claim to have given competitive coverage. Moreover, the structure of the program was entirely modern, shorn almost entirely of commentary. It focused on political personalities rather than issues or delegate counts, and was dominated by field reports rather than live coverage from the anchor desk. The 1968 broadcast showed not only the professionalism that Reynolds added to the organization, but the evolution of the news product into a recognizably modern form.

Reynolds Versus Agnew

Throughout 1968, Reynolds continued to put together respected broadcasts that won the admiration of his peers, but he made little headway in the ratings. To an extent, the blunt, conservative Reynolds was out of step with the times—too liberal to be embraced by the crowd applauding Governor Agnew's 1968 description of Democrats as "troglodytic leftists," and too straight for the sophisticated city audiences still watching the *Huntley-Brinkley Report*.

In late 1969, Vice President Agnew singled out Reynolds in his stinging Iowa speech regarding the influence of the news anchors. He lashed out at anchormen in general for the "narrow and distorted picture of America" that they provided, and Reynolds in particular for describing Nixon as possessing a "natural instinct to smash the enemy with a club or go after him with a meat-axe."

Agnew's focus on Reynolds reflected the preoccupations of the White House, not the public's houses. For the Nielsen books confirmed that Cronkite and Huntley and Brinkley continued to dominate in the ratings. ABC executives pressed Howard K. Smith to join the broadcast as co-anchor because they felt that he would shore up the commentary. And perhaps Smith's uniquely good relations with the Nixon White House would help, considering Agnew's comments about Reynolds.

On December 4, 1970, Reynolds made his last appearance in

the anchor chair for a long time. He made it a memorable one. Commenting to Smith on the switch to the new co-anchor, Harry Reasoner, Reynolds said, "Due to circumstances beyond my control, the unemployment statistics rose yesterday."

Network executives were aghast, but, in any case, Reynolds was out. However, he continued to work as a correspondent for ABC. Like Peter Jennings, Reynolds's stature grew during his period of exile. He did excellent work with the opportunities that he had.

In 1976, Reynolds was one of the panel members asking questions at the first presidential debate between Jimmy Carter and Gerald Ford. Carter later admitted that he got off to a rough start from the very first question in that debate. That question came from Reynolds. He asked Carter about his plans to reduce unemployment because the candidate had named that issue a top priority in an Associated Press interview. Carter became rattled and quoted too many arcane statistics. Using AP reports to extract straight and challenging questions was typical of Reynolds's interview style.

The Roone Years

During the debate, Reynolds was calm, collected, and a real professional while Carter dodged his verbal bullets. Roone Arledge watched the debates and noticed that Reynolds, whom he always liked, was on his game. Arledge was in charge of sports for ABC, but, in 1977, he became the president of the news division.

Author Michael Thompson wrote of the ABC Evening News:

> One of the first things Arledge did as president of ABC News was address the anchor problem of the evening newscast. It was obvious that Harry Reasoner and Barbara Walters [Howard K. Smith's replacement], the anchors of the evening

newscast, not only had little chemistry, but also had little regard for each other. When Reasoner left the network in 1978, that left Arledge free to revamp the newscast. Walters, who had an unpleasant experience anchoring the news, was assigned to do various news specials and interviews, and Arledge redesigned and renamed the evening newscast. *World News Tonight*, as it was now called, featured three anchors: Peter Jennings in London, Frank Reynolds in Washington, and Max Robinson in Chicago.

While the anchor format didn't work out, other elements Arledge devised for *World News Tonight* did. ABC, due to its huge success with its entertainment programs, supplied Arledge with a hefty budget, and he made good use of it. He decided to instill graphics and theme music onto *World News Tonight*, neither of which had ever been done before on any newscasts, and both of which soon became standard on the other network newscasts. Also, slowly but surely, *World News Tonight's* ratings began to rise.

In the summer of 1978, the ABC anchor team took over, with Barbara Walters doing special assignment reports and the three main anchors in their respective cities.

One of Reynolds's most chilling broadcasts of this period was an October, 1978, profile of young suicide bombers in Palestine. It was called *Terror in the Promised Land*. At the time, communities of Palestinian refugees proliferated in South Lebanon, and the PLO, under Yasser Arafat, used the area as a base from which to launch terrorist and Katyusha rocket attacks against northern Israel. The suicide bomber was supposed to be the unstoppable weapon that would bring Israel to its knees. The report opened with 8 mm footage of three armed civilians. Reynolds narrated: "These three young men are dead. When this film was taken by their friends, they knew they were about to die. Twenty-four hours later, they blew up both themselves and eighteen other people in an Israeli apartment building."

Reynolds also covered the presidential election in 1980. Sometimes he was more involved than he wanted to be. During the North Carolina Primary, Reynolds told one of Reagan's close aides, Marty Anderson, that Reagan won the primary. Marty was standing in the back, and Reynolds came up to him all excited with a piece of paper in his hand that read, "55–45." Anderson thought, "Oh, we're losing by ten." And Reynolds said, "You're winning by ten!" Reagan was told, but he would not react or celebrate until he was back on the plane and the pilot got the latest results. Then, with half the vote in and a solid lead, he finally acknowledged victory in North Carolina with a plastic glass of champagne and a bowl of ice cream.

In late 1979, when Iranian students stormed the United States Embassy and seized fifty-one American hostages. Arledge persuaded ABC to air a limited series of late-night, fifteen-minute reports on the crisis. Anchored by Reynolds, *The Iran Crisis: America Held Hostage*, debuted on November 8, 1979, and soon had more than twelve million viewers. Reynolds had almost as much audience in late night as he had in the early evening. Sensing a largely untapped late-night audience for hard news, Arledge made plans for a regularly scheduled half-hour show and selected Ted Koppel, a rising ABC star with extensive experience as a diplomatic correspondent, as anchor. On March 24, 1980, at 11:30 P.M. EST, the newly retitled *ABC News Nightline* became a permanent fixture on the late-night television landscape.

"Damn It, Somebody Get Me . . . "

"Damn it, somebody get me the correct information." These words will be associated forever with Frank Reynolds, the nonswearing, conservative anchorman at ABC. It was Monday, March 30, 1981. Ronald Reagan was just departing the Washington Hilton

after making a speech. Outside the hotel waited a troubled young man named John Hinckley. He believed that shooting Reagan would impress Jodie Foster. Shots rang out. Reagan was pushed into the limousine, and three other people were hit. One of them was James Brady, the president's press secretary.

The networks jumped into action, and Frank Reynolds broke into regular programming on ABC. He reported that President Reagan escaped harm and Brady was killed. When it became apparent that there was conflicting information, a very frustrated Reynolds stammered, "Damn it, somebody get me some correct information." He pounded the desk with his hand and looked off camera as if to say, "Let's get it right, let's nail this down."

Within the hour, Deputy Press Secretary Lyn Nofziger told the press that Reagan had been shot and was undergoing surgery and that James Brady was in critical condition fighting for his life, but was alive. Reynolds then said, "We apologize for telling you before that the president was saved and had not been struck, but that was the immediate information that came in to us."

It was a graceful wording for an embarrassing moment for the news anchor. However, better news for him was the outstanding performance of his son, Dean Reynolds, as a rising United Press International (UPI) reporter covering the assassination. For his efforts, young Reynolds won the Merriman Smith Award for Outstanding Coverage of a Breaking News Story.

Reynolds's Wrap: A Hollywood-Style Sendoff

In the spring of 1983, Reynolds began to suffer serious health problems that caused him to miss a number of telecasts. A blood transfusion was ordered in April, and Reynolds contracted acute

viral hepatitis from the transfusion. While in the hospital re-
covering from the hepatitis, he was informed that he had bone
cancer.

During his absence from the anchor desk, however, ratings
of *World News Tonight* dropped precipitously. Then Reynolds
passed away on July 20, 1983. President Reagan issued this
statement after Reynolds's passing:

> Frank Reynolds was one of America's foremost broadcast
> journalists, trusted and respected by millions of his fellow cit-
> izens, Nancy and I among them. To us he was also a warm,
> considerate friend who will be missed for his outstanding
> human qualities as well as for his many contributions as a
> newsman. Our prayers and sympathy are with Frank's family
> in their bereavement.

A World War II veteran, Reynolds was buried at Arlington Na-
tional Cemetery. His resting place is in the same section as Joe
"Louis" Barrow, the heavyweight boxing champion, Colonel
"Pappy" Boyington of Black Sheep Squadron, and General
Maxwell Taylor, the former chairman of the Joint Chiefs of Staff.

On May 23, 1985, President Reagan awarded the Presidential Medal of Freedom to the 1985 recipients at a White House
luncheon. Count Basie, Jacques-Yves Cousteau, Jeane J. Kirk-
patrick, Mother Teresa, Frank Sinatra, Jimmy Stewart, and
General Charles E. Yeager were among the honorees. Reynolds
won the award posthumously. Among news broadcasters, only
Edward R. Murrow and Walter Cronkite received the award before Reynolds, and only David Brinkley has received it since. It
is interesting to note that the two broadcasters who succeeded
in driving Reynolds off the airwaves in 1970—Cronkite and
Brinkley—are his fellow inductees.

What made the difference? The success of *World News
Tonight* was important, as was Reynolds's prime position in
Washington during the hostage crisis, the last turbulent Carter

years, and the first years of Reagan's administration. But Reynolds's lasting reputation is more than that. Much of it rests on the two-second comment made in the heat of the moment that, by all accounts, was completely out of character. A viewer wrote:

> In our memory, the most memorable coverage of events is when the commentator became "human" for a moment. Frank Reynolds of ABC News had a breakdown when he was reporting on the attempt on the life of President Ronald Reagan. He had just been given copy which told him that James Brady had died. Moments later, he received word that Brady was alive. "God d— it, somebody get me some correct information." Or Walter Cronkite reporting on the passing of President Kennedy, taking off his glasses, and wiping away a tear.

Reynolds's breakdown was a real moment, when the veil of the Teleprompter lifted, the artifice of performance collapsed, and the viewer saw the anguish of the nation written on the face of the anchor. In such instances, the more reserved the broadcaster, the more powerful the public reaction.

It was left to Frank Reynolds, in the end, to demonstrate for us the power and importance of breaking through the fourth wall. For anchors who have earned the public trust, the fourth wall melts away, leaving us in our living rooms watching the television not only for reaction from the White House, but for reaction from the anchor. Without empathy—*real connection*—to the viewer, the anchor is just a well-known face. Alternatively, viewers form connections with organizations instead of individuals, a process that got underway in Reynolds's time with the establishment of CNN.

Chapter EIGHT

Howard K. Smith, ABC

Courtesy of ABC

To look at their resumes, Howard K. Smith has an awful lot in common with Walter Cronkite. They were both born in small towns along the great inland river system: Cronkite alongside the Missouri, Smith by the Mississippi. Both relocated to lively

163

jazz towns as small boys: Cronkite to Kansas City, Smith to New Orleans.

Both worked as local newsmen before joining United Press. Both served as war correspondents in Europe. Edward R. Murrow recruited Cronkite, and Murrow appointed Smith as his own successor in Europe in 1946. Both went on to long careers at CBS and served as network anchors in the 1960s and 1970s.

Both were proud men—and prickly. Both were committed to high standards in broadcast journalism. But they couldn't have been more different. Cronkite was the reporter's reporter, the Unipresser, the steady and trusted midwestern "Uncle Walter," the irreplaceable fixture on the network newscast, and "the most trusted man in America."

No one made the mistake of thinking of Howard K. Smith as "Uncle Howard". Smith was not interested in being anybody's uncle; he was interested in being a conscience. He had the southerner's penchant for taking strong stands on controversial issues, and he had the southerner's inability to run away from a fight.

When you heard Howard K. Smith, there was no doubt of a southern origin, for he always carried the light drawl of a long-gone Louisiana boyhood. But there was less of the South in his voice than in his personality. He was as high-minded and stubborn as old John C. Calhoun, and he went toe-to-toe with some of the toughest professionals in the industry—like William S. Paley—without giving an inch.

He was the strongest commentator and analyst among the anchors since Murrow. Arriving at the anchor desk in Brinkley's waning years, he carried that standard forward. It was his penchant for outspoken commentary, for courting conflict that, without question, kept him so long out of the anchor chair. He was the oldest to ascend to that throne. He reached it with his appointment as ABC co-anchor with Frank Reynolds in 1969 at the age of fifty-five.

Smith made it to the top late in his career, but in two key respects, the timing was perfect. First, his perfect foil, Harry Reasoner, was ready to leave CBS. Second, he fit the times. For the darker the age, the better he was. He made his reputation during World War II and sealed it in the Watergate years.

The Story Man from Storeyville

Howard K. Smith was born May 12, 1914, in the rural town of Ferriday, Louisiana. It was a time of incredible change in Louisiana. Nick LaRocca's Original Dixieland Jazz Band just made the first jazz recording, *Livery Stable Blues*. Louis Armstrong, Buddy Bolden, Jelly Roll Morton, and King Oliver made their starts and played the nightclubs of Storeyville, the flourishing red-light district. The naval base was a major staging site for the Marine invasion of Mexico at Vera Cruz, aimed at toppling the dictatorship of Pancho Villa.

The Marines brought back Villa's marching song, *La Cucaracha*, which swept the nation, and marijuana, which swept the bordellos of Storeyville. Few of the Americans who hummed the catchy tune guessed that the lyrics described the adventures of a marijuana-obsessed cockroach. But the Latin rhythms added another dimension to a town already the most cosmopolitan in the South. Although thoroughly segregated, New Orleans offered a window into a life beyond the South.

Smith's family moved to Storeyville when he was very young, and he lived there through college. His grandfather had been a prosperous landowner near Ferriday, but lost his lands late in life. Smith's father worked a series of jobs, but was not much of a success at any of them; he was traumatized by the loss of the lands and, like Ashley Wilkes in *Gone with the Wind*, incapable of adapting to the new world order. Howard K. Smith Jr. grew up poor, restless, resentful, and bothered.

He worked as a journalist for the *New Orleans Item* before winning a scholarship to study German and journalism at Tulane University. He distinguished himself not only as a scholar, but also as a track star. He set the Tulane high-hurdles record and, in his senior year, placed second to Forrest Townes in an All-South track meet. Townes later won selection to the Olympic team and went to Berlin.

Smith made it to Germany as well, but athletics had nothing to do with it. He was awarded a scholarship to Heidelberg University and arrived in the summer of 1936. He was appalled by the Nazi regime and became an ardent opponent of appeasement. His reaction to appeasement was typical of the man. He came home, applied for a Rhodes scholarship, won one for 1937, went to Oxford, and spent every possible free moment in Germany. His holiday activities included taking an anti-Nazi newspaper across the border, for which he was arrested and held for several hours.

At Oxford, he joined the Labour Club. He was active in the campaign against the appeasement policy of Neville Chamberlain and the Conservative government. He frequently participated in parades and protests in London and coordinated activities across the country. In his second year, the students elected him club chairman. He was the first American to hold the honor.

Upon completing his studies in the summer of 1939, he decided to remain in Europe and was able to pick up a job with the United Press in London. He was sent to Berlin within three months and was there for the outbreak of the Second World War. When Bill Shirer left Berlin, Paul White in New York hired Smith to replace him. Smith later wrote, "I was alarmed at suddenly having top responsibility in a warring capital for a great network. When we knew one another better, I asked Paul White how he came to have faith in an unknown. He said, 'I know you were well brought up, from a top school.' I said, 'Oxford?' He said, 'No, United Press.'"

Smith didn't care much for the assignment. His talent for radio was immediately apparent, however. His light southern accent and pared-down writing style honed at United Press proved popular, but he chafed at the restrictions placed on journalists.

Lost in Love

By November, 1941, Smith ran afoul of the Germans because of his reports and virtually was shut out of the radio by censorship. He requested a transfer out of Germany, and CBS executives reluctantly agreed.

Earlier, he was introduced to *Fröken* Benedicte Traberg. She was a tall, nineteen-year-old Danish beauty working as a dispatch writer for a Danish paper. At dinner, they found themselves strongly attracted to one another and traded their stories rapidly, in the rushed manner typical of wartime romances. She told him that her first job had been in the Berlin office of *Berlingske Tidende*, where she was promoted from gofer to a dispatch writer. As they talked, Smith learned that she became a full correspondent and was transferring to Stockholm.

"When I kissed her good night at the door to her apartment house on the Kurfurstendamm, I was lost in love, with a rather strong feeling that she was, too. This one I resolved I was going to keep. It was not one more Berlin affair. It had to be managed with delicacy and respect."

Smith waited on his exit visa and expected to transfer to Switzerland, but his papers took so long and war was looming between Germany and the United States that he did not know whether he would go "to Switzerland or to Dachau".

Then, George Kennan, who went on to one of the most famous careers in the Cold War, came up with a strategy to get Smith out of Berlin. Kennan told him that when the Germans cut off Smith's broadcasting privileges, it was directed against him personally, and not CBS. Kennan theorized that if CBS appointed a successor, then the Germans would let Smith leave.

It worked. Smith was not told when his visa would be ready, but that he would be able to leave on forty-eight hours notice once it arrived. "So, I had no time to lose," wrote Smith. "I looked at my love of four days' acquaintance and decided I could not live without her." He proposed and was accepted. However, as a legal minor under the age of twenty-one, she needed her parents' permission to marry. The couple needed to make a trip to Copenhagen. Smith wrote:

> On December 1, 1941, I saw her off to Denmark at the Lufthansa office. . . . But five days later, I was called to the Foreign Office, and the liberating document was stamped in my passport. I immediately reserved a berth on the night train to Basel, Switzerland. The U.P. boys improvised an alcoholic farewell party, then took me to the Anhalter station and poured me into the train. That was December 6. I was so pleased with the celebration and so happy at the favorable turn my life had taken that I considered partying on for a day longer and leaving Berlin on the second night of my forty-eight hours, which would be December 7, 1941. I shudder to think how events might have transpired, had I done so.

Smith wrote about his experiences in a 1942 bestseller, *Last Train from Berlin: An Eyewitness Account of Germany at War*. It was considered successful enough as a thriller that it optioned for a Hollywood film. The film was not made, but Smith's reputation was. Although he spent two years trapped in Bern with very little to report, he made it to France with the liberation in 1944. There he established a very distinguished war reporting record, including the French liberation, the crossing of the Rhine, the first reports from Dachau, and the surrender of Germany. He made one of the first and best broadcasts from "bombed-out Berlin" on May 9, 1945.

After the war, Murrow transferred back to the United States. After unsuccessful attempts to lure Charles Collingwood or Bill Shirer into taking the London correspondent job, he appointed Smith to the position. At a leap, Smith gained the central correspondent's position in Europe, and from there, he covered the late 1940s with distinction. He also participated in Murrow's famed, annual, year-end round-ups and at the 1948 conventions.

In the late 1940s, television began to figure more and more importantly in the minds of the CBS correspondents. Smith's initial attitude was emphatically negative. When New York executives sent movie cameras to each of the correspondents with a suggestion to learn the device, Smith blasted the move. He said it was as "absurd as asking a surgeon to fill a few of his victim's teeth after an appendectomy".

However, when Edward R. Murrow moved *Hear It Now* to television and called it *See It Now*, Smith made a report on the first show, saying that developments in disarmament talks were a brief "peace scare" and that "mutual ill will is entirely unimpaired".

"We felt it was kind of unmanly to go onto TV and perform," Smith said, "just as it was in an earlier era somehow unmanly for a newspaperman to go to radio. When Ed went into it, of course, he showed that real men could take part in it without damaging their masculinity."

I Pledge Allegiance?

In 1952, Smith and fellow CBS correspondent Alexander Kendrick were named in the booklet Red Channels as "Communists or Communist sympathizers." A primary reason was a broadcast Smith made regarding the Soviet administration in

Courtesy of ABC

Eastern Europe. The publication of Smith's name, among other developments in the Red Scare, led to a request of CBS correspondents to sign a loyalty oath. He signed under protest, but escaped the clutches of the blacklist.

For several years, Smith remained in London, where he built up an already considerable reputation as a correspondent of the first magnitude. He returned to the United States in 1957 as chief Washington correspondent. The highlight of those years was his selection as moderator of the first 1960 Kennedy-Nixon debate in Chicago. It capped a season in which his CBS Reports documentary, *The Population Explosion*, won the Emmy for best documentary. The following season, he won the Peabody Award.

However, he ran into significant trouble with CBS during this period over civil rights. Smith was not in Europe offering reports and blistering commentary about Communism and the failings of various European allies; he was at home, attacking the political beliefs of entire populations of southerners, who formed the core audiences of powerful southern CBS affiliates and bought the products of powerful CBS advertisers.

Smith was a southerner, but he was appalled by segregation and the Jim Crow laws. Smith was a bestselling author with several books under his belt, and he had strong opinions on just about everything. After 1958, Bill Paley ordered an editor to review Smith's commentaries before they went on their air.

The matter came to a head over a documentary Smith took over when Murrow left the network. The program was about the Freedom Riders and the racial unrest rocking the region at the time. He arrived as the Freedom Riders were approaching town. "The head of the [local] KKK phoned me while I was having lunch in a hotel," Smith told the *Naples Daily News* in 2001. "He said, 'You want action, we've got action.'"

Not long after, Smith witnessed an ugly, vicious beating of

several of the Freedom Riders by members of the Ku Klux Klan. He was struck by the parallels to what he had witnessed with the Jews in 1930s Germany. To conclude the CBS news broadcast, he quoted philosopher Edmund Burke: "All that is necessary for the triumph of evil is for good men to do nothing."

The editor ordered the line cut, Paley backed the editor, and Smith asked to see Paley. The disagreement devolved into a shouting match and, at the penultimate point, Paley thundered, "If you want to report like this, then go somewhere else." Howard K. Smith got up, left the room, and within a few months, he was at ABC.

It wasn't the first time that ABC found itself with an A-list television correspondent on the lot, and as with John Daly, it didn't know what to do with him. The problem was that Howard K. Smith was a star of such magnitude, with such a defined personality within news broadcasting, that cutting back on his commentary made no sense at all. Why have Howard K. Smith without the commentary? On the other hand, his commentary was apt to land any network in hot water with advertisers, affiliates, and viewers.

Howard and Harry

Smith began doing a prime-time weekly show, *Howard K. Smith—News and Comment*. His program took on the controversial subjects expected of a Howard K. Smith program, and it won the predicted amount of critical praise as well as some decent if unspectacular prime-time ratings.

Predictably, Smith ran into trouble. This time, the problems arose over a documentary about Richard Nixon following his loss in the 1962 California governor's race. Smith included an interview with Alger Hiss, who was convicted of perjury in Richard Nixon's earliest political score. Protest about Hiss's appearance was loud and insistent. Smith lost his sponsor in the ensuing controversy, and the show was cancelled.

Between 1963 and 1969, Smith worked at ABC in a kind of semi-retirement; his primary job was hosting a little-seen Sunday afternoon program, *Issues and Answers*. In 1966, he was named the anchor of *Scope*, a weekly documentary program focused on coverage of Vietnam.

Unlike many other newsmen who became progressively disillusioned with the war, Smith became more and more hawkish as the war progressed. Among other things, he advocated bombing North Vietnam's dike system, bombing Haiphong, and invading Laos and Cambodia. Indeed, in one of his commentaries shortly after the Tet Offensive, Smith said, "There exists only one real alternative. That is to escalate, but this time on an overwhelming scale."

Smith's conservative drift on foreign affairs also was reflected in his domestic views. He was vociferous in his support of Vice President Spiro T. Agnew's 1969 "Des Moines speech," in which the vice president accused the television networks producers, newscasters, and commentators of a highly selective and often biased presentation of the news. Smith concurred, and in strong language for a broadcast of that day, he criticized network newsmen as being, among other things, "conformist," adhering to a liberal "party line," and, at least in some cases, as lacking "the depth of a saucer."

ABC still broadcast fifteen-minute news, and it felt it had no room for him. In 1968, ABC bit the bullet and went to a full half-hour, a big decision for the network at that time. They needed to compete with CBS and NBC and continued to struggle for an identity. Frank Reynolds was the anchor for the half-hour show, *ABC Evening News,* which included a spot for commentaries. Smith got the occasional slot, but ABC used a number of guest commentators, ranging from Bill Moyers to Gore Vidal. ABC paid these guests a good deal of money at a time when it could barely afford to keep the news on the air. The feedback from viewers was positive, but the accountants at ABC pressured the news division to stop hemorrhaging money to these people. So, ABC decided to do something unheard of for network news. It put two anchors who held radically diverging views on a variety of subjects on the program. The unintended consequence was that the program became best known for the running disagreements between the anchors as they all but attacked each other's views on the air. The anchor team of Frank Reynolds and Howard K. Smith was born in 1969.

It was an awkward match. A low point of the program came when Vice President Spiro Agnew said the press was biased, and Smith and Reynolds—on air—took opposing views. However, the lowest point came after ABC top management lured Harry Reasoner away from CBS. ABC announced a team of Howard K. Smith and Harry Reasoner as nightly news anchors, and Frank Reynolds spontaneously announced his own dismissal on the air.

But the move to hire Reasoner paid off handsomely. The combination of the two broadcasters was a dream match. Smith's acerbity was balanced by Reasoner's wit, and Reasoner's flashes of glibness were balanced, in turn, by Smith's sobriety. Within eighteen months, "Howard and Harry" on *ABC Evening News with Howard K. Smith and Harry Reasoner* was a fixture in American television, and although it did not overtake either CBS or NBC in the ratings, it drew mighty close—close enough to prompt NBC to reshuffle its line-up.

For the first time, there were three legitimate news choices— the trusted Cronkite, the thoughtful Chancellor, and the spice of Reasoner and Smith. The ABC team was entirely different from Huntley and Brinkley, but it came from an authentic news background and had undeniable chemistry onscreen.

Smith, based in Washington, was sober, critical, opinionated, and sometimes haughty. He had a light Louisiana drawl and a polished delivery that only thirty-five years of practice could bestow. Reasoner was sunny, literary, beguiling, and discursive. Viewers who would not accept thirty minutes of either were delighted with thirty minutes of both.

Neither man saw personality or character as the focus of the broadcast, but rather as a focal point and a filter through which the daily news could be shared effectively. Smith and Reasoner were celebrities, but they used their celebrity to communicate their vision, not only in the substance of the news, but its style.

One highlight of the Reasoner and Smith program's run was the coverage of Watergate. The multi-part coverage of Nixon's departure in 1974, featuring reports from Reasoner and Smith, as well as from future luminaries John Palmer and Ted Koppel, were especially good. But those were choice years for television reporting because of several historic events: the moon landings; Nixon's imposition of wage and price controls; the passing of Eisenhower, Johnson, and Truman; the Yom Kippur War; the oil embargo; and Chappaquiddick, to name a few. They were years of memorable triumphs and desert-like stretches of gloom.

Why did the broadcast end? Not because it was beaten. Lincoln once said that the United States could never be conquered by a foreign power, that it would have to fall because of self-annihilation. So it was with "Howard and Harry".

As the Network Turns

The two anchors disliked the dual-anchor format and wanted the sole anchor job. Neither would have succeeded; both failed in their solo shots early and late in their careers, Reasoner famously and immediately. But stars have clout, and clout forces choices, so somebody had to be chosen. Top management went with Reasoner. The announcement was made in mid-1975 that Howard K. Smith would, in future, become a commentator on the broadcast, rather than an anchor.

The axe fell. Smith accepted the move with public good grace. He continued to serve as commentator on the broadcast as ABC went into a disastrous nosedive with Harry Reasoner alone, and then with Reasoner and Barbara Walters. Then when new ABC News president Roone Arledge announced a multi-anchor approach with Reynolds, Walters, Max Robinson, and Peter Jennings, Smith called it quits. He pinned a one-page resignation letter to the ABC bulletin board and walked out.

Smith continued to be active. He was selected as moderator of the 1980 Reagan-Carter debate, where he reassumed the role he played in the 1960 Kennedy-Nixon debate. He also prepared a highly lauded four-part documentary, *Every Four Years*, about the presidency.

Like many aging stars, Smith made cameo appearances in film and television, appearing as a news commentator in *V*, *Escape from Sobibor*, and *The Best Little Whorehouse in Texas*, among other films. He continued to narrate documentaries from time to time. He published his memoir, *Events Leading Up to My Death: The Life of a Twentieth-Century Reporter*, in 1996.

Smith died after a bout with congestive heart failure at his home in Bethesda, Maryland. He was eighty-seven years old. He is survived by his wife of fifty-five years, Benedicte Traberg Smith—the Dane he married after that four-day acquaintance. His legacy is one of unblinking insistence on the primacy of informed opinion as a necessary part of the anchor's trade. Like all anchors, he built up a character over the years, in his case, an acerbic, almost strident commentator whose positions could not be easily defined as "liberal" or "conservative," but which were strongly felt, eloquently worded, and delivered with candor and courage. He was the last of the original Murrow Boys actively on television, and he served the Murrow vision admirably, adding in a considerable amount of Louisiana-style cayenne pepper along the way.

Chapter NINE

Harry Reasoner, ABC

Courtesy of ABC

The geography of the United States is dominated in its center by a great triangular watershed that feeds the Great Lakes and the Gulf of Mexico. Although the population center of the country is in the east, the central area is known as the heartland.

Of all the stars who served as regulars behind the nightly news anchor desk, only six hail from outside the heartland: John Charles Daly, David Brinkley, Barbara Walters, Max Robinson, Peter Jennings, and Connie Chung. Of those six, all are associated in some way with calculated gambles made by ABC to counter-program against the once-dominant news organizations at CBS and NBC.

When we think of classic heartland anchors, like Walter Cronkite, John Chancellor, Tom Brokaw, and Harry Reasoner, we associate them with an often warm, sometimes wry, but never arch personality. In every case, a certain solidity of character and gentility of spirit made him welcome in that crucible of network news success—the American living room.

Harry Reasoner was one of the last great heartland anchors. We rightly associate his wry, relaxed, insightful, "emperor-has-no-clothes" outlook with that of the heartland and the Mississippi River system because he is the authentic descendent of the voice and outlook of another son of the Mississippi, Huckleberry Finn.

Gary Paul Gates described Harry Reasoner's style in his book *Air Time* and called it "the sunny side of the street". Why was the sunny side of the street so popular with viewers in the 1960s, versus the tougher, tell-it-like-it-is style of the 1940s? In both decades, Americans faced crises, but, to a far greater extent, the crisis came from outside the United States in the 1940s, and external threats require less delicate handling. By the late 1960s, when the South and the cities were crumbling under racial tensions and Vietnam brought the carnage of war into American living rooms, a softer style found a place.

But Harry Reasoner brought more than a soft, warm style to the television screen. More than any other anchor, perhaps, he realized the paradox of television anchoring. Viewers can be thousands of miles from the network studios in New York, and yet be beguiled into believing that they know anchors. Television is not only a medium of pictures, but also of tone. It is a medium of prose, but, more importantly, cadence. Anchors speak to a audiences large enough to fill three hundred stadiums, and can move them with a gesture as subtle as a wink.

Reasoner knew that the borderline between mawkish, hackneyed performance and storytelling laced with humanity could not be mapped by science. It is an art form; it is personal; it is directly from the eyes of the anchor to the eyes of the viewer. It is for that reason that Reasoner resisted focus groups, rehearsals, and teamwork with other anchors. He viewed anchoring as an unusually personal occupation.

Along with David Brinkley, Reasoner was considered to be one of the best writers. He brought a writer's eye and a real grasp of the literary culture to his material. Like Brinkley, he was subject to the criticism of being facile, flippant, or glib; he developed a reputation for, from time to time, winging a broadcast with literary skill rather than solid preparation. Yet no one, except Brinkley, could so light up a broadcast with his wry wit.

Brinkley, however, had the considerable advantage of recognizing the strength of the tandem format, and as much as he detested the "Good night, Chet; goodnight, David" routine, he recognized that it was good for business. Harry Reasoner didn't want to say goodnight to Chet Huntley, Howard K. Smith, Walters, or any of the others with whom he was teamed. He wanted to say goodnight to the viewer, to us.

Reasoner's destiny was to work in a team, but he labored mightily for independence and control. He found his true home on the magazine show *60 Minutes*, where the correspondents rule over their own commonwealths, freely associated with each other under the general aegis of the overall program and the specific aegis of Don Hewitt, but otherwise independently self-governing.

The culture of *60 Minutes*, with its star correspondents, its producers, and its complete absence of an anchor, was an anomaly at CBS, albeit a hugely successful one. In the culture of CBS in the 1960s, all roads in broadcast journalism led to the one true Rome, and the emperor of Rome was, without question, the anchor of the nightly network news: Cronkite ruled.

By contrast, NBC had no particular emphasis on one emperor or another, or even a one-emperor format. It was content, on occasion, to permit two or even three emperors in multiple-anchor or revolving-anchor formats. It also was happy to accommodate competing princes, as long as the effort paid off commercially, with higher ratings and strong critical reception. No one faulted *Huntley-Brinkley* for straying from "the storied tradition of John Cameron Swayze," and Chancellor was expected to succeed Brinkley, not become him. Yet no one stuck by Chancellor the way CBS stuck by Edwards and, in his early days, Cronkite.

ABC, as the third network in a two-network race, was willing to grant the imperial purple to anyone in any format who could win battles in the field. It had the most experimental approach to anchor selections. Thus, ABC was the network that typically landed the anchoring "firsts": the first anchor younger than thirty years old, the first woman, the first African American, the first foreign-born anchor, the first anchor to host a game show on a competing network, the first anchor formerly fired by another network, the first anchor formerly fired by the same network, and so on. There was little continuity between regimes.

Reasoner was a CBS man. He bested a number of possible rivals and became second only to Cronkite. However, he realized that by the time Cronkite was ready to go, he would be passed over as too old, so he bolted the network.

ABC was glad to give him a seat at the anchor desk, albeit on a shared basis with Howard K. Smith. When ratings went up, ABC also was happy to grant him a sole anchor job. When ratings went down, ABC paired him with Barbara Walters. When ratings went down again, they moved to a three-anchor format and bumped Reasoner down to commentator.

"I would rather be first in a little Iberian village than second in Rome," Julius Caesar said, and Reasoner would have understood. But in refusing to be second in "Rome," Reasoner ended up no better than fourth at ABC by 1979. He then went back to CBS as a *60 Minutes* mainstay who was not seriously considered as Cronkite's successor in 1981.

Instead, Cronkite was succeeded by Dan Rather. How had Rather started up the ladder of success? He succeeded none other than Harry Reasoner, an irony that Reasoner might have appreciated more than any other person.

Lou Grant

Courtesy of ABC

Reasoner was born in Dakota City, Iowa, in 1923, on the banks of the Des Moines River. The child of two schoolteachers, he grew up in the small town of Humboldt. His family relocated to Minneapolis in 1935, where he lost both his parents by the time he was sixteen.

He entered the University of Minnesota in 1941. He took journalism classes and wrote for the *Minneapolis Times* on the side. His newspaper days were halted when he was drafted into the army in 1943. He served until 1946. When he returned to the United States, he wrote a well-received novel, *Tell Me About Women*, but it sold modestly. Reasoner did not pursue a career as a novelist. Rather, he married and began what became a large family of seven children.

He took a series of media-related jobs between 1946 and 1956 that gave him broad experience. He was a rewrite man and drama critic at his old paper, the *Times*. He spent two years in public relations for Northwest Airlines before coming back to news for WCCO radio in Minneapolis. He went to work for the United States Information Agency in Manila for three years, returned to the United States, and became a news director at a Minneapolis television station. Lou Grant would have been proud to know that Harry Reasoner was a working news director at a real Minneapolis television station. But Reasoner left his version of Mary, Ted, and Murray behind and headed for New York.

He was hired at CBS, where he initially worked at a desk job in camera assignments. Under the tutelage of Don Hewitt, he branched out into field producing and reporting before he became a CBS correspondent in 1958.

Reasoner was frequently compared to a younger, but equally new, Charles Kuralt. What separated Reasoner from his colleagues was his writing style. Compared to many newsmen, it had real flow and style, and he could write terrific narration for himself.

In 1957, Reasoner catapulted into high favor at CBS because of his reporting of the desegregation crisis at Little Rock, Arkansas. In 1954, the Supreme Court ruled 9–0 that segregated schools violated the Fifteenth Amendment, and schools were ordered to integrate. President Eisenhower allowed time for the schools to integrate in an orderly process, but, in 1957,

Eisenhower stepped up the pressure on recalcitrant school districts in the South.

On September 2, 1957, the night before school was to start, Arkansas governor Orval Faubus called out the state's National Guard to surround Little Rock Central High School to prevent any African-American students from entering. He claimed that protesters were headed in caravans toward Little Rock, and he was protecting citizens and property from possible violence. A federal judge granted an injunction against the governor's use of National Guard troops to prevent integration, and they were withdrawn on September 20, 1957.

When school resumed on Monday, September 23, Central High was surrounded by Little Rock policemen. Approximately one thousand people gathered in front of the school. The police escorted the nine African-American students to a side door. When the mob learned the African Americans were inside, it began to challenge the police and surge toward the school with shouts and threats. Fearful the police would be unable to control the crowd, the school administration moved the African-American students out a side door before noon.

Congressman Brooks Hays and Mayor Woodrow Mann asked the federal government for help. On September 24, Mann sent a telegram to President Eisenhower to request troops. They were dispatched that day. The president also federalized the entire Arkansas National Guard, taking it away from the governor. On September 25, 1957, the nine students entered the school under the protection of one thousand members of the 101st Airborne Division of the United States Army.

Reasoner reported the events with uncanny style. Audiences connected with the way he wrote the story. Reasoner recalled in his book, *Before the Colors Fade*, that the Little Rock event was a turning point in television news. "The thing about Little Rock is that it was where television reporting came to influence, if not to maturity. As in the case of the Vietnam War a decade later, things might have been very different if it weren't for the new impact of television news: you could not hide from it."

He went on to cover such events as Nikita Khrushchev's visit to the United States in 1960. Khrushchev made extraordinarily good television, with gestures like taking his shoe off and banging it on a desk to make a point. He provided Reasoner with incredible opportunities to shine. And shine he did. By 1963, he was given the anchor slot on *Calendar*, a weekend magazine show with a literary edge. He also substituted for Cronkite and anchored the Sunday evening news. It was Reasoner who wrote and produced the CBS obituary on President Kennedy after the assassination. He substituted for Walter Cronkite during the days of coverage, and it was Reasoner who was on the air on CBS that Sunday afternoon when Jack Ruby shot Lee Harvey Oswald.

Reasoner met Andy Rooney on *Calendar*, which Reasoner co-hosted. Rooney wrote a bunch of lighthearted documentaries for CBS, which Reasoner narrated. Rooney had an extraordinary way of writing for Reasoner; in turn, no one delivered a Rooney script like Reasoner. Their distinctive partnership paved the way to stardom on *60 Minutes*.

Don Hewitt decided to build the *60 Minutes* concept around Reasoner's trademark wit and the range of soft and hard news stories for which he was celebrated. Ever since critic John Lardner identified *See It Now* as "higher Murrow" and *Person to Person* as "lower Murrow," Hewitt was intrigued by the idea of a news magazine show that combined the two. He thought Reasoner alone had the range. But, having received the green light for the show, Hewitt had second thoughts. Could Reasoner actually pull it off alone? Hewitt, along with Bill Leonard, began to think in terms of two correspondents, and he brought in Mike Wallace because of his facility with the heavier stories.

It was prescient, but, at the time, Reasoner's major focus was on his Sunday evening newscast and his role as "permanent guest host" for Walter Cronkite. It was easy for Reasoner to see that, in 1970, Uncle Walter wasn't going anywhere except up in the ratings, and that if he wanted the top job, it would have to be elsewhere.

Reasoner took the assignment at ABC, even though it meant joining an established anchor, Howard K. Smith, in a two-anchor format. He reported for work in December, 1970.

Eric Sevareid said Reasoner brought to the field of journalism "a certain grace and reflectfulness". To ABC, he brought a twenty-two share—a nose behind NBC and up from fifteen before his arrival. The program was a hit, and because Howard K. Smith had been at the anchor desk when the show was mired in third place, Reasoner received the lion's share of the credit.

His timing was fortuitous. As American involvement in Vietnam wound down, there was less emphasis placed on the war correspondent and more on the anchor back in New York. Yet the tribulations of the Nixon Administration ensured a strong focus on news. Plus, NBC was in temporary disarray in the aftermath of Chet Huntley's retirement.

But the reason for the show's success was more than Smith. It was more than Smith and Reasoner. It was, in large part, Harry Reasoner's skill. What did he do that was different? His primary device was the closing story. He used offbeat material to shape unusual pieces.

Reasoner and Smith and Walters

Smith and Reasoner never hit it off, never achieved a personal chemistry, but the television never showed it. Their team clicked like no team since Huntley and Brinkley; and no team since has equaled their impact on the American news scene. Reasoner in New York and Smith in Washington had the same locations as Huntley and Brinkley, but the polarity was reversed. Instead of the witty observer in Washington who commented on the foibles of government folly, Smith's solid but often "smash mouth" stories came from the capital, with Reasoner's wistful, "catcher in the wry" stories coming from, of all places, cosmopolitan New York.

Smith, "the heavy," was in the right place at the right time during Watergate. His presence in Washington gave them a strong voice in the capital during the years when Dan Rather was making his national reputation as CBS White House correspondent. David Brinkley's reputation suffered greatly during this period, and Reasoner, who had held the CBS White House job in the 1960s, would have been in a quagmire.

Most importantly, the combination clicked with the public. Contrast was in. *All in the Family*, *Sonny and Cher*, and the *Mary Tyler Moore Show* gave us Archie and Edith, Sonny and Cher, and Mary Richards and Lou Grant. Differences won the ratings then. Combative partnership was hot. News teaming is far more closely related to entertainment programming than perhaps we like to think. Reasoner and Smith benefited from the prevailing interest in contrast. ABC, in pairing them, shrewdly guessed the spirit of the times.

By 1975, Reasoner had enough. His contract was up, and it was time for him to strike for the solo anchor slot he felt he needed and earned. He was fifty-two years old and at the zenith of his popularity. Smith was duly relegated to the commentator's slot, and Reasoner went it alone.

The same year, *Sonny and Cher* made their television comeback in a we're-divorced-but-we're-still-together format. Both pairings had the same fate: ratings plunged. Although the

broadcasts were some of Reasoner's best, the network panicked. Then along came Barbara Walters with a celebrated
salary of one million dollars.

The partnership of Reasoner and Walters never worked,
and the responsibility lay primarily with Reasoner. On many
occasions, Reasoner walked off the set without saying a word.
It was reported that Reasoner felt Walters got a free ride on
her *Today* show celebrity. Reasoner thought of her as a host,
not a serious journalist. The incompatibility revealed the incredible gap perceived by the staffs of the morning and
evening shows. Walters and Reasoner managed to keep it together on air, but barely. No hint of friendliness ever crept
across the set and out into Middle America, and the bottom
fell out of the ratings.

ABC decided to make a change in 1978, and the change
brought Reasoner to the same commentator's post to which
Howard K. Smith had been relegated just three years back.
Reasoner made the move back to CBS and *60 Minutes*.

The Stopwatch Winds Down

He was home. Gone were the days of sharing the desk and reporting on the major dramas of the times. Now, with his "calm,
analytical, and introspective persona," according to the Museum of Broadcasting profile of *60 Minutes*, he "became part of
his 'new form' of storytelling, allowing the audience to watch
their intimate involvement in discovering information, trip-
ping up an interviewee, and developing a narrative. As a result, [he was] often central to Hewitt's notion of stories as
morality plays, the confrontation of vice and virtue."

An interview with snake oil salesman Doc Willard and one
of the devotees of his "Willard Water" in Rapid City, South
Dakota, exemplifies Reasoner's broadcasting style:

REASONER: So, what's in it that could make so many things happen? Well, a little liquid road salt, that's what melts snow and rots your car, and sodium silicate and magnesium sulfate and sulfated castor oil, and then Doc Willard mixes some of it with powdered lignite. What you have finally are various mixtures called by different names: LA Water (it has nothing to do with that town in California, it means lignite activated water) or CAW water, catalyst activated water. But it's all Willard Water, whatever it is.

DOC WILLARD: Well, it's the calcium magnesium, polysilicate polymer with a castor oil . . .

REASONER: Now that's chemist talk. You've already lost me.

DOC WILLARD: All right. It's a catalyst that alters the structure of the water, making water behave in a manner that heretofore has not been reported in the literature.

REASONER: Whatever "real" Willard Water is, we set out to visit some folks around Rapid City who talk about what it has done for them. On burns, for example, producer Paul Loewenwarter talked with Chauncey Taylor, who scorched his leg doing some welding on an old oil drum.

CHAUNCEY TAYLOR: The fumes in it, I guess, ignited and blowed out a hole and melted my overalls. I had a pair of poly . . . polyester overalls on, and it melted them and melted my shirt and burnt my leg.

PAUL LOEWENWARTER: So you looked down and just saw your leg charred?

TAYLOR: I looked down and the skin was just hanging all different ways there.

LOEWENWARTER: Well, what did you do to treat it?

TAYLOR: Oh, I had a bottle of this LA Water and I just started squirting it on there and just kept pouring it on, a fine mist.

LOEWENWARTER: And what does it do?

TAYLOR: It heals it, I guess.

Reasoner spent twelve years on *60 Minutes* before his retirement in 1991. His work continued to cover a wide range of subjects, from hard news to soft. He retired in 1991 with the same boss at CBS as he had started out with in 1956, Don Hewitt. Reasoner worked with long-standing colleagues Andy Rooney (since 1963) and Mike Wallace (since 1968) and continued to hang out with the writers.

Reasoner underwent surgery for lung cancer in 1987 and 1988. He retired from CBS in May, 1991. In August, 1991, he tumbled down stairs at his Westport, Connecticut, home and developed a blood clot on the brain. He passed away on August 6, 1991. True to his heartland roots, he was laid to rest in Humboldt, Iowa.

Although his fame rests on his work on *60 Minutes* and he did his best work there, his influence remains on anchoring style. The rich, reflective end-piece is his legacy, and those who use the device are in his debt. Further, with Howard K. Smith, he succeeded in putting ABC News firmly and forever on the ratings map.

John Chancellor, NBC

Chapter TEN

Courtesy of Globe Photo/NBC

Among the many glittering prizes awarded in journalism, the one with perhaps the most personal story behind it is the John Chancellor Award for Excellence in Journalism, granted annually since 1996.

The prize was endowed at the University of Pennsylvania by Ira Lipman, the chairman of a security services firm and a member of the Board of Overseers of the Wharton School. In 1957, Lipman was a sixteen-year-old high school senior in Little Rock, Arkansas, when the desegregation crisis exploded in his own school district.

On the night before school started, the newly elected governor, Orval Faubus, a segregationist, called up the Arkansas National Guard to prevent nine black high school students from enrolling at Central the next day. It provoked a crisis that led President Eisenhower to call up the National Guard to assume federal control and ensure the safety of the children and their integration into the high school.

The crisis brought the networks down to Little Rock, and NBC sent John Chancellor. Lipman was a friend of one of the nine students. Attending another city high school, he followed the events on NBC.

Lipman later recalled, "The world simply had to know the truth of what was going on inside Central High. I looked up to John Chancellor and knew that he was a fair man—a good man—and that through his reporting, he was certain to have a profound effect on the entire nation."

Chancellor was not allowed inside the school, but Lipman, because of his position as editor of his high school's yearbook, which was printed at Central, did. He became a source for Chancellor inside the school, and he relayed reports to the NBC correspondent about the conditions inside Central High. The two began a thirty-nine–year friendship, and Lipman ultimately established the journalism award in Chancellor's honor.

John Chancellor has been called one of "a few who stand as columns supporting the standards set by Edward R. Murrow" by the *Providence Journal*'s Tom Mooney. Robert MacNeil, former co-anchor of the *MacNeil-Lehrer News Hour*, has said that he modeled his reporting style after Chancellor.

Not every viewer becomes a source, and not every source endows a university with a prize named in the anchor's honor. But it was just the sort of thing that, if it happened to anyone, it would happen to John Chancellor. Urbane without being pretentious, warm without becoming cloying, a communicator without a trick, a humorist without a shtick, a commentator without an axe to grind, he never achieved Cronkite's remarkable reputation as "the most trusted man in America," but he was, for many viewers, a close second. In short, he was the Rock of 30 Rock (the NBC studios at 30 Rockefeller Center)—a solid television news anchor. Noted not so much for how he changed the role of a classic anchor, but for how well he personified the standards he inherited.

His base for many years was Washington—at the epicenter of that political establishment—but during his tenure as anchor, he saw politics and national news diminish in their importance to the national culture. During nearly eleven years as NBC anchor, the nation saw the end of the Vietnam War and Watergate, the flowering of televised national sports, blockbuster movies, FM radio, the rise of cable television and the superstations, and the introduction of VCRs. All those cultural milestones challenged news and network television for the central position in the "did you see that?" derby around the nation's water coolers.

Honest John

When Chancellor inherited the anchor role, there was disarray at NBC because the network executives did not know how to structure the news after Chet Huntley's retirement. But everyone knew what the news was, and all the networks covered it, more or less, in the same manner with varying degrees of success. Each network had thirty-minute newscasts augmented by national and foreign correspondents with major operations in Washington and New York.

The always-quotable Chancellor defined news as "a chronicle of conflict and change," knowing from the outset that there was no margin in covering the status quo. The conflicts and the change were essentially political, and the story of his time was freedom—the preservation of freedom from foreign threat and the promotion of freedom both foreign and domestic in the expansion of civil rights both economic and political. The backdrop for his time was the awesome specter of the Cold War. Everything paled in comparison to it, and the capitals of the Cold War—Berlin, Saigon, Moscow, and Brussels—were Chancellor's proving ground.

He became known for his civility, forthrightness, humor, and a bottomless fund of common sense. He flourished in an era when top reporters and anchors seemed always to be on the edge of politics. Indeed, Murrow and Cronkite were approached to go into politics. Chancellor and Bill Moyers worked in the Johnson Administration. The Nixon Administration employed Diane Sawyer, Pat Buchanan, David Gergen, John McLaughlin, Ben Stein, and William Safire.

When Chancellor arrived at NBC in 1950, the issues were the Soviet Union, the faltering economy, and civil rights. The competition was CBS and ABC. When he left the anchor desk in 1982, the issues were the Soviet Union, the faltering economy, and women's rights. The competition was CBS and ABC. The competition was as precisely defined as an Olympic sport, and the challenge was, simply and profoundly, to be the best.

Chancellor once recalled a story that underscored the dominance of the three networks:

> Lyndon Johnson was what they now call a media freak. He had the ticker tapes in his office. Frank Stanton [of CBS] used to give to people in the administration these little arrays of three television sets and a box. You pressed various buttons on the box and you could get the sound coming from any one of the three networks.

It is remarkable to us now that a president watched only three channels in order to have a sense of the coverage of the news. Then there were the three network evening news telecasts; now there are one hundred shows. Back then, viewers could start watching at six o'clock EST, when the early evening ABC telecast began in Baltimore. By 7:27, when the CBS evening news signed off and went to the mid-hour commercials, viewers knew where the country stood. Today, viewers would have to watch television twenty-four hours a day.

Chancellor's particular challenges were to somehow follow the hugely successful Huntley and Brinkley regime and to compete with Walter Cronkite, who had a nine-year head start in building rapport with the viewers. Chancellor also had to survive the challenge posed by the rising popularity of Howard K. Smith and Harry Reasoner at ABC.

When Chancellor left the anchor desk in 1982, Cronkite, Reasoner, and Smith were all gone. Jennings was at the desk at ABC, Rather was at CBS, and Tom Brokaw was his co-anchor at NBC. Already, the epochal shift in television was underway— there was a rise in cable (and especially CNN) viewership and an increased focus on prime time news programming. Chancellor met the challenge without arrogance or overt showmanship, just news. His delivery and on-camera dynamics were classic and understated. His voice was warm and friendly. If Cronkite was "Uncle Walter," then Chancellor at least qualified for "Honest John".

Big Dreams, and Then . . .

Courtesy of Globe Photo/NBC

John William Chancellor was born on the north side of Chicago. His parents were in the hotel business and lost their chain of small properties during the Depression. He was an only child, and his parents were divorced when he was twelve. He dropped out of a Catholic high school when he was fifteen. He wanted to be an author or even a journalist, but he knew that would come later, as he had to earn money to survive on his own. He began a string of jobs that included a hospital orderly, a lab assistant, a parking attendant, a job interviewer, and even a deckhand on a riverboat. All the while, he wrote on his lunch hours and at night. He remembered:

I was working as a hospital orderly and waiting to be drafted at the time of V-E Day. I recall that everybody felt very good when V-E Day came. Thank goodness, we had won in Europe and now it was time to beat the Japanese. Everybody in my age group was waiting for a letter saying: "Greetings."

I had poor eyesight, so the other services had turned me down. But, about four months after V-E Day, my letter came, and I went into the army. I ended up at the Army Information School at Carlisle Barracks, [Pennsylvania].

After the army, he was picked up by the *Chicago Sun-Times* as a copy boy. He worked his way up to reporter and moved to the NBC station in Chicago in 1950 as a film editor and reporter. Two years later, he received a good deal of attention for his coverage of the 1952 Democratic National Convention in Chicago. NBC President William McAndrew was favorably impressed, and Chancellor was signed by the network. So, it was off to New York City, where they started him off as a writer for the *Camel News Caravan*. It was during this period that NBC strengthened its ranks of correspondents. David Brinkley became the correspondent in Washington, and Chancellor began covering the Midwest and South. Reuven Frank molded this team into what eventually became the *Huntley-Brinkley Report*, which began shakily in 1956, but by 1957, was on its way to an unprecedented ten-year run atop the ratings.

The year 1957 brought desegregation in Little Rock, and Chancellor's reports on Central High School led the *Huntley-Brinkley Report* day after day. That year also brought him a coveted foreign assignment, and Chancellor moved to Vienna in 1958. Between 1958 and 1961, he was in London, Brussels, Moscow, and Berlin. Chancellor sat down with almost all of the presidents in his day, and foreign dignitaries often were seen in the seat across from the NBC anchor. His low-key style and the way he crafted his words won him praise along the way. In 1960, he was on the panel for the Kennedy-Nixon debates. In 1961, he sat across from Dave Garroway to do the *Today Show*. He called that experience "awful". He told CNN's Larry King, "I found myself introducing musical acts at 7:45 in the morning, and that was just too much for me. I wanted to get back to work."

The morning show experiment lasted less than two years. Chancellor was not the first of the anchors to work on the morning programs; Cronkite, Chancellor, Walters, and Brokaw all took their turns. Only Brokaw was successful in both assignments. Mixing show business and news underscores the fundamental entertainment element that is essential to morning success, but which tends to undercut the credibility of the evening anchor.

"I've Been Promised Bail"

The Associated Press remembers when Chancellor became a news story himself during the 1964 Republican National Convention:

> Chancellor blocked an aisle while conducting an interview, and the convention had police escort him off the floor. Television viewers watched Chancellor led out of the hall, giving a play-by-play into his microphone: "Here we go down the middle aisle. . . . I've been promised bail, ladies and gentlemen, by my office. This is John Chancellor, somewhere in custody."

In 1965, Chancellor was elevated to White House correspondent. He was one of the few anchors to develop a close relationship with any president, and he developed keen insights into Johnson and his administration:

> I remember one day, one of our lads here at NBC got the story that Maxwell Taylor was going to leave Saigon. He was then ambassador in Saigon. I got a call from our desk here in

Washington that we were going to go with the story—could I check it? And I tried to check it with Jack Valenti. . . . The broadcast was going on the eleven o'clock morning newscast on radio, and at about ten minutes to eleven, I got Valenti, and I said, "We're going to go ahead with the story that Max Taylor is leaving Saigon," which was a piece of important political news at the time.

And I said, "I just want you to know this." This is kind of a reporter's device. I said, "I want you to know this; we're going to go ahead with it, and do you have anything else to tell us about it?" He said, "No, I don't have anything else to tell you about it." And I said, "But you would say, Jack, that this wouldn't mean any change in American policy as far as Vietnam is concerned." He said, "No, absolutely not." And so I thought, well, that's just great because Valenti has just told me that this is true.

Parenthetically, it wasn't true.

It did take place about four months later, but I think I had foxed Jack. In any case, I went on and did what we call a little shirt-tail, and I said that the White House would not confirm nor deny this, but "if it is true,"—and I'm happy I said that because it didn't turn out to be quite true—"if it is true, it does not mean any change in American policy."

Then I went back to my little cubicle there in the press room and the phone rang, and it was the president. . . . He was furious! He said, "That's not true. Why didn't you ask me? I'm a hundred yards away from you right now. Why didn't you just come in and ask me?"

You know, you just don't go in and ask presidents questions like that. I remember answering, I thought for a minute, and I said, "Well, Mr. President, I can't come and ask you that. You're running the country."

The *Voice of America*

Although Chancellor initially attempted to turn down the appointment he received to work on *Voice of America*, he received pressure from NBC, as well as President Johnson, to accept it. Chancellor said, "My wife and I spent quite a bit of time that spring with the Johnsons, and this culminated in my being appointed to the *Voice of America* job."

He was the first professional journalist to hold the post, which combined telling the truth with a point of view. "Nothing that we said at the [United States Information Agency] USIA was ever untrue—but it was the arrangement of the truthful information that made the point," Chancellor once said.

Henry Loomis had just resigned his post with *Voice of America*, and many felt it was over increased pressures of government interference, censorship issues, and politics. Chancellor perhaps did not know what he was getting into. He told an interviewer for the Johnson Library:

> I remember having a conversation with the president in which I said, "If I do this (I guess I'd said by then I would), you're going to have a lot of trouble with me if we get into any policy disagreements." And he said, "I want you to go down there and run it the way you want it run, and I'll give you all the backing-up I can. So will everybody else in the White House. You're my man down there." He was then going to appoint Leonard Marks as the head of the USIA. He said, "You go and talk to Leonard and tell him I said that, and if you can't agree, then all three of us will get together and we'll agree on the standards."
>
> So I went to Leonard and I said, 'If I do this, I want the same freedom I would have if I were running NBC news. I can't take it on any basis narrower than that."
>
> And Leonard said, "Fine." Now, neither one of us then knew how you ran a thing like that, so that we were both being fairly innocent. But I give the president his due and Leonard Marks his due.
>
> They never broke that rule with me. We had policy disagreements about specific things, about small things, but in terms of general news policy at the *Voice*, which included

commentary, I was responsible for it, and I decided on its tone, and Leonard backed me up, and it never involved the White House. So Lyndon Johnson kept his word to me, and the *Voice*, if you'll go back through the records, was relatively serene in that period. There was no trouble. There was no public worrying about the quality of the *Voice* in terms of its freedom.

Riding Off Into . . . Well, Not Yet

Returning to NBC in late 1967, Chancellor increasingly was seen along with NBC space correspondent Frank McGee as a successor to Huntley and Brinkley, if the need arose. In July, 1970, Chet Huntley retired to his ranch in Montana, and NBC did not quite know how to structure its anchor package.

So the network decided to rotate anchors using Chancellor, McGee, and Brinkley seven nights per week. The instability drove the ratings down, and there was pressure for the news division to make up its mind and move on. So it did; it cast Chancellor in the role of anchor. He went back to New York and decided to stay a while. It was a decision that kept him there for the next eleven years. For three of those years (1976–1979), Brinkley appeared as co-anchor with Chancellor. NBC thought it would help boost unstable ratings, but it had little effect.

When Chancellor took the anchor chair, he had more experience than any other anchor before him—twenty years of experience. Only Cronkite, with twenty-five years of reporting experience, but only twelve years of television experience, rivaled him for mastery of the television arts.

The primary story during Chancellor's first years was Vietnam. As he had done in 1965, with a documentary on Lyndon Johnson at the Johnson Ranch, Chancellor arranged with the White House for *A Day in the Life of a President* documentary. It was filmed in December, 1971. H.R. Haldeman wrote:

All in all, it was quite a tour de force. He had the TV cameras in the office much longer than they had planned or we had planned to give them, which is, of course all to the good. His attitude was a little snappy at the start of the day, but it picked up considerably, and when he had me in at 9:30 for the staff period, he was cranking under full steam.

John Chancellor and the NBC people were ecstatic with the way the whole day went, particularly with the amount of time the president was letting crew have in his office.

Chancellor once said:

Television news, in my judgment, when looking at presidents, tends to be very much of a passive medium. The president makes a speech, we cover it. The president has a news conference, we cover it. The president signs some legislation, we cover it. And there is, I am sorry to say, not yet on television the room for the kind of commentary you get in newspapers and the kind of critical judgments you can make in magazines. So I think television was not unkind to [President] Johnson, in that it transmitted to the country Johnson—for good or bad—but it was Johnson.

Two Years and Eighteen Minutes Later

By 1973, relations between the White House and the press corps collapsed under the pressure of Watergate. Chancellor's handling of Nixon's resignation crisis was typical of the man:

CHANCELLOR: Good evening. President Nixon stunned the country today by admitting that he held back evidence from the House Judiciary Committee, keeping it a secret from his lawyers, and not disclosing it in public statements. The news has caused a storm in Washington, and some of Mr. Nixon's most loyal supporters are calling for his resignation. . . .

Chancellor's broadcast was profiled by Theodore H. White in his book *Breach of Faith: The Fall of Richard Nixon.* White wrote:

"And from there, the networks let the situation speak for itself. . . . The voices were all the same—bearing hurt, anger, contempt, incomprehension all through the night."

By 1976, Chancellor still was not successful in making significant headway in his ratings battle with Cronkite, and the network paired Chancellor with Brinkley, who had delivered commentary. In 1977, the network launched a new format featuring longer stories on a shorter list of subjects. It presaged the long-form focus introduced in later years at countless prime time talking head shows on CNN and also the *MacNeil-Lehrer News Hour*. At the same time, ABC moved in the other direction, offering a "whip around" the world at a dizzying pace not seen since John Cameron Swayze had gone "hop-scotching the world for headlines" back in the 1950s.

For the first time ever, the three networks offered differently packaged products, but neither ABC nor NBC could take the lead from Cronkite. Chancellor asked to be re-assigned to commentaries long before he was released from the anchor role, but the network—while agreeing in principle—did not have a successor groomed. Chancellor stuck it out until 1983, losing Brinkley as co-anchor in 1979 and gaining Brokaw in 1982.

Chancellor found his calling with commentaries. He appeared three days per week from 1983–91 with ninety-second capsules. They became famous.

Knowing His Left from His Right

Chancellor gave views that were on both sides of the political line in a sort of one-man *Crossfire*.

[FROM THE RIGHT, I'M JOHN CHANCELLOR]: The Soviets have been modernizing their submarine fleet for the last ten years, and [it] has continued under Gorbachev . . . more than nine hundred missiles are on Soviet subs. Each missile contains several warheads, which means that thousands of nuclear weapons are aimed at American cities right now. . . . The Soviets have kept the world's largest submarine fleet in place within striking distance of American targets.

[AND FROM THE LEFT, I'M JOHN CHANCELLOR]: [on postage rates] Thirty cents is a bargain when you compare it to what other countries charge. . . . It is a little like the price of gasoline, which is cheaper here than almost anywhere. A bigger federal tax on gasoline would bring down the deficit, but our leaders say it is politically impossible to raise the taxes.

On the same topic a few months later, Chancellor said, "The federal government desperately needs more revenue, but the Republican president has been saying no new taxes, and the Democrats have been going along. West Germany and Japan have higher tax rates, and they're in better shape than the United States. What is striking about this is that some of the smartest, toughest people in the country say taxes ought to be raised."

According to Media Watch: "Chancellor was equally surprising on Central America, where the networks often samba past the misdeeds of the left. He blasted Ortega five days later as a 'crook . . . [whom] Al Capone would have cheered'. . . ."

Happier Trails

In 1991, Chancellor retired after more than forty years in the industry. Along with his retirement from NBC went his commentaries. Network evening news has not seen them since. Nor have the networks had someone with John Chancellor's insight.

He shared his thoughts about the evolution of television news with the *Christian Science Monitor*. Chancellor told the *Monitor* that a television reporter must file his story as quickly as possible. With today's satellite transmission, it means instantaneous reporting. "I don't want to sound like an old geezer complaining, I do think that (the new technology) has changed the manner of a lot of reporting. It's too bad, because it detracts; it just means that you have people turning up for a lot of stories who aren't as well-grounded in those stories as maybe they ought to be."

He was treated for stomach cancer, and a *Boston Globe* reporter asked him if he feared death. He answered, "I've been an agnostic for as long as I can remember . . . so I don't know where we go. But if it turns out that the lights are just turned off and nothing happens, well, that's okay."

John Chancellor, who will always be known as not only a solid journalist, but also as one of television's first reporters, died two years later at the age sixty-eight, just two days before his birthday.

Of all the final words on John Chancellor, from tributes to critical assessments, the most eloquent was written by Chancellor himself on his last night as a commentator in 1991:

> It was a privilege to be in your home all these years. Thanks for your letters, not all of which I was able to answer. Some of those letters, you realize, were not complimentary. That goes with the territory. Commentary sometimes works best when it makes people angry. I owe a great debt to a multitude of colleagues at NBC News who encouraged me, instructed me, and put up with me. I've seen some of them become accomplished broadcasters, and Tom Brokaw is certainly a fine example of that. It's been a lot of fun. There's a little secret about journalism. We would do it for free if that were possible, but they actually pay us to do it.
>
> Finally, I want to thank those of you in the audience for your patience, courtesy, and hospitality over these many years. It was an honor to be a guest in your home.

Part Three

The Changing of the Guard

Associated Press

Chapter ELEVEN

Barbara Walters, ABC

Courtesy of ABC

Barbara Walters was to television news what the moon landing was to NASA. She was the first woman to grace a weekly evening news anchor desk, and her arrival there was the culmination of years of effort, both personal and by other women in news. Yet, having served as anchor, she left a mixed legacy, for it was seventeen years before Connie Chung followed her, and there have been none since.

However, Walters's turn as an anchor is quite significant. Walters was, in many ways, the first of the "modern" anchors. Her clash with Harry Reasoner can now, with time, be seen less as a battle of the sexes and more as a battle between two schools of thought concerning the role of the evening news within the news division and within the network organization.

Just a few years back, ABC News launched an aggressive promotion of its major network news personalities: David Brinkley, Peter Jennings, Walters, Hugh Downs, Sam Donaldson, Ted Koppel, and Diane Sawyer. They were dubbed the Magnificent Seven. One journalist wrote of the promotion, "A dyspeptic critic might seize on that photograph as a metaphor for how television news has evolved in forty years. Downs, after all, makes no claim to being a journalist, and he, like Brinkley, is a part-timer at the network. Walters and Sawyer have been called—not altogether justifiably—"personalities," "dabblers," and not real journalists engaged systematically in the thorny geopolitical issues of the day."

It must have been sad for Barbara Walters to find herself described as a dabbler after a forty-year news career that included work as a news writer, producer, morning show host, network anchor, news magazine show host, and celebrity interviewer. However, it cannot have been a shock to find herself described in those terms. Even Edward R. Murrow faced criticism over his popular program, *Person to Person*, from colleagues and critics who found it beneath his dignity to host a program so obviously lacking in stature. Walters, for all her substantial credentials, made such a specialty of celebrity interviews that she became indelibly associated with the role early in her career.

In the eyes of many colleagues, this association diminished her. Likewise, it colored her reputation in the eyes of many senior executives at news organizations who envied her ratings, but disparaged her means of garnering them. Further, she was diminished by a perception of "cat-fighting" with Diane Sawyer over key interview subjects. Some of this was warranted, but some was plain, old-fashioned competitiveness

Yet news, taken as a whole, is moving in Walters's direction. Now, multitalented anchors host in multiple formats. There is a focus on building shows around key news people with the stated goal of cracking into prime time. Nightly half-hour news programming is de-emphasized in favor of weekly, or even occasional "event" programming via specials. There is a convergence of sports, entertainment, and news features and techniques. All viewers are not focused onto one evening broadcast, but instead picked up through a studied programming mix of magazine shows, "event" journalism, morning shows, late night shows, and traditional evening broadcasts. And there is a pursuit of "chemistry" in co-anchors.

Practically every major trend in news today is expressed in Barbara Walters's career. She is a pathfinder for news organizations and news professionals seeking an understanding of how news careers will be shaped in years to come.

Today and Tomorrow

Nevertheless, if Barbara Walters was known for one thing above all else in her storied career, it was her 1976 appointment to the job of co-anchor, with Harry Reasoner, of the *ABC Evening News*. Her hiring was a landmark not only for the fact that she became the first female evening network news anchor, but even more for the creativity of her deal, the strategy behind it, and the role it outlined for her. The deal changed news, and changed it forever.

In 1974, Walters reached the top at NBC's *Today* after fifteen years on the show and a sometimes arduous climb out of obscurity. When she was appointed co-host in 1974, the promotion rewarded her fourteen years on *Today*, the last ten of which were spent in an all-but-host role. She was particularly known, even then, for her interviews (she penned the book *How to Talk with Practically Anybody About Practically Anything*, Dell Publishing Company, 1970, along the way). In terms of reputation and "heat," she was at the top of her game. At the same time, ABC was mired in third place and falling quickly in the nightly news ratings because its sole-anchor format with Harry Reasoner was not able to find the audience for which the network had hoped.

The president of ABC television was Frederick S. Pierce, and under his guidance, ABC began its storied rise out of third place with entertainment programming. A commentator wrote:

> The network's strategy stemmed from innovation, experimentation, risk, and diversity, words he frequently employed. He introduced the "living schedule," the practice of testing five to eight new series in late winter and the spring, each for a month or more, in preparation for fall scheduling. Pierce also referred to this practice, to be adopted by the other networks, as "investment spending," and thought of it as a way of respecting and responding to audience feedback. When the "family-viewing hour" was instituted, Pierce scheduled comedies and other fare from 8:00 to 9:00 P.M., and followed with action adventure programs, Monday through Friday. The strategy, called "clotheslining" or "ridgepoling," succeeding in holding viewers.

Pierce, who rose to the presidency after a twenty-year career in research and sales, was one of the first to approach the job with a grand strategy. His entertainment strategy began to pay off huge dividends in 1975–76, and by 1976–77, ABC became the most-watched network overall—a stunning result for the perennial bottom-dweller.

The strategic style of programming made it possible for shows like *Happy Days* to develop. It began as a short, one-shot segment of an ABC Friday night show, *Love, American Style,* called, "Love and the Happy Day," featuring Ron Howard as Richie Cunningham. After Howard's phenomenal success in the film *American Graffiti* and the emergence of a wave of 1950s nostalgia, a series was developed. *Happy Days* debuted as a mid-season replacement in 1974 and became the most highly rated show in 1976–77. (Another spin-off from the series, *Laverne and Shirley,* was the most highly rated show from 1977–79.)

This developmental culture featured an almost organic approach to growth. Aspects of programs were picked out for spin-off development, using the mid-season as a launching pad for smaller, riskier shows with great promise. Pierce inaugurated a greater emphasis on "event" programming, such as the Olympics or mini-series like *Roots* and the *Winds of War*.

When Walters was lured to ABC in 1976, the public focused on her million-dollar salary and her assignment as network news anchor. But Walters, however, understood at the time, and we can see with hindsight, that equally important were the four celebrity-interview specials she agreed to produce per year for ABC. They were exactly the sort of "event" programming ABC was looking for—news "events" that were planned and promoted like entertainment specials. Advertising led to premium rates, prime-time profits, and drew viewers away from NBC and CBS. The platform also was used to promote other ABC News and entertainment programming.

It was a wholly new way of approaching the news as a

business, and it was little understood at the time. The public focused on Walters in her new anchor role; the interview shows were perceived as pleasant add-ons. Consequently, what the public saw was Walters and Reasoner not getting along five days a week on the evening news. What the network saw—from its profit perspective—was four Walters financial block-busters every year.

In retrospect, we can understand the network's motivations. The news managers at ABC had to do something fast. The idea of a woman anchor might have been the shot in the arm the network needed to get the ratings up. But it was more than a case of panic when Reasoner's ratings began to fall. While the ABC newscast fell seven points since Howard K. Smith was rel-egated to commentator, and although it was obvious to most that Reasoner could use a straight man, it was not at all obvi-ous that Barbara Walters was the choice. In fact, ABC seriously considered pairing Roger Mudd with Harry Reasoner in 1975, but Mudd backed away because Reasoner, who was a close friend, badly wanted the solo anchor assignment. However, Reasoner gladly would have taken Mudd in 1976 over Walters. So why was she chosen?

The overwhelming impact of Roone Arledge and *Monday Night Football* must be taken into consideration because of the way they totally changed the way ABC thought about every-thing. *Monday Night Football* was an annual autumn monster that wiped out NBC and CBS in the very arena, NFL football, they had dominated for years. It did not just win its time slot, it consumed Monday nights and delivered unheard of ratings spikes with young adults and men—the ultimate prizes in early 1970s prime time. Previously, people joked that the best way to end the Vietnam War in thirteen weeks was to schedule it on ABC.

But *Monday Night Football* was more than a ratings

phenomenon. Like *All in the Family*, which debuted in the same season, it was a phenomenon for the way it broke taboos and shook established broadcasting traditions. It broke every rule. It put sports in prime time. It had three commentators in the same booth. It was a monumental breakthrough not in spite of its unusual packaging, but precisely because of it.

Frederick Pierce was one of the first executives to see the underlying connection between news and sports. This connection was amply demonstrated during the hostage drama at the 1972 Summer Olympics, at a time when rival network executives openly laughed at such ideas. But *Monday Night Football* proved that divisions such as sports and news did not have to be relegated to inferior time slots. The *ABC Evening News* show lacked imagination, promotion, and packaging. The logic of pairing Walters and Reasoner, flawed though it turned out to be, flowed from the phenomenal success of the "impossible" combination of Howard Cosell, Frank Gifford, and "Dandy" Don Meredith, who gave ABC a three-hour hammerlock on Monday night prime time. Roone Arledge, as head of ABC Sports, created a weekly "event" program, the appeal of which rested as much on the antagonisms and edgy camaraderie of the commentators as it did on the action on the field itself. Many football purists were appalled by Cosell, who was not a football expert. However, the grouping brought new viewers to professional football.

Pierce and other executives were not stupid; they looked way beyond the traditional audience for evening news. They wanted realignment. They were willing to take a risk. They knew that the CBS morning show audience among adults twenty-five to fifty-four was 55 percent women, but *Today* was 75 percent women. They knew that all three networks' evening news had a combined eight rating, which was equal to 8 percent of the available viewing audience in the time period in 1974, for two and one-half hours of programming per week. *Monday Night Football*, by contrast, brought in a mid-twenties rating among twenty-five to fifty-four year olds for three hours per week. (This was a 50 percent premium over the audience that CBS and NBC generated on weekends with their own NFL coverage.)

The stakes were high. Realignment, they knew, could bring enormous dividends in terms of bringing new viewers—especially women—to the evening news. Realignment could bring news programming back into prime time if the package was right. So, Walters was more than their "golden girl". She was the way forward. They were not only chasing women for the evening news, but also for some kind of an entry into prime time via Walters's specials.

It was a gambit, a gamble. The evening news strategy self-destructed because Harry Reasoner was essentially an old-school anchorman in the CBS tradition of solo anchors. He could not adjust either to the new concepts or, famously, to Walters herself. However, the specials prospered mightily.

Ultimately, Pierce followed up on the series of moves he made with by appointing Roone Arledge, head of ABC Sports, to head up ABC News. Arledge revamped the *ABC Evening News* and turned it into *World News Tonight*. He developed *20/20*, *Nightline*, *Prime Time Live*, and *This Week* and turned ABC into the "world news leader". He did as much as anyone, save perhaps Don Hewitt, to move news into prime time with packages that are seamless blends of entertainment, sports, and news production concepts. This created the Magnificent Seven of network news personalities; only a few years prior, there was only a Magnificent One, or maybe Two.

Arledge eventually moved Barbara Walters off the network news. He realized that she was wasted on the time slot. Instead, she focused on her prime time celebrity specials, which became exactly the "event" broadcasts that ABC had hoped when they brought her on board. The specials earned monster ratings, tons of publicity, and premium sponsorship rates. In 1984, Walters took over co-anchoring duties with Hugh Downs on *20/20* and helped make that show into the serious competitor that *60 Minutes* had never had and a mainstay on the hitherto uncelebrated ABC Friday night lineup.

Music Up, Dissolve to the Biography

If Barbara were to write her own biography piece to be included in *20/20*, it would probably read something like this. Barbara Walters was born September 25, 1931, in Boston, Massachusetts. Her father was Louis Edward Walters, and her mother was Dena Selett Walters. A brother died young; she has one sister. Her sister, Jacquilene, was mentally retarded. Her parents were involved in the night club business. Barbara moved a lot as a child, so she had few friends and only her sister with whom to play.

She started the first grade in Brookline, Massachusetts, and later schools were in New York, Fieldston, and Birch Wathen. She earned a Bachelor of Arts degree at Sarah Lawrence College in Riverdale. She focused on English, dramatics, and creative writing.

After college, Walters married and gave birth to her only child, a daughter. She had a series of jobs in New York during the 1950s. She worked as a secretary at an advertising agency, followed by assistant to the publicity director for NBC's WRCA-TV. Then she became a WRCA-TV producer and writer. Later, she moved to WPIX Radio and CBS-TV as a writer.

In the late 1950s, Walters went to work for Jerry Finkelstein, and she remains one of his best friends. Finkelstein knew everybody. He worked both sides of the political street—

including Senator Jacob Javits, Mayor John Lindsay, Mayor William O'Dwyer, and Governor Tom Dewey. William Safire worked for Finkelstein before opening his own public relations shop. Finkelstein was a close friend of Roy Cohn, the former Chief Counsel to Senator Joe McCarthy. Cohn became a close friend of Walters while he became one of the most feared power-brokers in New York City. Cohn used to tell *New York Post* columnist Sid Zion that "one day he'd marry, he'd probably marry Barbara Walters". Cohn's orbit included Cardinal Spellman, Ronald Reagan, the John Birch Society, George Steinbrenner, Ian Shrager and Steve Rubell, a number of private financiers of the Contras, and just about every New York political insider in the 1960s and 1970s.

So, when Barbara Walters was hired as a writer by the *Today* show in 1961 and promoted to reporter-at-large in 1962, she already had moved into a society far more interesting than that for which most people give her credit. Certainly *Today* host Hugh Downs underestimated her when he introduced her as the "the new *Today* girl."

Walters's first big test was Saturday, November 23, 1963, when she and Hugh Downs co-hosted a Saturday edition of *Today* on the day following President Kennedy's assassination. They had the first of what William Manchester described in *Death of a President* as "the nonstop broadcasts of that weekend." Their task was to write the "first draft of history". They covered the arrival of President Johnson back in Washington overnight, the bulletins on Governor John Connally, the arraignment of Lee Harvey Oswald, the arrival of the coffin at the White House, world reaction, and a complete recap of the events of Friday.

Throughout the 1960s, Walters honed the interview skills and air of extreme solicitousness which were to make her famous; as Elizabeth Peer noted in *Newsweek*: "Her questions pounce and probe; whether tart or thoughtful or perplexed, they are always fiercely eager. Even in silence—and some viewers contend that isn't nearly often enough—Walters resembles, as one critic has observed, 'energy looking for a lightning rod down which to dissipate.'"

Journalist Susan Leland wrote: "According to Walters, she was not allowed to write for the male correspondents or to ask questions in "male-dominated" areas such as economics or politics, and she was forbidden to interview guests on camera until all of the men on *Today* had finished asking questions." According to the famous story that Walters tells, when she was paired with Frank McGee on the *Today* show in 1971, McGee insisted—and NBC management agreed—that he would ask the first three questions in any hard news interview before Walters could talk.

Yet, Walters stayed with the show, continued to build a strong reputation as an interviewer, and barriers began to crumble. She was offered a chance to cover Richard Nixon's historic 1972 visit to China. When McGee died of cancer in 1974, NBC talked to Walters about who would be named as the show's new host, and she corrected them: "co-host." Her career with *Today* was then in its fifteenth year. She began there as writer and became a national celebrity. When ABC approached her in 1976, it offered her one million per year for five years.

It's Getting Harry

Howard K. Smith remembered those days leading up to their first newscast together:

> I liked Barbara and readily joined in speaking a message of greeting to her at a small dinner given by ABC news executives when she came over. But Reasoner was offended by the arrangement, since it suggested he had failed. He refused to

BARBARA WALTERS JOINS HARRY REASONER ON ABC!

Barbara Walters and Harry Reasoner —the news team America has been waiting for! The news team America is watching!

Barbara Walters has earned the admiration of millions of Americans for her incisive interviews with newsmakers all over the world. Time magazine hailed her as one of the hundred most influential leaders in America.

Harry Reasoner, with over two decades' experience in television journalism, is one of America's most trusted broadcasters. In his six years with ABC News he has reported every major news story in the nation and the world.

This combination of experience and ability forms the center of television's most dynamic and informative news team. And of course, Howard K. Smith continues his special commentary which reveals and clarifies the issues behind the news.

So whatever you do this week, don't miss Barbara Walters and Harry Reasoner.

ABC EVENING NEWS WITH HARRY REASONER & BARBARA WALTERS.

ABC ⓐⓑⓒ **NEWS**

ON THE NETWORK MORE PEOPLE ARE WATCHING.

Courtesy of TV Guide

rehearse a new format with her. "I already know how to read a Teleprompter," he said to me. He behaved like a peeved child on and off the air.

Walters's salary alone was enough to garner criticism not only from the press itself, but from colleagues. Similarly, the press extensively covered the announcement that Katie Couric signed a sixty million dollar contact with NBC in 2001. But Walters was always quick to point out that her salary was actually split in two. As she told *New York Magazine*:

> In 1976, when I came to ABC, there was all the hoopla about my making one million dollars a year for doing the news. It was considered practically a crime. But actually, I was getting five hundred thousand dollars for co-hosting ABC News (the same salary Harry Reasoner was getting) and five hundred thousand dollars from the entertainment department for doing four one-hour prime time specials. It was the bargain of the year for them! Those specials have been on for twenty-one years now, and they've made a fortune for ABC. But we news people were considered so *pure*. To give you some perspective, Mike Douglas was making something like ten million dollars that year, while I was making one million dollars, and nobody criticized him.
>
> Then there was the question of my being the first female co-host of a news program, and there were all those stories about me. How I had a pink typewriter. I mean, what are they, insane? And that I had a bookcase taken in through the window. I mean, I have a nice office. Hugh Downs has a bigger one, and I'm happy for him. I'm not going to die over this.
>
> What did I do that was so terrible? But there was all this terrible stuff, stuff that I know, in my heart, would not have happened had it been a man. Imagine it happening to Ed Bradley or Mike Wallace. In retrospect, though, it probably was a very good thing; I remember going to Poland, and people knew who I was: "Oh! She's the one who got the million dollars!" So in a silly way, it made me famous way beyond America.

Although Walters looked at what happened with a chuckle, it was anything but funny in the days following her debut. Newspapers across the country had a field day with it. It was leaked to the press that she made contract demands and got many of them, including equal billing, equal size of type used for her name, the word co-anchor always to be used, a researcher, a private secretary, a makeup consultant, a wardrobe person, a private office, and first-class accommodations wherever ABC sent her.

ABC saw a small increase in the ratings due to all the publicity, but then ratings fell. The third place news operation was even farther behind than before. There was no question that Walters and Reasoner did not get along. Bill Sheehan, the news division president, was beside himself. Roone Arledge lurked around the corner with a desire to take over the news division. Walters knew her skills were in the interview area, and she honed them. She received widespread drubbing, however, when she closed a 1976 interview with president-elect Jimmy Carter with the astonishing words, "Be wise; be good to us." But she scored a remarkable coup when she arranged a joint interview with Anwar Sadat and Menachem Begin because many assumed the men would never speak to each other.

Walters became one of the world's greatest interviewers. It seemed like celebrities were not truly famous until they sat down with Walters for an interview. *Saturday Night Live* used to parody the ABC star, who could never pronounce her *R*s. Indeed, Gilda Radner's biting "Baba Wawa" characterization is now part of the public consciousness.

A Little Ditty 'bout Barbara and Diane

Today, Walters campaigns to get interviews with show hosts and news people from other networks. Perhaps one of the great competitions happens within ABC itself. One day, sitting on the set of my weekly show, *This Week in Saint Louis*, one of the big stars of ABC told me about the all-out war going on within the news division between Diane Sawyer and Barbara Walters.

I asked some of my colleagues who work there, and they told

me stories of two distinct camps, the "Diane camp" and the "Barbara camp." Sawyer and Walters fight to be first to interview famous people. Both of them flew to California and went to the Los Angeles County Jail to visit with Robert Blake in an effort to convince him to talk to them. Sawyer, in an attempt to beat Walters at her own game, reported on *Good Morning America* that she visited him. "Through the Plexiglass, he said to me, 'I didn't do this horrible thing,'" Sawyer said, adding that Blake also told her, "Don't believe all you're reading."

A famous example of their rivalry was the push to get Monica Lewinsky. *The Columbia Journalism Review* reported it this way:

> *20/20*'s Barbara Walters, tipped off when Ginsburg was in Washington that he had expressed a yen for a lunch of bran flakes and skim milk, showed up at the Cosmos Club with a shopping bag full of—guess what? One rival network news executive I spoke with complained that ABC's Diane Sawyer entertained the lawyer and his wife for an entire weekend at her house in the country.

The Tough Question

"But in general, I'm very peaceful with myself," Walters told *New York Magazine*. "It sounds terrible. I'm supposed to have a lot more neuroses. I'd love to be able to tell you I'm driven, unhappy, that my private life is a mess, that there's another mountain to climb. But I am happy; I've climbed all the mountains. This plateau is very nice. I don't know how long I'll stay on it before I'll want to climb down a little bit and plant some trees. But not yet."

When she does climb down a little bit, her reputation as an interviewer par excellence will be solid. However, it would be better if she were remembered for the role she played in the fundamental shift of news strategy that occurred in 1976.

ABC's shift to a "star" strategy, looking to a new way of packaging news, was the cornerstone of their strategy over the next ten years. It recruited Brinkley and Sawyer, in addition to Walters; Downs, Donaldson, Koppel, and Jennings already were at the network. It went after Dan Rather in 1980, touching off the 1980 succession crisis at CBS.

It was a new kind of news—a wider range of news packages, a wider range of anchors' skill sets and backgrounds, and an infusion of sports and entertainment concepts. But the new news was much in keeping with no less a figure than Edward R. Murrow, who avoided the television anchor desk. He focused, instead, on his magazine show, *See It Now* and his interview forums, *Person to Person* and *Small World*. The next person to come along with that focus was Barbara Walters, with her network specials and *20/20*. She pulled off those assignments and remained viable in the ratings for a far longer period than Murrow did.

Walters's contributions since the controversial days of her anchor experience are many and widely acknowledged. However, she remains quiet or gracious on the subject of her anchoring experience with Harry Reasoner. It was not a happy time, when two completely different practitioners of the news art briefly sat together at the anchor desk. One represented the last of the old guard, and the other the first of the new wave. The new must defeat the old; it is natural and inevitable— perhaps regrettable, but certainly unavoidable.

Perhaps Barbara Walters will not be remembered in history books as an evening news anchor, but she should. Because she has interviewed presidents and kings and has sat across from movie stars and convicted criminals, Walters undoubtedly will be remembered for her interviews because there is an art to what she does.

Television viewers look to Walters for that "big interview," so

Larry King once asked her if, given the chance, she would have interviewed Hitler:

WALTERS: I would have shot him.

KING: But you might have interviewed him? Better we know than we don't know or we draw a line?

WALTERS: See, I don't want to read in tomorrow's paper, "Barbara Walters said, 'Yes, I would interview Hitler!'" So I think I will abstain, but you know what I would have said, you know. These are tough questions. You know, we always hear this thing about, "Are they using you or are you using us?" It doesn't have to be Osama bin Laden or Adolf Hitler, which are pretty hideous, and you have to make decisions as to whether I'm going to give these people air time.

As Emerson once said, "When we arrive at the question, the answer is already near." Barbara Walter seems to sense that, and when she enters a room and sits down for an interview, those answers are sure to emerge.

Chapter TWELVE

Max Robinson, ABC

Courtesy of ABC

When Roone Arledge was named head of ABC News in 1977, the network knew that it was bringing in a revolutionary who was going to shake things up. For twenty-five years, ABC News languished in third-place, and it was time for dramatic changes. Arledge was prepared to make some.

His belief in talent is legendary, and his technique of building strong shows around marquee personalities is well known. What was less publicized was his knack for plucking his stars from local stations, outposts, retirement, or various broadcasting twilights into which great talents sometimes manage to fall.

At ABC Sports, he elevated Howard Cosell and Keith Jackson from ABC local stations. He kept Jim McKay at the helm of the 1972 Olympics broadcast even after the terrorist capture of the Israeli team closed the Games down and turned the sports story into a tense international political drama. At ABC News, he coaxed Hugh Downs out of a six-year retirement and into the co-host's chair for *20/20*.

When it came to restructuring the ABC evening news in 1978, a move prompted by the departure of Harry Reasoner and a ratings slide for the newscast, Arledge opted for a three-anchor format with desks in London, Washington, and Chicago. Arledge reached back into ABC history and brought back former anchor Peter Jennings for the London desk, and he placed former anchor Frank Reynolds at the Washington desk. Neither had anchored the evening news in more than nine years, and the new anchors themselves were surprised by the move.

For Chicago, Arledge made an even more startling move. He tapped Max Robinson, the long-time co-anchor of WTOP, the CBS affiliate in Washington, for the job. Robinson became the first anchor ever to be elevated directly from a local station. (Chet Huntley was appointed after only a few months with the national network, but even Huntley anchored the 1956 convention coverage before the launch of the *Huntley-Brinkley Report*.)

In Max Robinson, Arledge selected a crusader as well as a seasoned, proven news anchor. In his audacious, outspoken commentary on the industry, Robinson evoked memories of Edward R. Murrow and, in particular, the blasting Murrow gave the industry in 1958 at the Radio-Television News Directors Association and Foundation convention. That speech just about finished Murrow, and a similar speech in 1981 just about finished Robinson. Within three years of their speeches, both left their networks.

At ABC, Robinson was a man in a hurry, as if he knew that his time was to be limited by an illness that ultimately claimed his life at a young age. He became a network anchor before his fortieth birthday, joining Edward R. Murrow, David Brinkley, and Peter Jennings among that elite group. Yet, his tenure at ABC was not marked by quiet perseverance and gradual improvement. He pushed for rapid changes and improvements in the opportunities for African Americans and the coverage afforded to their issues. He did not have a major impact in this effort because his time was cut short. Yet, to the end, he retained his anger and passion about the difficulties facing African Americans, but was remarkably calm about his own medical crises.

But what made Robinson the focus of so much attention was not the leap he made from local to national in a single bound, it was the fact that he was African American. Like Jackie Robinson in 1947, he broke the color barrier, and, in so doing, he became the object of a great deal of attention he neither wanted, nor felt he particularly deserved.

To be selected for a significant "first" places incredible and almost unbearable stress on individuals. Jackie Robinson wrote of how difficult his situation became for him. Buzz Aldrin, the lunar module pilot of *Apollo 11*, wrote about the years it took him to recover from the honor of the first moon landing. For Max Robinson, his "first" inaugurated a series of life crises that ended only with his early death in 1989 at the age of forty-nine.

Although there is no specific record of Robinson's race being a factor in his selection, it makes sense. The industry was overdue for diversity, the perennially third-place ABC had the most to gain, no one had more courage than Arledge in picking talent, and Robinson was, by far, the most experienced African-American anchor in the country.

With *World News Tonight*, Arledge sought not to refine ABC's evening news; he sought to redefine it. Upon his arrival in 1977, he altered the balance of coverage on the broadcast, bringing down the on-camera time of the New York–based anchors, Reasoner and Walters, to just three minutes. He favored a "whip around" the world format, not entirely unlike the CBS "round-up" format that transformed radio news in the 1930s. His introduction of *World News Tonight* eliminated New York as an anchor base for the first (and only) time in network history. The three-anchor format promised more face time for the anchors, stability for viewers, and preserved the around-the-world approach of the production.

It was easy to conclude that ABC would not win the ratings war by competing head-to-head with CBS and NBC because the leaders had too many entrenched advantages. Arledge chose to fight depth with breadth. The graphics were enhanced, music was introduced, and production values were enhanced in every way. The crucial factor was the anchor talent, and Arledge's three choices all had significant reporting and anchoring experience. It was the freshest and yet most experienced team ever assembled.

Hiding Behind a Slide

Max Robinson was born on May 1, 1939, in Richmond, Virginia. In 1959, he began his journey in the broadcast industry by applying for and winning a job at a Portsmouth, Virginia, station. The job was for on-air news reading. It had been "whites only," and Robinson later recalled how, in those days, the station hid his face behind a slide bearing the station's logo. "One night," Clarence Page wrote in *Chicago*, "[Robinson] ordered the slide removed so his relatives could see him. He was fired the next day. The station manager told him, 'Portsmouth isn't ready for color television.'"

Robinson eventually regrouped and found a job at WTOP-TV, the CBS affiliate in Washington, D.C., where he was hired as a cameraman-reporter trainee. His work included an assignment operating a puppet on the children's show, and thus he joins Walter Cronkite, among major news anchors, as the only ones to have worked with puppets. His opportunities at the station improved gradually, and, by the end of his first year, he rose to traffic reporter. However, rival station WRC offered him a role as a full-fledged reporter, and he switched stations.

"He had a great presence on the air," WTOP news vice president James Snyder told Burt Folkart of the *Los Angeles Times*. "He was very meticulous about his on-air performance. He rarely made a mistake. He was very conscious that he was a role model."

He stayed at WRC for most of the 1960s and made a mark for himself with his coverage of the riots that followed the April, 1968, assassination of Robert Kennedy. He won awards for his documentary, *The Other Washington*. But it was a difficult time for him within the WRC offices. "I can remember walking down the halls and speaking to people who would look right through me," Robinson told Peter Benjaminson in *Contemporary Authors*. "It was hateful at times . . . I've been the first too often, quite frankly. We firsts ought to get extra pay."

After several years as a leading reporter, he felt he was ready for the anchor job, but the position at WRC was not opened to him. In 1969, he moved back to WTOP as midday anchor. In 1971, a new evening news team was assembled at WTOP, and Robinson was named co-anchor. WTOP was a glorious period for him and a prestigious berth. It was one of the top ten television markets in the country, and WTOP had been home to some of the biggest names in the industry: Walter Cronkite, Sam Donaldson, Arthur Godfrey, Max Robinson, Eric Sevareid, Howard K. Smith, and Lowell Thomas.

During this period, WTOP was noted for its innovations in the news field. The head of the news operation, Ray Hubbard, persevered with Robinson even after the Ku Klux Klan burned a cross on the station lawn. He innovated in other ways during Robinson's tenure, adding newscasts at noon, 4:00 P.M., 5:00 P.M., 5:00 A.M., 5:30 A.M., and 6:00 A.M., to the main broadcasts at 6:00 P.M. and 11:00 P.M.

Robinson flourished with his anchoring partner, Gordon Peterson, and later called Peterson the best partner he ever had. The rapport between Peterson and Robinson was strong. Peterson said of him: "Max's story is heartbreaking. I often wish that he had stayed with us, and perhaps we could have helped him work out some things." Many of those who worked with Robinson in those years felt the same way. "On camera," Bart Barnes of the *Washington Post* wrote, "Robinson had a quiet, authoritative delivery, a deep resonant voice, and a serious demeanor that inspired trust and confidence in his viewers."

Robinson moved to the network and Chicago in 1978, and he was welcomed as a hero in his new city. However, he began to crumble under the twin pressures of being the first African-American anchor and one of three anchors in an untried and unwieldy three-anchor, two-continent format. During this period, Robinson fell victim to alcoholism and showed many of its classic symptoms, including behavior changes and missing work.

Some of the show's difficulties fell hardest on the Chicago team. Although the concept of a national desk makes sense on paper, when the Washington stories were subtracted because there were only twenty-two minutes of content in the show and there was more pressing national news, it became more difficult to determine exactly what the "national" desk should cover. For many years, the evening news focused on Washington and international coverage. During the Cold War years, that was a successful formula, but success proved more elusive when the focus moved away from the Cold War. The difficulties Robinson experienced as he tried to define a national desk in Chicago were advance signs of the approaching difficulties.

The news log, however, for April 25, 1980, covering the failed attempt to rescue the American hostages in Iran, shows a balanced, authoritative approach to covering international crisis. And, despite the fact that Robinson easily could have been frozen out of most of the broadcast because it was a Washington or international story better suited to Jennings in London and Reynolds in Washington, the broadcast stayed true to its world news format and balanced time between the anchors.

The broadcast began with an opening from Reynolds, who summarized the major news of the failed rescue, with detailed reports from John McWethy and Sam Donaldson out of Washington, including President Carter's acceptance of responsibility for the failed mission.

The coverage then moved to London and Jennings, where the London studio ran a remote from Tehran that summarized the Iranian reaction. An addendum from the United Nations by Reynolds rounded out the first act of the broadcast.

Reynolds then introduced the national reaction stories, including stories from Ann Compton in Washington with Capitol Hill reaction and Robinson's report that primary campaign activities were suspended by the Carter and Kennedy camps. As ABC went to commercial, viewers had an excellent overview of the main story.

In the second half of the broadcast, Jennings introduced a foreign reaction piece about the hostage crisis. Routine economic news summaries were followed by Robinson introducing segments on a plane crash in Tenerife, the Cuban refugee crisis, and a note that the second part of a special on Interferon was postponed due to coverage of the rescue attempt. Finally,

Robinson introduced a segment by Bob Brown on reaction from the hostages' families.

It was a classic round-up broadcast. It showed the potential of the three-anchor format. The major story was presented. In this case, the primary reporting came from the foreign desk, followed by national, foreign, and Washington reaction to the main story with a round-up of the other major stories of the day.

The Crooked Mirror

Despite the success of the hostage crisis reporting and the apparent balance of the news that was achieved on many evening broadcasts, Robinson launched a blistering public attack on ABC at Smith College in February, 1981. Network anchor Carole Simpson recalls:

> Max Robinson got into some difficulty when he gave a speech at Smith College and criticized ABC and the other networks, but he included ABC most prominently in being racist because he was not called upon to do the inauguration. They would give him lesser roles to perform. Of the three major anchors, Peter Jennings and Frank Reynolds, he would get whatever was the less important role. They would be anchoring the actual inauguration; he would be on the street talking to people in the crowd. . . . We were still in this other category: you're still not seen.
>
> He got into a lot of trouble for making that speech, not because it perhaps was not true, but because it reflected badly on his employer. . . . His big mistake was nailing ABC and how he was treated at ABC in a public venue, apparently without ever having gone to them to complain ahead of time.

"He told [the] audience," wrote Jeremy Gerard in the *New York Times*, "that the news media were 'a crooked mirror' through which 'white America views itself,' and that 'only by talking about racism, by taking a professional risk, will I take myself out of the mean, racist trap all black Americans find themselves in.'"

ABC executives were dumbfounded and remained bitter until Robinson departed. Most industry observers familiar with the facts say that Robinson never overcame the bad feelings his speech created.

Reynolds's Funeral Was Robinson's

Aaron Freeman later wrote about the problems between Reynolds and Robinson: "[Robinson] told me about his ongoing feud with Frank Reynolds. Reynolds, it seems, was arrogant and inconsiderate to janitors, secretaries, and maintenance people. This outraged Max. So whenever Reynolds came to visit Max's office, he was made to wait outside in the reception area for a minimum of fifteen minutes before being allowed an audience."

The end for Robinson as anchor came in 1983. Frank Reynolds died after a six-month illness, and Robinson did not attend the funeral, even though he was scheduled to attend and sit next to First Lady Nancy Reagan.

After the funeral, ABC took the opportunity to revamp the broadcast. It named Peter Jennings as the sole anchor and appointed Robinson as the weekend anchor and Washington correspondent. The grand experiment of having the national news anchored from three locations—New York, London, and Chicago—was over. It hadn't worked well in the ratings, and the controversies over Robinson finally brought matters to a head. The balance of coverage issues and now the funeral controversy was more than Robinson or ABC wanted to handle.

Robinson made the decision to leave ABC and became the local anchor for WMAQ in Chicago. But by then, personal stresses and alcoholism had taken their toll. Robinson missed newscasts and, in one memorable gaffe, he vented his frustrations on the crew. An observer recalled, "While the credits were rolling, Max lit into the crew in language that would curl a sailor's hair. But the [sound] had 'accidentally' been left open, and those choice words went out all over Chicago."

He left the station in 1985 and went into semi-retirement, battling various illnesses and stress. He died on December 20, 1988. To the end, he retained many of the strengths that had made him one of the most successful anchors ever in local television. His friend Aaron Freeman wrote in *Chicago* magazine:

> [Max] produced a big blowup of a *Washington Post* feature on his career as America's most famous black anchorman. . . . It included recent pictures of him and I remember thinking, damn, the camera still loves this guy. . . . I could hardly believe Max was terminally ill. He was thin, but not frighteningly so. His face seemed not hollow but craggy and full of character. His eyes spoke not of disease but weariness. His trademark voice, the voice that carried him so far, was clear, strong, rich, and musical.

Bernard Shaw, former anchor at CNN, said, "His impact will go on for generations. He was Engine No. 1."

It's Not Always Black and White

Robinson's passing led to one immediate and major innovation at ABC. Carole Simpson recalls being asked to meet with Roone Arledge shortly after Robinson's death:

> Roone started thinking about the discussions that he had had with Max over that other incident [the Smith College speech], and apparently Max had told him, "You'll never understand what it's like to be a black man in America. You'll never understand it."
>
> And he [Roone] said that he realized he [Max] was probably right, and he said, "That gave me an idea. I'd like to turn

over an hour of prime time television on ABC to the black employees at ABC to do a documentary on what it's like to be black in America today."

Well, this was just—I mean, we were awestruck. It was like, "What?" What an incredible opportunity to have and to turn it over to the black employees. As I say, it grew out of his thinking about Max and that it's true, probably white people do not realize how we see things and how we view things as black Americans.

We also began the program with the famous University of Chicago study. Do you remember this study about the black dolls and the white dolls? It turned out I had participated. My mother told me that I had participated in that original study as a child. I must have been six years old, but I don't remember it at all.

But she told me that I picked the white dolls for the pretty dolls, for the good dolls, which I'm sad to admit, and I did admit in this program later, that I was one of the children that picked the white dolls. What we did was go to Atlanta where there was another academic who was working with pictures with children today, to show that blacks still have poor self-esteem.

If you ask little children, "Who's the good boy and who's the bad boy?" and they look at pictures of white boys and black boys, the black boys are the bad boys. "Which is the pretty girl and which is the ugly girl?" And still too many children are picking the little black girl as the ugly girl and the bad girl.

The documentary started with that, that we still have this low self-esteem. Then my particular portion that had to do with the black middle class showed you that a man who is an executive of Xerox still has women pass him on the street and clutch their bags. No matter how successful you are—I mean, it really brought home the color thing, the badge of color which does not go away.

Credit, thus, in part for the documentary, *Black in White America*, goes to Max Robinson. It aired in August, 1989, on ABC, which promoted the program by saying, "Tuesday, August 29, for one hour, the ABC television network will go black."

The paradox of Max Robinson is the struggle between the very low self-esteem featured in the documentary and the phenomenal success he had during his short career. His inability to reconcile the two may well have been a primary underlying cause of his early death.

What is clear is that Robinson went to Chicago to help ABC change the way network news was done. He pushed hard for the network to go a step beyond Little Rock. Rather than reporting stories on the problems of the black experience or putting a black face on the national news, he hoped to persuade the network and viewers to look beyond facile assessments and cosmetic repairs. He wanted to get people out of the easy chair and onto the hard road of doing something about the troubling iniquities that still were plaguing the South and the nation.

It is a position of public advocacy with which some anchors and all networks are uncomfortable: controversy breeds difficulties. But Robinson never was one to finish a broadcast with, "And that's the way we would have liked it to be." Like a classic newsman, he told the story in plain words for anyone who tuned in. That approach took Robinson from the back of the bus to the head of the newscast, and he thought he could help others get out of the back of the bus, too.

Gordon Peterson of WTOP, his favorite co-anchor, perhaps best captured the attitude of the man. "I remember," he related, "[promotional] pictures of Max and me on the back of the buses in town. On one occasion, a nephew of mine was in Washington—he was quite young at the time—and he kept saying to his mother, 'Mom, Uncle Pete is on the bus!' And she would keep saying, 'No, don't be silly, he's not on the bus.' Max's line about that was, 'I don't like riding on the back of the bus, even if it's only my picture.'"

Chapter THIRTEEN

Peter Jennings, ABC

Associated Press

With the arrival of the millennium, Peter Jennings became the first network news anchor to sit at the anchor chair during five decades. In doing so, he broke his own record. Several anchors have worked across three decades, and anchors of the first order of magnitude, such as Walter Cronkite and David Brinkley, served over four or five decades, if one includes convention and election night anchoring. But Jennings has set a longevity record on the order of Joe DiMaggio's fifty-six–game hitting streak; it may be equaled one day, but it is difficult to conceive under what circumstances that might happen.

Jennings grew up with the news. He first became an ABC anchor in 1965, when the network was mired in a far-distant third place. It had little to lose by experimenting with the twenty-seven-year-old phenomenon from the Canadian Television Network in 1964. Now, in the late years of his career, he approaches his senior years just as the networks have changed their notions that anchors should retire at age sixty-five. It is just conceivable that he still will be anchoring in 2010, and thus anchor in a sixth decade—a record which, if set, is likely to stand for all time.

His career an anchor and journalist is far more significant than can be conveyed simply in longevity records. When an anchor is on the nightly news thirty-seven years after he first began in the role—even allowing for an eleven-year hiatus as a foreign correspondent—he is perhaps the most monumental anchor figure of all. Such a statement even allows for Chet Huntley, David Brinkley, Walter Cronkite, Tom Brokaw, and Dan Rather. Jennings was voted the second-most trusted newscaster of all time after Cronkite, and his anchoring experience has exceeded Cronkite's own longevity marks.

Jennings acknowledges the role of the anchor to be the rock of stability. However, he takes care to define it in precise terms. "There are a lot of people who think our job is to reassure the public every night that their home, their community, and their nation is safe," he says. "I don't subscribe to that at all. I subscribe to leaving people with essentially—sorry it's a cliché—a rough draft of history. Some days it's reassuring, some days it's absolutely destructive."

His rough draft of history, now some forty years in the making, covers a wide enough swathe of American history that it surprises many that he retained his Canadian passport. It bedeviled him from time to time with detractors who rolled out charges of un-Americanism whenever Jennings offered pointed or perceived criticism of American leadership or adventures at home or abroad. It is arguably a factor in the lackluster sales of his recent book on the American experience.

Jennings is, in fact, one of the most uniquely qualified individuals to comment on the American experience, for he is the only anchorman to undertake that single most defining American journey, the journey of immigration. Furthermore, his long experience and travels at home and abroad make him not only the most internationally experienced of major news personalities, but also one of the most grounded in the American experience and way of life. This country is so wide and varied that Americanism cannot be a product of birthright only, but it also must be the product of pilgrimage and study.

Jennings is celebrated for a cool, intellectual style. He avoids the pitfalls of overt emotion and its evil twin, cynicism, to provide a nightly broadcast that could be retitled *Worldly News Tonight*. But he brings more than sophistication. When John Cameron Swayze said, "It takes a licking, but keeps on ticking," he came as close to capturing Jennings as he did the marvels of the Timex watch.

Jennings's record for longevity is remarkable for his unrelenting commitment to the daily task of reporting the daily news. Whether it is a slow news day or there is a veritable tsunami of swirling events, the task remains the same: twenty-two minutes of information reported, checked, selected, combined into a cohesive whole, and presented every day from scratch.

The Early Years

Peter Jennings was born in Toronto, Canada, on July 29, 1938. At nine years old, he got what could be considered as his very first anchor job on a Saturday morning radio show that showcased young talent. He earned twenty-five dollars for each show, but his father took the money away to remind his son that radio was a public service. Jennings reflects:

> Lots of people had an influence on my career. I'm certainly aware of the abilities of people like Murrow or Cronkite, but the only anchorperson, though we never would have called him that, who had a real affect on my career was my father. He was a radio broadcaster and pioneer in Canada in the '20s and '30s. He imparted to me, taught me, which I hope I learned the basic value, the basic notion that whether you're in a commercial broadcasting system as I am, or in a public broadcasting system as he was, that it is a public service.

Charles Jennings, in fact, was perhaps *the* pioneer in Canadian news broadcasting. He broke new ground for our neighbors to the north as the first announcer for a nightly national news program dubbed the *National*. The late news broadcast on the Canadian Broadcasting Corporation (CBC) network has the same title today. He eventually moved up the ladder and became vice president of news at the CBC. He was head of the CBC news division, in fact, during Jennings's first years as an ABC anchorman. It was a remarkable father-son achievement in news that never has been duplicated, the closest example being Mike and Chris Wallace or Frank and Dean Reynolds.

By all accounts, Peter Jennings was bored in school. His fascination for the world and its problems, the news and its impact, and sheer curiosity caused him to drop out in the tenth grade, later to attend Carleton University and Rider College. At times, he had little regard for formal education, a decision he looked back on with some regret. "I would have wanted to go to school longer," he reflected recently. "I say that as something of an automatic reaction. Whenever I'm working on a big important project, I'm sometimes reminded that I did not have the great reading experience that's there for someone to have when they are at college. My two children are in college now, and they are both much better read than I ever was, either then or for many years afterwards."

Jennings's own broadcasting career began almost immediately after his decision to leave school. He became a disc jockey and news reporter for a small radio station in Brockton, Ontario. One day, there was a major train wreck, and, as the broadcaster on the spot, he covered it for the CBC. His performance attracted the attention of a news manager at Canadian Television (CTV, Canada's first private television network), and Jennings was offered a position as an on-air reporter. His popularity was so quick and so universal that the handsome young correspondent was named CTV anchor in 1962.

The Americanization of Peter

As a CTV anchor, he became known to Elmer Lower, the head of ABC News at that time. Lower saw something in Jennings that he didn't see in any of the people he had at the alphabet network at the time: good looks, a certain charm, and solid reporting skills. ABC made him an offer to come aboard as a correspondent. Jennings accepted and arrived in New York in late 1964.

Since 1960, when it brought back John Cameron Swayze in an ill-fated attempt to jump-start its news ratings, ABC News was a nonstarter in the network news race in terms of ratings and prestige. Although ABC never was a major factor in the ratings, John Daly won major awards, such as the Peabody and the Emmy for his work in the 1950s. But ABC experimented in the 1960s with a broad range of broadcasters without success. From 1962 to 1965, it had Ron Cochran in the role to host an obscure fifteen-minute newscast. Cochran took over the broadcast at almost exactly the same time as Walter Cronkite succeeded at CBS, and, in fact, the two looked very much alike.

It was Elmer Lower's assignment, when he started in 1963, to do something about the poor ratings. He stayed with Cochran for some time, but one of the reasons he did so was because he couldn't find anyone else. He did have Howard K. Smith and Edward Morgan on to anchor President Kennedy's assassination, which, curiously, did nothing to stimulate thinking about having Smith do the job, but was the beginning of the end for Cochran.

The fact that Lower didn't go with the well-known and available Howard K. Smith says less about Smith than it says about ABC News's commitment and attitude toward the evening news at the time. It was committed to near-zero spending. CBS and NBC spent more than thirty million dollars on their news divisions at that time, and ABC spent 3.5 million. ABC had approximately two hundred employees world wide, and the other networks had more than five hundred. NBC had 203 affiliates, and ABC had 117. ABC also was committed to keeping its bigger news personalities focused on documentaries and specials and to figuring out a way to carve an audience without challenging NBC and CBS on their own terms and own turf.

Not Ready for Prime Time

It was a matter of months into Jennings's new correspondent role that Elmer Lower called him and offered him the anchor position. Jennings turned it down. It was reported that Howard K. Smith was a driving force, perhaps put up to it by Lower, in changing Jennings's mind. Smith talked with Jennings on more than one occasion in an effort to persuade him to take the seat.

Jennings relented and become the youngest person ever to grace a network anchor chair when he was put on ABC's fifteen-minute program in February, 1965. The program went head to head with CBS and NBC, but at fifteen minutes and with a young, yet-unpolished Jennings, the ratings didn't budge. Many of his coworkers resented Lower's decision and treated Jennings as an outcast. Magazines treated him as a male model instead of a newsman. All that weighed heavily on him as the months on ABC's anchor desk ticked by. "This was a very young news division that decided they were going to try to appeal to a younger audience, and I was the only guy here who had all my hair and teeth. For three years, I was the anchorperson in the sixties. I didn't enjoy it very much at all! I hadn't wanted to do it in the first place and left after three years in 1967".

Frankly, Jennings was hired in the anchor slot more for his appeal than for his qualities. He was still forming as a journalist, and the great growing experience of the Middle East and London was well ahead in the future. He was a newsreader with matinee-idol looks, and it was for that reason that he was given the assignment. ABC had, for many years, experimented with taking the youngest slice of the audience. It was ABC that launched the *Disneyland* program with the original Mickey Mouse Club. It was ABC that aired the *Lone Ranger* and other younger programming. It went heavily for sports, *American Bandstand*, and developed shows like the *Partridge Family* and the *Brady Bunch* in the late 1960s; such shows locked down Friday nights and a generation of syndicated reruns. ABC's strategy inspired the Fox network when it debuted in the 1980s, but, back in the 1960s, it was ABC on the outside looking in. When it came to news, the network rightly surmised that there was a younger audience that hadn't adopted Huntley and Brinkley or Cronkite.

It was a sensible idea, for the British invasion of 1964 shifted attention onto youth culture like never before, and it was absolutely the right thing to do to aim younger. But, rapidly, it became clear that the limited ABC network, with its miniscule news budget, was not going to capture the audience.

It tried one last time with Jennings by moving to a thirty-minute broadcast in January, 1967, but the ratings needle did not move. ABC abandoned the effort by the end of the year and replaced Jennings with Bob Young in 1968 for a few months while it negotiated a deal with Harry Reasoner. Instead, Frank Reynolds took the reins.

The World Tour

That was fine with Jennings, who wanted to report anyway. He was sent to Rome to polish his reporting skills, and he also reported from Vietnam. The Rome assignment was successful in terms of invigorating Jennings, but the limitations on Rome as a base were substantial. First, in those days, the reports were shot on film, and while the difficulties of developing and transporting film were substantial everywhere in those days, Jennings's reports from Italy were delayed sometimes up to a week. Second, the pace of European events slowed considerably by the late 1960s. The front that supplied much of the news and almost all of the drama since the late 1930s finally entered a period of considerable stability.

However, the Middle East was hot and got hotter. After eleven years of a difficult peace, war erupted in the region in

1967. The Six Day War began, and Israel won a famously sweeping victory. Meanwhile, American dependence on Arabian oil increased at a phenomenal clip, and the Nixon Administration became the first to initiate an extensive set of ties with conservative Arab states as a bulwark against Soviet encroachment. As a result of the ties, American foreign policy in the Middle East, which, for twenty years was predicated on support for the young Israeli state, became more difficult.

Matters grew even more delicate in 1970, when the new Egyptian president, Anwar Sadat, forged closer relations between Egypt and the Soviet Union to obtain aid for his Aswan High Dam project. Pan-Arab nationalism, fueled by the personality of Egypt's Gamel Nasser, splintered in a series of disputes between Egypt and Syria and in the general aftermath of the Six Day War. The Ba'ath Socialist party, a pan-Arab party with Soviet leanings, came to power and brought Saddam Hussein to the international scene.

Jennings was reassigned to head the Middle East Bureau for ABC. He recalled those days when talking with Michele Stanush of *Rolling Stone*:

> I was the first television correspondent to formally open a bureau for an American television network in the Arab world in Beirut in 1969. It was really the first exposure the Arab world was getting. It was in the wake of the Arab-Israeli War, in which the press corps had altogether gone overboard in cheering for Israel, in terms of defeating the Arabs. I felt very strongly, and still do, that there is much more to the Israeli side to the Middle East story. There are nineteen countries in the Arab world, and I worked in all of them. I did a lot of stories in those days, which said, "Hey, hold it folks, Arabs are people. They don't all ride camels, they don't all live in tents, they drive Mercedes." Of course, as we went though the seventies, we found they had a considerable amount to do with our economic destiny.

The days of traveling in that region were memorable for Jennings. He met and married his second wife there. When we talked one day, he recalled a small event that had a lasting impact:

> I covered the 1971 war between India and Pakistan, and I remember getting very deeply affected by a man in a refugee camp. It was a huge refugee camp outside Calcutta, and he believed that I was his salvation, of course I wasn't. That's always very hard for a reporter because you realized that, in some measure, your craft is conducted based on other people's unhappiness and misery. That encounter has stuck with me for much of my professional life.

Jennings was hardly the first anchor to gain considerable experience and a wider perspective while working as a foreign correspondent, but he was the first to go *after* years on the anchor desk. His growing experience and considerable reporting skills made a strong impression on ABC management. But there were other factors that helped him along in those years, not the least of which was the magic of a Canadian passport. Although he had difficulty explaining it back in the United States in later years, he reaped a significant benefit during the Beirut years, when Americans were viewed with incredible suspicion in many quarters of the world, and Canadians widely were welcomed. Jennings believes that his Canadian citizenship rescued him from innumerable tight spots in the Middle East during those years.

Munich, 1972

Jennings's next great assignment took him back to Europe, where his European and Middle Eastern experiences twisted tragically together when he was called on to cover the 1972 Summer Olympics in Munich.

The 1972 Olympic Games were advertised as a rapprochement between Germany and the world, for the Games returned to Germany for the first time since 1936, when the Nazi regime made the Berlin Games a showcase for the fascist ideology. Television played a major part and was a focal point of the 1972 Games, as symbolized by the 930 ft. high television tower called the Olympic Tower and the extensive press and television center facilities. ABC had the United States broadcast rights, as it had since the 1960 Summer Games in Rome. With each succeeding Olympiad, the preparations became more elaborate. The Olympics, in fact, eventually supplanted the political conventions as *the* quadrennial network showcase event, and much of the ground-laying credit goes to Roone Arledge and his ABC Sports team for the manner in which they approached Olympic coverage in that era. More than eight hundred million viewers were expected to tune in to the Summer Games.

Jennings was brought in to add to the coverage team, although his beat was the non-sporting events that were considered minor. Instead, Arab commandos stormed the Israeli compound and took the Israeli Olympic team hostage.

Jennings hid inside the compound with his camera crew and impressed everyone by getting the now-famous pictures of the attackers on the balcony of the Israeli building. Jennings communicated by walkie-talkie with Howard Cosell during the ordeal:

> JENNINGS: This is Peter. Do you have something to report to us from where you are?
>
> COSELL: I certainly do, Peter. Police officers in armored, platoon-like numbers have been running passed us and are now staging in front of us. We are building up, I think, to a climax.

Jennings watched the tapes of the events of that day on *Good Morning America*. Jennings recalled, "The Italians hid me in their building when the police sweep came along across from building thirty-one, and I was lucky to stay there all day."

The coverage was amazing. The tragic news event was carried live as it happened. "At one point," Jennings recalled, "the German police came into the ABC control room with their guns and said stop taking pictures. We had a camera up on a tower, and it could see what was happening on top of the buildings as the German commandos prepared to storm the terrorists. Then we realized, of course, that the Palestinians inside the building could see it on television as well."

All the hostages were killed, some in the compound, the rest at the airport when the terrorists were surrounded while trying to board planes for which they had negotiated. The Germans had no intention of letting them escape.

Jim McKay won the first Emmy ever awarded to a sports commentator for his news coverage of the tragedy. Eventually, Roone Arledge took over the news division. Because of the 1972 coverage, he formed an impression of Jennings's growing talents that brought Jennings back to the anchor chair in 1978.

After Munich, Jennings returned his attention to the Middle East bureau and a newfound American interest in the region. The Yom Kippur War broke out in 1973 and, as in 1967, the United States supported Israel. The Arab countries responded with a crippling oil embargo in 1973–74 that shocked the United States economy into a steep recession and temporarily pushed Watergate off the top of the news.

Jennings was in the right place at the right time. He had his defining moment as a Middle East correspondent in 1974: "I went on the Anwar Sadat visit, the first visit to Israel. I was a party to that visit from almost the moment Sadat thought about it. So, that was a very exciting prospect those several days." Jennings landed the coveted Peabody Award in 1974 for his interview with the Egyptian leader.

Jennings's work also received recognition from the ABC News division. In its cast-off anchor, it had a star reporter. So, Jennings was brought back to the United States and temporarily installed in Washington as the news reader for *A.M. America*, a new program that was transformed into *Good Morning America*.

In 1975, Jennings was ready to move back out to the field as chief foreign correspondent for the network. He moved to London. In 1975, London was the only location from which ABC could report live. ABC set up a bureau complete with a newsroom-type set, as the satellite link over the Atlantic was then in place. Jennings was based in London for some momentous phases in its history: the dramatic 1976 election, the 1978–79 "Winter of Discontent", Margaret Thatcher's rise to power, and the historic win of the Tories in 1979, which ushered in a decade of increasingly conservative governments in the United States and Europe.

During that period, he worked with numerous anchoring teams back in the United States:. Frank Reynolds solo, Frank Reynolds with Howard K. Smith, Harry Reasoner with Howard K. Smith, Harry Reasoner as anchor with Howard K. Smith as commentator, and, finally, the difficult pairing of Harry Reasoner with Barbara Walters. The Reasoner and Walters pairing prompted a management shuffle at ABC, and Roone Arledge was handed the opportunity to run the news division.

Three's a Crowd

Arledge brought a level of experimentation and innovation to the news division unseen since the birth of network news in the 1940s and 1950s. *Nightline, 20/20,* and *World News Tonight* were his creations—all long-running hits still in production today, although much changed over the years.

Arledge's key innovations were to move Barbara Walters to *20/20* and to change to a three-anchor format for the network evening news with the name *World News Tonight*. Previously, two-anchor formats were based in New York and Washington. Arledge opted to place Max Robinson in Chicago, former anchor Frank Reynolds in Washington, and Jennings in London.

Arledge's third anchor concept was revolutionary. Not since the 1940s, when Murrow broadcast from London, had there been regular nightly anchoring from there. But Arledge saw an opportunity to provide a broader coverage than the rival networks. Rather than beat them with depth, he aimed to fight them with breadth. And Jennings's combined anchor experience and substantial credentials as a European correspondent were vital to the Arledge strategy. Jennings remembers:

> After there had been a number of anchor experiments at ABC news, Roone Arledge, the president of the division, devised a system where we would have sub-anchors. We had a Washington anchor, a Chicago anchor, and an overseas anchor. I was then the chief overseas correspondent and became the overseas anchor. The Washington anchor, Frank Reynolds, got ill and died, and, subsequently, so did Max Robinson, who was the Chicago anchor—he also died, and I ended up here, one could argue, accidentally and alone.

The anchor experiment of which Jennings spoke began in the summer of 1978. Three anchors were in three different cities with Barbara Walter doing occasional pieces from New York. Of the three anchors, Frank Reynolds in Washington was accepted the most quickly. Robinson and Jennings faced the most criticism. Jennings's keen insight into foreign affairs gave his segment of the program a particular flair, although many critics claimed that the average American viewer didn't want to see so much international news. Jennings felt that Robinson was misplaced in Chicago. As he told *Rolling Stone*, "Max never approached the Midwest as if it were a real nation state. And, therefore, what Max ended up doing a lot of the time was floods, snowstorms, and traffic jams. Frank and I had very defined jobs."

The ratings were not impressive. Cronkite continued to run well ahead of both ABC and NBC, and although there were significant breakthroughs for ABC during this period—the establishment of *20/20* and the launch of *Nightline*—Arledge did not shake up the news frontier as he had hoped to do with the three-anchor format.

When Reynolds died and Robinson left the broadcast in the early 1980s, Jennings was asked to solo anchor, "My first instinct was to say no altogether. Kati, my wife, was the one who convinced me this was a very important job, and you didn't just say no idly. We had a long difficult time deciding to come." Jennings said yes, and they came back to New York. He once told a reporter for the Berkeley college paper, "The sad thing about being an anchor is I no longer get to be a reporter. If it was raining in London, I went to Africa looking for a story."

Musical Chairs, Jennings Wins

In August of 1983, Jennings was named the solo anchor for the broadcast, and he began anchoring out of Washington, D.C. Jennings had a way with words, he had style and flair. During the early 1980s, when the television landscape shifted more than it had since the early 1960s, Jennings was able to grab a substantial share of audience.

Walter Cronkite was in the process of leaving CBS, and his replacement, Dan Rather, had a folksy style that did not immediately connect with all of Cronkite's loyal following. NBC was in the midst of a transition that began with Chancellor and Brinkley at the desk and ended with Brokaw after four years with various changes in between. CNN was in the midst of its launch, and did not, for some time, win its audience, but it made an impression and influenced the competition very quickly. PBS began its preparations to move toward a one-hour broadcast and away from its half-hour, in-depth supplement to the nightly news. By 1983, the transitions were complete, and Brokaw, Rather, and Jennings were the solo anchors at the three networks.

By then, Jennings had five years in the anchor chair, established his cool, cerebral style, and found an audience that put ABC first into equal competition, and then, finally, brought ABC into the lead. The great forty-year odyssey of the ABC evening news ended; it found the format and the anchor.

In 1984, Jennings anchored the conventions with David Brinkley. Although conventions ceased to have the kind of television interest and drama that sustained the public's interest over several days, the 1984 conventions did feature one of the last dramatic entries into national politics. It came as the result of a single political speech; Mario Cuomo's electrifying address put him at the forefront of potential presidential candidates in 1988 and 1992.

In 1986, Jennings had his first major crisis news event when the space shuttle *Challenger* blew up within moments of its January, 1986, launch. The commission investigating the disaster placed considerable emphasis on the perceived media pressure that NASA was under to get a rocket off the ground. Not only was the *Challenger* launch delayed several times, but the *Columbia* launch was delayed seven times by various factors. The multiple delays led to significant questioning on the news and across the nation of NASA's competency, and, more specifically, of its stated goal of twenty-four shuttle launches in 1986. In 2003, NASA's competency came into question again, following *Columbia*'s breaking apart on reentry and the subsequent death of the shuttle crew.

Jennings was widely cited in all the various inquiries and commissions for his on-air comment after one of the *Challenger* delays, "Once again, a flawless lift-off proved to be too much of a challenge for the *Challenger*." The context for the remark was the problems with *Challenger*, the heavy launch schedule, the significant attention NASA brought to the mission by scheduling the schoolteacher Christa McAuliffe as a crew member, and the January launch, which made winter weather delays more common. Further, NASA was behind on its launch program, and was trying to hang on to the responsibility of placing military satellites in orbit that it had just won from the Air Force.

Jennings's remark is not unique in its perspective because there was widespread dissatisfaction with the continuing, last-minute mechanical and weather delays. What is significant is that Jennings found the words that were remembered. That is part of his considerable anchoring appeal, for better or worse. Among the anchors, he is more often than not the one who comes up with the phrases we remember. For example, it was Jennings who referred to the coverage of the World Trade Center attacks of September 11, 2001, as "the national campfire", which is exactly what television becomes when the immediacy of the news disaster fades, and yet the public still channel-scans, anxious to work through shock, horror, or grief.

The Lockerbie terrorist bombing of Pan Am 103 littered an entire plane over northern Scotland, and Jennings won the Peabody Award for his coverage. However, the invasion of Kuwait in 1990 and the subsequent Gulf War showed Jennings at his best. For this most international of anchors was well acquainted with the personalities and issues of the region from of his years in Beirut. Jennings was better qualified than any anchor before or since to put the awful events in the Middle East in context: the bombing of Tripoli, the explosion of a Marine garrison in Beirut, and the stream of kidnappings of Americans that beset the region, beginning with the Iranian hostages. Jennings was arguably in the front rank of experience, exceeding many of the war correspondents on whom he depended at ABC or with whom he competed on other networks. In addition to his nightly news chores, he anchored more than one hundred hours of special reports during the war, as well as three award-winning prime time specials.

Then, his international experience in the Middle East took a backseat to his European experience during the crises that beset Eastern Europe during the late 1980s and early 1990s. Of all the anchors, except for Howard K. Smith and Edward R. Murrow, Jennings had the most personal reporting experience in Europe, and the news from Europe was more dramatic than it had been since the late 1940s, when the Cold War commenced. The fall of the Berlin Wall in 1989 was something on which he reported as a witness to its construction in the early 1960s. He also anchored coverage on the fall of Communism in Romania, Hungary, Poland, Yugoslavia, Czechoslovakia, and Bulgaria as one who reported extensively from each country during the Communist years. He reported the disintegration of the Soviet Union and the Gorbachev coup as one who was the chief European correspondent of ABC and reported from London when Gorbachev first joined the *Politburo*.

Those were perhaps his grandest days, for when the attention turned to Oklahoma City, it was Dan Rather who knew the region intimately from his days as a Texas news director and Dallas bureau chief for CBS. When attention was focused on California in 1994 in the aftermath of the Rodney King riots, the Northridge earthquake, and the O.J. Simpson murder "trial of the century," it was Brokaw with the intimate knowledge of the region from his many years as an NBC correspondent based in Los Angeles.

Throughout the years of their competition, Jennings has appealed to a more sophisticated crowd than Rather and Brokaw have. They have three very different approaches—folksy Rather, urbane Jennings, and smooth Brokaw—and each developed a following. ABC's programming helped to bring people to the network, and by the end of the 1980s, the once-youngest face on network news passed CBS and NBC and became the leader.

Although the business offices at the networks nessarily look at the ratings as the primary measure of success, many of us in the business use other gauges. Jennings was as solid a reporter as he was an anchor. Very few journalists travel to every corner of the world and meet the number of people that Jennings did over the years. In the five years that the *Washington Journalism Review* gave an award for the country's best anchor, Jennings was named each time. In 1995, the *Boston Globe* noted "the passing of Edward R. Murrow's mantle to Peter Jennings". Jennings also won Harvard University's Goldsmith Career Award for excellence in journalism and the coveted Radio and Television News Directors Paul White Award, chosen by the news directors of all three major networks. In 2001, he was awarded the Sol Taishoff Award for Excellence in Broadcast Journalism from the National Press Foundation. Jennings discussed the role of an anchor:

> I think it's changed somewhat over the years, from Douglas Edwards on CBS through Bob Trout into Cronkite, Huntley, Brinkley, now into we three and whatever comes next. . . . I don't really know the answer to the question of how anchoring has changed over the years, but the difference between the U.S. and other places is that you expect the journalist to be the anchorperson. That hasn't always been the case, but you

certainly expect a journalist, at the very least an editor, to be the anchorperson. It would be self-important to say so, but I think in some respects, it's been the transition has been a fairly logical one. Those of us who are anchoring now were reporters beforehand and had been given pretty rich opportunities by our news divisions, at least in my case, to see the rest of the world and get plugged in over time to the various beats and assignments that become important to you as an editor, mainly national, Washington, and overseas.

A Front Row Seat for History

Jennings, like others who came before him, was on the front line of television journalism, both in the field and in the studio:

I think that most of us who do this for a living appreciate how fortunate we are to have such good seats for history. So, it's not something you turn on and off in any eight-, ten-, or twenty-hour day. But that doesn't mean that I carry the immediacy of the shop home with me because if you did that, and worry about the moralities of what you did every day, you wouldn't be out discovering all those things about life which a good journalist must appreciate and absorb every day. You cannot do this job or any other job in journalism, in my view, if you aren't in constant contact with the world. I'm working on a book project about how provincial journalists in Washington and New York can get in terms of searching for America. You need to be on the road. You simply need to be on the road sharing people's experiences, otherwise it's very hard to report on them in any meaningful way. It's one of the great drawbacks of being an anchorperson who doesn't go anywhere. People ask why do anchors go on the road? The answer is you go on the road to absorb experience, context, geography, culture, etc.

When he found himself hiding behind a wall in Munich, looking into the camera and reporting that President Reagan was shot, or on September 11, 2001, he remained calm. No one keeps his cool under pressure better than Jennings. But it may the very few times he lost that rock solid control or became emotional on camera that brought out the critics. There is a group of people in this country who are paid to find fault in our craft—after all, it sells newspapers and magazine. For every article that's positive about television news, you can find ten that aren't. Jennings said:

> Certainly I pay attention to the critics, but not all of them. Some I pay no attention to whatsoever. I don't read criticism as a general rule. Television has this slight case of pencil envy. There's a daily bundle that goes around here with what's been said in print about the network, and I never read that. But, there used to be a guy named Walter Goodman who wrote for the *New York Times*. He was quite conservative politically, and he often wrote criticisms of the documentaries which I did, and I thought they were very intelligent. If he got something or didn't get something out of a program that we had done, then, yes, I took it very seriously. There's a difference between criticism as in theater or ballet or literary criticism and television columns. Television columnists, writers for newspapers, very often have to fill space every day, so what they write is often not criticism—it's more news.

A Sterling Success

As his record approaches the twenty-five–year mark in continuous network anchoring, Jennings's attitude and response to the widespread charges of liberal bias and a "Washington–New York" "axis of myopia" are worth studying.

He rejects the charges of liberal bias, which originated in the right-wing confines of the John Birch society and the pages of *Red Channels* in the 1950s. The charges spilled back into the Republican Party in the early 1960s, courtesy of the conservative movement that gave Barry Goldwater the 1964 presidential nomination. The charges gained White House endorsement when Nixon and Agnew raised traditional executive complaints about the Fourth Estate to the level of an organized conspiracy. They were enshrined in the national debate after southern conservatives switched to the Republican Party. Lingering regional resentment over civil rights joined with western suspicion over eastern elitism to raise liberal bias to whole new plane of debate under President George H.W. Bush.

However, Jennings does subscribe to the concept that there is a "Washington–New York" parochialism to the news and has remarked on it. In earlier days, when anchors tended to have a longevity of five years or so, there always seemed to be a fresh point of view injected by a newly minted anchor coming in from Europe or the West. But Jennings acknowledges the problem of parochialism when the big three anchors—Brokaw, Jennings, and Rather—all have been working out of New York City for an average of more than twenty years each and give the rarified point of view of the anchor, rather than the beat reporter.

His prescription for the problem is to make the effort to get out: out of New York and Washington for foreign reporting, out into the country simply to discover the nature and temper of the American public. Each of the anchors took on significant book and documentary projects that brought them in touch with ordinary Americans, from Brokaw's *The Greatest Generation*, to Jennings's own, *The Century*.

Jennings, of course, has the greatest difficulty, for he is exploring his adopted country. Jennings, alone among the anchors, encounters nativist sentiment that borders on antiforeign paranoia. What does it matter that he was born in Toronto? John Charles Daly was born in Johannesburg. It is the citizenship issue that rankles, the suspicion of carpet-baggery that bedevils him, just as accusations of "scalawag" used to be hurled at Louisiana-born Howard K. Smith when he thundered against the evils of segregation. The evidence is overwhelming that Jennings is no carpetbagger, but it is an easy charge to hurl. Some of it has to do with his influence. Some of it has to do with the very public knowledge of how much money Jennings has made in the United States.

From Elmer Lower to Roone Arledge to David Westin, Peter Jennings was treated with respect, encouraged, and, on occasion, placated when it came to contract renewal. On the heals of a bad public relations blunder by ABC that involved speculation that ABC would replace Ted Koppel on *Nightline* with David Letterman, Jennings's contract came up for renewal. Speculation that he might or might not reach a new agreement made front page news in 2002. That was yet another time in corporate belt tightening, and Jennings was making between ten and fourteen million dollars per year.

The pay scale for the news anchors is hard to comprehend for most people. All the great fortunes accumulated in the past century have been predicated on the massive scale of the American economy, a wealth unseen in any previous time of history. Those few who have skills or products relevant in every community find themselves earning money on a massive personal scale. On the one hand, based on the profits their programs generate for the networks—profits that are uniquely tied to the hold of their personalities over a defined audience—they might be underpaid. Compared to the pay scales of their associates who provide the underlying nuts-and-bolts of the broadcast, not just its public face, the salaries are a scandal. But such pay inequalities exist in the corporate boardroom, professional sports, and in Hollywood, and they are unlikely to be resolved solely concerning national anchors. The anchors did not create the star system.

That system is under threat. Not only because of an under-lying weakness of the formula, but because its distribution point, the twenty-two minutes of electronic signal known as the evening news, is collapsing as a platform. The evidence abounds that it is irretrievable. In a twenty-four–hour news en-vironment, it is neither practical nor possible to focus news at-tention on a single program or anchor. Yet, as serious news viewers migrate to other time slots and channels out of con-venience or preference, where does that leave anchors such as Jennings? His reluctance to take the anchor job in 1965 stemmed from his view that the ABC Evening News was an in-substantial program. His successor may well come, necessar-ily, to the same conclusion.

Chapter FOURTEEN

Dan Rather, CBS

Associated Press

"He swept though the South like a tornado through a trailer park," Dan Rather said one night on the air when referring to a political candidate. He just as easily could have been talking about his own career. Little did anyone know, when Rather was born in Wharton, Texas, on October 31, 1931, that television would become the rage, Walter Cronkite would become the most trusted man in America, and Rather would be the one man on the planet to be considered to fill Cronkite's shoes. Assaulted by viewers, television critics, a United States president, and even muggers on the streets of New York, Rather rose above it all with his folksy wit and his journalistic fervor.

His roots were planted firmly in Texas. Rather's career in journalism began while he attended college in the early 1950s. He was first an Associated Press reporter in Huntsville, Texas, then he moved on to United Press International (joining the enormous alumni of Unipressers among the network anchors), and then to KSAM radio in Huntsville. He graduated from Sam Houston State Teachers College in 1953, where he received a bachelor's degree in journalism. He spent the following year as a journalism teacher. He went on to attend the University of Houston and then the South Texas School of Law. From 1954 to 1955, he worked for KTRH radio in Houston and the *Houston Chronicle*. He then became news director of KTRH radio in 1956 and then a reporter for KTRK-TV, the ABC station in Houston in 1959. Rather watched the network television news like a hawk, looking toward a "someday" when a job would open up for him.

He jumped across the street to become a reporter for the local Houston CBS television station, KHOU. Hurricane Carla gave him his big break. He was stuck on Galveston Island for three days, and his dramatic coverage caught the eye of Ernest Leiser and others at CBS in New York.

Rather joined CBS News in 1962 in New York, but, after a brief indoctrination, he was transferred to Dallas to open a new bureau. He cultivated a reputation as a hard news man in the Murrow tradition, but that tough image was challenged in 1962 on a flight from Memphis to Birmingham. In his 1988 book, *This . . . is CBS*, Robert Salter wrote:

> Sometimes a television correspondent like Rather had to apply his own makeup without the luxury of relying on a makeup person in the studio. That meant the correspondent would have to carry his own compact. Placing his coat on the overhead rack, he found himself in great embarrassment when the compact fell out and landed on the floor in the

aisle. A stewardess quickly retrieved it and asked to whom did the compact belong. Rather gave her a stare as if to say what would he be doing with a thing like that? She looked around at the other (female) passengers, but no one spoke up. Rather was panicky for the rest of the flight. He realized that he had to do a piece almost as soon as he landed, and he needed the makeup. But there was no way he was going to ask the stewardess for his compact back. So he walked off the plane and did the piece without the makeup.

In 1963, he became the chief of the southern bureau in New Orleans. He was responsible for coverage of news events in the South, Southwest, Mexico, and Central America. It was a time of racial conflicts in the South and the crusade of Dr. Martin Luther King Jr.

Rather's Career "Rockets Forward"

On November 21, 1963, he was in Dallas to file a routine story on the president's arrival in Texas. The report struggled for a hard news angle because Kennedy was in town on a less-than-glamorous peace mission to mend deepening divisions in the Democratic Party before the 1964 political season. Rather's report, in fact, did not dwell at all on the significance of the president's appearance in the motorcade. All eyes were on Jackie Kennedy's arrival, for it was her first appearance in front of large crowds since the 1960 campaign.

On November 22, 1963, in Dallas, Rather broke the news of President John F. Kennedy's death. Rather assigned coverage of the motorcade to a camera crew—although they did not catch the assassination on film—and Rather was simply on the scene because he was waiting for a film drop from them. One print journalist at the scene remembers that Rather literally stood next to the Triple Overpass Bridge in Dealey Plaza as the car with President Kennedy passed right under it and in front of him when the shots rang out.

Rather didn't hear the shots. What he saw was the presidential limousine speed away from the route to the Dallas Trade Mart, where Kennedy was scheduled to speak. Instead, it sped off in the direction of the airport. Rather realized something happened, although, in the confusion, it was not clear that the president was shot. Rather ran to the CBS bureau that was five blocks away, opened a line to New York, and called Parkland General Hospital (which he realized was on the route to the airport). Rather reached a doctor, who told him the president was dead, and, after crucial minutes, Rather was able to confirm the news with a Catholic priest who was available.

In New York, Walter Cronkite was delivering the UPI bulletin of the shooting when Rather called in and was connected to a radio editor. There was noise, confusion, and Rather was juggling the call to New York with a call to the Dallas Trade Mart. When he confirmed to the reporter at the Trade Mart that two people had told him that Kennedy was dead, the radio editor heard it and put it on the air. That is why CBS Radio reported the death of the president fifteen minutes ahead of the other networks.

Cronkite told the viewers that Rather's report was unconfirmed, but, less than an hour later, it was official. Cronkite took off his glasses and wiped a tear from his eye. Rather was Walter Cronkite's point man for the coverage for many days. It was a defining moment in both men's careers.

When the Abraham Zapruder film of the assassination became public knowledge, Rather reported that he saw the film. The executives at CBS, and even Cronkite, wanted to hear what Rather had to say. They were all glued to the screen with half of America when Rather described how he had seen on the film Kennedy's head "rocket forward" from the head shot.

Rather seemed to be one step ahead of NBC and ABC—after all, he was a Texan and had many local connections.

Don Hewitt, in his 2001 book, *Tell Me a Story*, describes the scramble that ensued over the Zapruder film:

> [Rather] phoned me from Dallas and told me that a guy named Zapruder was supposed to have film of the assassination and was going to put it up for sale. In fact, he eventually did, sold it to *Life* magazine for a reputed six hundred thousand dollars. In my desire to get a hold of what was probably the most dramatic piece of news footage ever shot, I told Rather to go to Zapruder's house, sock him in the jaw, take his film to our affiliate in Dallas, copy it onto videotape, and let the CBS lawyers decide whether it could be sold or whether it was in the public domain. And then take the film back to Zapruder's house and give it back to him. That way, the only thing they could get him for was assault because he would have returned Zapruder's property.
>
> Rather said, "Great idea. I'll do it."
>
> I hadn't hung up the phone maybe ten seconds when it hit me: What in the hell did you just do? Are you out of your mind? So I called Rather back. Luckily, he was still there, and I said to him, "For Christ's sake, don't do what I just told you to. I think this day has gotten to me and thank God I caught you before you left." Knowing Dan to be as competitive as I am, I had the feeling that he wished he'd left before the second phone call.

For his outstanding work in Dallas, CBS decided to make him its White House correspondent. He worked in Washington for a year before the network transferred him first to London and then to Vietnam. He returned to the White House beat in 1966 and remained until 1974.

It was during the Washington years that Rather became even more closely associated with the Murrow tradition at CBS. He cultivated the association and drew close to Eric Sevareid, in particular. He considered Sevareid not only a link to the days of Murrow, but a mentor and friend. Sevareid and Rather were closest during Rather's time in Vietnam. In later years, he related to several staff member at CBS that Sevareid counseled him to read Herodotus and the French essayist Montaigne. Rather passed along similar advice to young CBS reporters in the next generation.

It came as a stinging rebuke that Sevareid, several years after Vietnam, wrote a letter to Rather that was made public. In it, he denied that any such conversation about Herodotus and Montaigne ever took place. In the letter, Sevareid claimed not to have read Montaigne since college and that it was wholly out of character to recommend Herodotus.

The episode embarrassed Rather, but it should have embarrassed Sevareid. It is amazing that a famed commentator would have made such a specific denial of an anecdote which, when told, placed Sevareid in such a positive mentoring light. Moreover, Sevareid went to such lengths to deny the episode. He used curt language in the letter to Rather, despite the fact that he did not deny that he had many conversations with Rather about newsgathering and the art of the broadcast reporting.

The disagreement remains a mystery. It is not clear whether Rather exaggerated, Sevareid forgot, or whether there was a mix-up. After all, they were in Vietnam and not in a bar across the street from CBS headquarters. Memories are famously affected by the stress of war. But the situation sheds light on Rather's character—not only his great admiration for the Murrow tradition and Murrow's boys, but a certain desire, which perhaps reflects a youthful insecurity, to seek out mentors and emphasize, perhaps even overemphasize, his relationship and gratitude to them.

In his later career, Rather was criticized for what some critics termed "remote" or "wacky" behavior. He was widely criticized for walking out on a broadcast in 1987 because a tennis match ran long and cut into the news time. Later still, there were immense difficulties in his relationship with co-anchor Connie Chung, including accusations that Rather was two-faced while they served together at the anchor desk. In all these instances, a strong desire to please and be accepted appears to be mixed with extremely high professional standards and difficulties with some types of personal confrontation.

In 1968, Rather was involved in an altercation at the Democratic Convention. A security guard punched him in the stomach on camera as the security tried to remove a member of the Georgia delegation. It prompted one of the extremely rare outbursts of emotion the public ever saw from Walter Cronkite, who said, "I think we have a bunch of thugs here," as Rather picked himself up off the floor.

"Walter, I'm all right," Rather said. "It's all in a day's work."

"I Can't Be a Robot"

Nixon was elected, and Rather tagged along on one presidential trip after another, including the famous trip to China. During the summer of 1972, following the foiled break-in at the Democratic National Committee headquarters at the Watergate Hotel, details of the Watergate Conspiracy began to emerge. Rather and the White House press corps read the articles by Bob Woodward and Carl Bernstein, which featured an off-the-record source known as "Deep Throat". The articles highlighted a web of corruption and conspiracy that involved high-ranking members of the Nixon Administration. None of the electronic correspondents were able to break major aspects of the developing story, and the networks were forced to re-report the stories from the *Washington Post* and the *New York Times*, whose investigative teams began to uncover further evidence of the conspiracy.

It was a frustrating time for Rather. In 1972, he began work on an in-depth article for *Harper's* magazine about the grow-ing—and troubling—influence of John Erlichman and Bob Haldeman at the White House. A top CBS executive of the time, fearing a White House "freeze-out" given the climate of the times, told Rather to drop the story. It did not appear until 1974 in *The Palace Guard*, a book co-authored by Rather and Gary Paul Gates.

In the book, Rather traced the growing power of the White House staff at the expense of Cabinet officials following Nixon's first inauguration in 1969, with Chief of Staff Halde-man and Chief Domestic Policy Advisor Erlichman as the pri-mary beneficiaries. Nixon's wariness of the Washington press corps and the permanent bureaucracy—dating back to his days as an anti-communist crusader in the Congresses of the late 1940s and early 1950s—was exacerbated by opposition to his strategy to end the Vietnam War. Convinced that the war was unwinnable, and knowing that anti-war activities in the United States emboldened the North Vietnamese, he at-tempted to bomb the North Vietnamese to the negotiation table with a series of air strikes against Hanoi and secret oper-ations in Laos and Cambodia.

The strategy depended on a degree of secrecy not seen in American government since World War II, but the strategy was badly hurt by an ongoing series of press leaks, which Nixon blamed on the permanent bureaucracy and the press corps. He countered by centralizing his administration in White House staff in a manner unseen since the Roosevelt Administration and the national emergencies of the Great Depression and World War II. However, Nixon lacked Roosevelt's ability to domi-nate the press corps and Kennedy's deft handling of it, so his press notices (always unfavorable) became generally hostile.

As Rather traced the story in *The Palace Guard*, policy and direction became more the province of the White House under Haldeman and Erlichman. Nixon's key ally in the Cabinet, John Mitchell, left the government to head up Nixon's 1972 re-election campaign. Throughout 1971 and 1972, the nexus of the presidency moved more and more into the White House, where an increasingly desperate series of measures was undertaken to stop the press leaks. An always-adversarial relationship between Nixon and the Washington press corps dissolved into almost outright hostility. Nixon held fewer press conferences and opted for direct national addresses via television; the press corps engaged in hostile questioning and stepped up the pace of its investigative reporting to uncover stories from the White House.

The Nixon strategy eventually led the White House team to establish a "plumbers unit" to stop the leaks. It was that unit's operations that led to the Watergate break-in. Rather's book traces the growing conspiratorial climate in the White House throughout Nixon's first term and shows the underlying conditions that created Watergate itself.

In the press room, the tension between President Nixon and Rather became palpable. Rather's questions were among the most challenging and direct offered by the press corps, and Nixon could not find enough of the humor of a Kennedy, the high seriousness of Roosevelt, or the plain-spokenness of a Truman to deflect the questions gracefully. In a famed press conference, when Rather challenged Nixon aggressively, the president snapped, "Are you running for something?"

Rather snapped back, "No, sir, Mr. President, are you?"

Many of the news managers at CBS thought Rather was too much of a loose cannon. With the CBS Evening news on top, they didn't want to embarrass Cronkite, and they wanted the incident with Nixon to go away. Rather had this spin on a reporter's emotions:

I don't think you can be a first rate journalist and not be passionately involved in the responsibility of trying to produce quality journalism. If you care passionately about the quality of what you're doing, then you will be emotionally involved in the responsibilities. . . . I view it as like the Ten Commandments. We know that the Ten Commandments are excellent rules for life, and we also know that it's not humanly possible to live up to them in every way every minute of every day. In a miniscule way, so it is with trying to keep your emotions out of your reporting. Having said that, I think it's also an integral part of being passionately, emotionally involved in the responsibilities of trying to turn out good journalism that you don't seek to be a robot. First of all, no one can do that, either. I don't try to be a robot; I'm not a robot and can't be. This means that sometimes your emotions are going to well up and flood over. . . . To judge a reporter by how well he or she tries, and how well he or she succeeds in meeting the standard of what used to be called "objective journalism," a standard to which I still subscribe, and recognizing that an awful lot of people never believed in it and more people today just think it's an outdated notion, how hard you try and how often you succeed in doing it is a standard by which I'm prepared to be judged. I think any decent intending reporter should be.

CBS felt it was time for a cooling off period for Rather and reassigned him to the documentary unit. He prepared network specials on the assassinations, cancer, and politics. They were well thought out and well received.

Rather, by then, was the Sunday night news anchor; he inherited the broadcast from Harry Reasoner when Reasoner jumped ship to ABC. In October, 1975, Rather made his first appearance on *60 Minutes* as a regular. Two months into his tenure, he did a piece on Allied Chemical that revealed that it dumped insecticide. The report resulted in 153 indictments and almost fourteen million dollars in fines.

Rather continued to build a reputation as a tough, often confrontational, hard news reporter. He made a series of celebrated reports from Afghanistan in 1980 and became one of the most recognized news personalities in the country. Rather's image, at the time, was stronger and more indelible than either Brokaw's or Jennings's, which led to a number of public incidents where Rather was assaulted by complete strangers. The most famous incident was in 1986, when he was assaulted by a man later identified as Walter Tager, who later was convicted in the killing of NBC staff member in 1994. Tager assaulted him, knocked him down, and kicked him repeatedly in the back, shouting "Kenneth, what is the frequency?" It was an apparent reflection of Tager's paranoid belief that the media were beaming messages to him. The incident was memorialized in a hit song by the musical group R.E.M., titled, "What's the Frequency, Kenneth?" The encounter served as an early warning about the increasing impact of television, even news, on disturbed minds.

The Arledge Call

Rather wanted to do more. He wanted to be the main anchor, but Cronkite wasn't going anywhere, at least not yet. In late 1979, Rather received a call from Roone Arledge. ABC was floundering. Reasoner and Walters had, famously, not worked out, and so ABC tried multiple anchors in different cities. That did not work a ratings miracle either. Arledge laid out a convincing plan for Rather to join them. Rather remembers:

> A number of things had come together in mid to late 1979 to the very early part of 1980 that I had opportunities to go other places and anchor. One of the things that people who were closest to me, that I know really care about me and love me as a person, they expressed concern that following a legend such

as Walter Cronkite would be problematical, if not impossible. A very good friend of mine, who's now passed on, said to me that the first person in after Cronkite is going to get his head blown off! He was Texan, and Texans talk that way. What he meant was that that he felt it was what he called "a damned fool idea to try to follow Cronkite" and recommended strongly that I go someplace else, anywhere else, if I want to anchor.

In the end, for whatever it may be worth, and looking back on it, it's not worth very much, I signed with CBS for less money, quite a bit less money than was available elsewhere. It was mostly because I just couldn't bring myself to work anyplace else. I have never been sorry about that decision. It was a personal decision I had to make myself, and I tried to get myself mentally to envision working someplace else, and even under the extraordinary, positive circumstances that had been presented to me at other places as a genuine desire to have me come and succeed someplace else, I could never get myself mentally, and of the heart, any other place.

So he stayed, and, before long, it became apparent that Cronkite was getting tired and perhaps wanted to retire. Rather began to talk to Cronkite about his job and the future for both of them:

> Some of those conversations were very private and personal and will remain so. It's fair to say that Walter was very clear that he was ready to step into a new phase of his life and that he didn't want to continue having the responsibility. He loved being at the anchor desk for his five nights a week, most days and weeks of the year. That was important to me that he was ready to do this! It turned out that he expressed to me down the road that he was not only ready to do it, but he was eager to do it. We had a number of meaningful conversations about anchoring, about what he saw in the future, both positive and negative.
>
> Looking back on it, I'm not surprised, but I am impressed,

with just how right he was about any number of things, including that the competitive arena would become larger and more voracious. We had a number of these conversations.

By then, Cronkite had succeeded like no anchor before him. He decided to go out on top. In 1981, Cronkite retired.

Filling Cronkite's Shoes . . . or Not?

On Friday night, March 6, 1981, Walter Cronkite was asked by the network to mention Rather's name at the end of his final broadcast. Cronkite agreed, but some people say it was not an easy decision for him. Cronkite said that his colleague, Dan Rather, a good man, would be on the broadcast on Monday.

Cronkite's departure received so much attention in the press that it was even mentioned on the other networks. That Monday, all eyes were watching as Rather took the chair. Rather went on the air that night as if he had been there all along. The question was, "Could Rather be another Cronkite?" Rather hated that question. He didn't like being compared because it was a new day and a different person anchoring.

Rather told the publication *Cigar Aficionado*, "I wasn't sure I'd be in it more than a year or two. I had a good job at *60 Minutes,* arguably the best job in television news. And while I can be dumb as dirt about a lot of things, I was at least smart enough to know that."

Rather had to find his own identity. He struggled with it for weeks as the network experienced a drop in ratings. Everyone figured that when Cronkite left, Rather wouldn't be able to hold the fort. But that was the year that news numbers went flat, and television news viewership was as high as it was ever going to get. CNN was building, and new sources for news were beginning to emerge. So it just wasn't CBS that experienced the decline. It was also the time when the network news divisions were expected, for the first time, to be profit centers for the networks. Rather commented:

> Certainly, until the mid to late 1970s, no major network news division was expected to show a profit. The dramatic change, beginning in the mid to late '70s and no later than the mid '80s, has been that news divisions are seen as profit centers. The pressure was on to deliver ratings demographics and profits! When you work in commercial television and radio—and I'm old enough to have worked in radio—there's always been some of it, but now there's a much greater undertow created by those factors today than there's ever been before!

Rather went to work concentrating on news itself and the two things that he felt were paramount to the viewers:

> The first thing is, is it important? The second question is, is it interesting? The very best news stories are those that are both important and interesting. Sometimes things are important, but you say to yourself, how interesting can I make this? That's always a challenge. Then there are plenty of other things that are interesting, but not very important. The standard I use of is it important, I say to myself, well, if it really isn't all that important, then how interesting is it?

At the same time, Rather also worked intensively on his personal image, softening a tough manner that worked better on the confrontational *60 Minutes* and as a White House correspondent during the Watergate years. Rather learned that what worked well for a reporter did not always translate effectively in anchoring. Famously, he dropped his conservative business suits for sweaters—a device Jimmy Carter used successfully for his fireside chats in the first year of his presidency. As a result of Rather's wardrobe change, his ratings improved substantially. He reclaimed the ratings lead and held it for several years.

The cost to Rather was that in changing his on-air image and then switching back to suits, he acquired a reputation among some viewers as something of an anchoring chameleon. He got the reputation despite the fact that his Texas accent, folksy ways, and string of Texas slang expressions were characteristic of the actual man. In fact, the "tough guy" image was something that had been cultivated carefully as well, such as when he donned *mujahideen* garb for his reports from Afghanistan in 1980. Anchors, like movie stars, face the problem of typecasting. It's one of the reasons we had such difficulty accepting Walter Cronkite as host of the CBS *Morning Show* opposite Charlemagne the puppet lion.

Also, before 1981, the country was largely unaccustomed to Texans as anchors. Texans in earlier eras downplayed their regional accent and style. However, derision was heaped on the elder George Bush when the Yale-educated politician expressed his affection for country music and pork rinds. It smacked of opportunism, despite the fact that he lived in Texas for nearly twenty years. Rather never previously emphasized his Texan roots, and he was anything but folksy during his time on *60 Minutes* and at the White House. Consequently, he acquired a certain reputation for pandering for ratings when his Texan fondness for aphorisms and casual style asserted itself.

Rather's rating began to slide again in the mid-1980s. After *World News Tonight* and the NBC *Nightly News* both jettisoned their multi-anchor formats, the ratings war became a direct contest between Rather, Tom Brokaw, and Peter Jennings. Rather's ratings did not crumble, but they slipped enough that there was considerable tension at CBS headquarters. The tension was exacerbated by the fact that CBS went through a series of ownership changes and cost cuts that, in the view of most longtime CBS staff members, decimated the network news division and crippled its ability to be competitive.

On September 2, 1985, Rather tried a new innovation without

warning. He jettisoned the traditional "and that's the way it is" ending for the CBS *Evening News*, ending the broadcast with, "Courage!" There's no more important word in the Rather lexicon, but the new ending seemed simply bizarre to most people. When he repeated the ending on Tuesday, he had the same problem with Executive Producer Tom Bettag that Cronkite had with News President Dick Salant when he developed "and that's the way it is" in the early 1960s. Bettag asked Rather to check with him before changing the sign-off.

On Wednesday, Rather used the ending again, and considerable negative coverage erupted in the media. Several staffers met with Rather to dissuade him from using the closing. On Thursday, Rather used the closing, but seemed to give it a Spanish pronunciation—"cour-a-hey". He returned to "courage" on Friday. A remarkable study in courage itself, it was a failure as a sign-off and attracted widespread derision. Famously, on the *Today Show*, Bryant Gumbel satirized the situation by using "hot dogs" and "mazel tov" as sign-offs. Rather got the message, and "courage" disappeared the next week, but it signaled a new era in the public's relationship with Rather.

Behind the scenes, a new network news president, Van Gordon Sauter, arrived with a mandate to soften the news formats. Despite the fact that Rather was associated with a hard news tradition, he became a friend to Sauter. The friendship cost him considerable credibility within the CBS News organization because Sauter became a lightning rod for criticism among news staff, who resented the format changes and layoffs associated with his tenure.

Rather's difficult mid-1980s continued when, in 1987, long-simmering disagreements at the network over cutting into the CBS *Evening News* when sports programming ran long boiled over into public controversy. On September 11, 1987, a tennis match ran long. The decision was made to continue the tennis broadcast and to cut into the network news. Rather, completely fed up with the practice, stormed off the set moments before the news broadcast was set to begin. To complicate matters, the tennis match ended unexpectedly. CBS switched over to the news, and the network went to black. It remained black for six minutes. After Rather returned and completed the broadcast, a storm of protest erupted.

Rather was stunned that, although his move had been made in defense of the news, news executives, and even Walter Cronkite, criticized him publicly. "I would have fired him. There's no excuse for it," Cronkite said.

Phil Jones, the former chairman of the CBS affiliated advisory broad, said, "There's a reason people are called anchors: they should be anchored and not get up."

Rather issued a hasty and contrite apology and was allowed to continue in the anchor role, but his image was tarnished by the episode.

Bushwhacked

Four months later, Rather was still trying to live down those six minutes. One night, when he was interviewing Vice President George Bush Sr., Rather was fixated on trying to get Bush to answer questions about Iran-Contra. Bush got mad, very mad:

RATHER: Then how do you explain that you can't remember it, and the other people at the meeting say he was apoplectic?

BUSH: Maybe I wasn't there at that point.

RATHER: You weren't in the meeting?

BUSH: I'm not suggesting. I'm just saying I don't remember it.

RATHER: I don't want to be argumentative, Mr. Vice President.

BUSH: You do, Dan.

RATHER: No . . . no, sir, I don't.

BUSH: This is not a great night, because I want to talk about why I want to be president, why those 41 percent of the people are supporting me. And I don't think it's fair—

RATHER: And Mr. Vice President, if these questions are—

BUSH: . . . to judge my whole career by a rehash on Iran. How would you like it if I judged your career by those seven minutes when you walked off the set in New York? [Note: Rather actually was in Miami, and he was off the set for six minutes.]

RATHER: Well, Mr.—

BUSH: Would you like that?

RATHER: Mr. Vice President—

BUSH: I have respect for you, but I don't have respect for what you're doing here tonight.

RATHER: Mr. Vice President, I think you'll agree that your qualification for president and what kind of leadership you'd bring to the country, what kind of government you'd have, what kind of people you have around you—

BUSH: Exactly.

RATHER: . . . is much more important than what you just referred to. I'd be happy to—

BUSH: Well, I want to be judged on the whole record, and you're not giving an opportunity.

RATHER: And I'm trying to set the record straight, Mr. Vice President.

Throughout the 1990s, Rather's ratings continued to slide on the *Evening News,* but he found new audiences through the news magazine programs *48 Hours* and, later, *60 Minutes II.* He became entangled, during the 1990s, in a running dispute with the political right. The dispute stemmed from his years as White House correspondent and flared up again during the 1988 Bush campaign. His relationship with the Republican right reached its nadir in his tussles with 1996 Republican presidential candidate Pat Buchanan, who had served as a Nixon speechwriter.

"Are you, as some of your critics charge, interested in being a kind of moral dictator?" Rather asked Buchanan on *48 Hours* early in the 1996 primary season. His controversial "tough style" was never more evident than with figures like Buchanan. Perhaps one of the ironies of Rather's failed co-anchoring partnership with Connie Chung is that both wanted to be known as "tough" journalists who asked "tough" questions. Rather was reportedly embarrassed by the softer story lines that were pursued in those years, such as Chung's rink-side report from the 1994 Winter Olympics of the assault by Tonya Harding's bodyguards on Nancy Kerrigan.

As the 1990s progressed, Rather increasingly became associated with his "Texan-isms"—aphorisms that were often incomprehensible to the national audience, but were designed to reflect a more folksy, accessible Rather. For Rather knew that he lacked the natural on-camera warmth of many of the other anchors. For instance, he found it difficult to smile. But, to some extent, his attempts at accessibility backfired. Much of the national audience tuned out such an overtly regional personality. Others found Rather's aphorisms scripted and forced.

"Such embellishments," wrote Peter Boyle in *Who Killed CBS?*, "were meant to seem to viewers like a natural flair for colorful talk, but even they were taken by some as a sign of Rather's phoniness. Many of Rather's 'spontaneous' sayings were, in fact, written out beforehand, and some of them weren't even written by Rather, but by his writers."

The problem was phoniness, for it is far worse to be a phony, in network news terms, than it is to be perceived as a phony. So much of an anchor's appeal was, and continues to be, a perceived personal and truthful relationship devoid of artifice or manipulation that encourages us, as an audience, to believe and trust in the network evening news.

The combination of Rather's colorful talk and questions about the reliability of the network news operation came together in a potent combination on election night in 2000. It was a memorable night for the networks and for those who watched Rather.

Rather was tired. The networks—all of them—called the election results in Florida for Gore, then Bush, then they didn't know who won, and the coverage continued. There was an intense seesaw of results, and the coverage went deep into the night.

Also, that election night featured more "Rather-isms" than any other night by far. He made remarks like, "This race is tight like a too-small bathing suit on a too-long ride home from the beach," "this race is as tight as the rusted lug nuts on a '57 Chevy," and "Texas: thirty-two electoral votes, another of the so-called big enchiladas or, if not an enchilada, at least a huge taco."

Later, when answering questions after a lecture at Brown University, Rather talked about how the networks handled that famous election night in 2000:

> This year, we made some serious mistakes. Unfortunately for us, the worst mistakes we made happened in the worst possible place, the state that turned out to be decisive. The mistakes that we made were not emphasizing enough what we know to be true, which is that we make estimates. When we say George Bush carries Louisiana, that is an estimate. No one knows until the votes are counted. We need to repeat that hour after hour, which we don't do.
>
> At CBS News, we have called something like thirty thousand national races since exit polling came in during the 1960s. Our record is the best in the business. We don't have the best in the business record on everything, but, on this, we do. I believe we have called them wrong fourteen times out

of thirty thousand. So, statistically, we have been very good. That does not take away from the inaccuracy of this election night in this particular place. We had lulled ourselves into believing the statistics. . . . The information we put out early in the evening was flawed. We should have caught it, and we didn't. Whether it changed the outcome of the election or not, I would like to give a definite answer. But, in all candor, I don't know. I have heard no persuasive evidence that has convinced me that it made any difference in the election whatsoever. But I respect those who have a different view.

Dan Rather has his critics, and, on election night in 2000, I was one of them. But he told me he takes it all in stride:

I do pay attention to criticism. I try to separate out criticism that I think has, as its source, some highly political and/or ideological or special agenda. That can often be orchestrated to try to influence ones reporting. I do listen to criticism, and I take my attitude about critics is I don't rule out the possibility that the person criticizing or organization may be correct. Depending on the source, I tend to take it seriously and say to myself, let me, as objectively as possible, consider this criticism. Sometimes it's warranted, and I give myself lectures about how I think this criticism is valid and I need to address it. What I don't do is tailor my reporting or our broadcast to fit criticism over my own standards. . . . You can't always be right. My principle editing rule of thumb is the first thing I want to do is make it compatible with my journalistic conscience.

The Viciously Competitive Pit

Rather always stuck with what he believed, and, many times, it got him a front row seat in the boss's office. Even off-the-wall tabloid-style journalism creeps into the network newscasts from time to time when the media gets into a feeding frenzy.

He blames it on the competitive nature of the news business, as he told PBS one day:

> Well, I'll tell you how it happens. But it's really important you understand this is not my way of making excuses. I don't have any excuses. I am not the vice president in charge of excuses here. I'm trying to help explain how it happens.
>
> You're in this, you know, viciously competitive pit, where day to day, week to week, month to month, it's a matter of survival, that is, you know, to keep your program on the air, keep yourself on the air. And somebody says—let's take the Gennifer Flowers case. When it first came up, you say, well, gosh, I don't have any stomach for doing that. They'll say, "Come on, Dan, you can't live back in the days of spats and the hominy wagon. These are the 1990s. These are the late '80s and early 1990s. Things have changed. And when this kind of story breaks, you've got to go with it."
>
> Here's the point. The pressure builds. Because somebody else is doing it, you've got to do it. And too often, we succumb to that pressure. Too often, I succumb to that pressure. You see it all the time in political coverage.

Rather is a defender of the craft, a self-made newsman with a flare for the dramatic and an odd sense of humor. The journalism of news has suffered over the years in a quest for ratings. When Edward R. Murrow was on the air, ratings mattered, but getting the story on the air seemed more important than determining who was going to watch it. In speaking to members of the Radio Television News Directors Association, Rather talked about that very issue:

> In the constant scratching and scrambling for ever-better ratings, and money, and the boss's praise, and a better job, it is worth pausing to ask—how goes the real war, the really important battle of our professional lives? How goes the battle for quality, for truth and justice, for programs worthy of the best within ourselves and the audience? How goes the battle against "ignorance, intolerance, and indifference"? The battle

not to be merely "wires and lights in a box," the battle to make television not just entertaining, but also, at least some little of the time, useful for higher, better things? How goes the battle?

Rather reaches back to Murrow to find that beacon of integrity still intact:

Ed Murrow had faith in our country and in our country's decision to emphasize, from the beginning, commercial broadcasting. He recognized commercial broadcasting's potential and its superiority over other possibilities. But even as he believed in the strength of market values and the freedom of commercial broadcasting, Ed Murrow feared the rise of a cult that worshipped at the shrine of implacable, idle ratings. He feared that the drive to sell, sell—and nothing but sell—was overwhelming the potential for service of radio and television.

Rather has said that he's afraid television news is shifting away from its intended purpose. "Murrow was concerned about it in the '50s; Cronkite was concerned about it in the '60s and '70s. The difference between now and then is that now, in some ways, news values have been overwhelmed by entertainment values!"

Will There Be Life After Dan Rather?

So what is to become of Dan Rather? What is to become of the evening news broadcasts on network television? What will be said about Dan Rather when he steps down?

"I don't think about what will be written about me when the time comes," he reflects. "Quite honestly, I have had so many more good things happen to me than I could ever possibly imagine, that whatever anybody wants to write or say, it will be okay with me."

He reflects further on the nature of mistakes, learning, and recovery—the very topics that his nemesis, Richard Nixon, wrote about in the splendid book of defeat and renewal, *In the Arena*. Rather said:

> In the end, anchors and presidents, who make their mistakes in the full glare of the public eye and take their blows immediately afterwards around the water coolers of the nation and on shows populated by media pundits and political pundits. These folk know what Teddy Roosevelt wrote of, "The credit belongs to the man who is actually in the arena; whose face is marred by the dust and sweat and blood; who strives valiantly; who errs and comes short again and again; who knows the great enthusiasms, the great devotions, and spends himself in a worthy cause."

It is ironic that Nixon and Rather remember the same quote from Teddy Roosevelt in reflecting on their respective careers, but it should not surprise. They share an immense admiration for personal courage and personal toughness. That admiration connects them despite their adversarial relationship. Rather himself struck a decidedly Nixonian tone when reflecting on the mistakes of his career: "I would like to think," he said, "that while I know that I have wounds, all of them are from the front and honorably earned."

Chapter FIFTEEN

Tom Brokaw

Courtesy of Globe Photo/NBC

Among the network news anchors, Tom Brokaw and Chet Huntley wrote memoirs about their childhoods. Brokaw's is titled, *A Long Way from Home*, and in the introductory material, he acknowledges that he resisted writing the book for a long time because he feared it would be seen as "simply an exercise in vanity, rather than what I hoped it would be, an attempt to document . . . the character of life in the American heartland from which I have drawn so much."

Brokaw was born to a family of French Huguenot descent, which settled on the banks of the Missouri, one of the three great rivers of the Louisiana Purchase, France's massive land transfer that gave the United States the left bank of the Mississippi and all the land between the Mississippi and the Rocky Mountains. The Brokaws then made their way to eastern South Dakota.

South Dakota retains more of a sense of the frontier than almost any other state in the Union. Part of this stems from underpopulation and underdevelopment. The landscapes of the state are, in many areas, undisturbed. Part of the frontier-like feel also stems from the landscape itself, with the Missouri River system, the Black Hills, and Mt. Rushmore offering tangible links to the older days. Mostly, though, it's in the personalities of the South Dakotans—low-key, without being laid back like Californians. Perhaps it is because South Dakota is primarily a farming state, and there is hardly a more hopeful yet sanguine profession than one that depends on a certain abundance of rain in what is essentially dry prairie country.

"I am particularly attached to the Missouri River," Brokaw wrote. "Whenever I return to my native state, I always try and swim in the river channel, just to feel its restless currents again." His family moved between several major dam and construction projects along the Missouri, and Brokaw's childhood was lived in the shadow of Lewis and Clark, who pushed through that country in 1804 en route to the Pacific Coast. Brokaw even graduated from high school in Yankton, South

Dakota, where Lewis and Clark had their first encounter with the Sioux.

But for all of the rich history of the region, Brokaw was raised in a family that looked forward and was deeply interested in progress. He recalled that Pickstown, where he lived during much of his childhood, "was no ordinary small town in a remote location. The combination of round-the-clock construction on the dam . . . and the unique layout of the new town . . . drew a steady stream of visitors. . . . *Life* magazine and regional newspapers such as the *Des Moines Register* did extensive features on the Missouri River development, and I remember the pride we felt at being part of something important enough to be noticed beyond our provincial borders."

Brokaw turned to broadcasting in his teenage years, working in local Yankton radio. But his family did not have television until the late 1950s. "Evenings, our family's appointment with Chet Huntley and David Brinkley was, for me, a magical experience. That fifteen-minute broadcast magnified my view over the spare prairie horizons that framed my physical existence . . . television was a godsend to those of us in remote areas."

Brokaw recalled his experiences in local radio in a 2002 speech at the Radio and Television News Directors Association:

> It was there that I learned firsthand the great commercial pressures that exist within broadcasting operations. The fine line that exists between commerce and news. Because I was on the air at the age of sixteen, having had no other experience, thinking this is the way it was done everywhere in America.
>
> In Yankton, South Dakota, they had a volunteer fire department, and when the phone rang and the siren went off and the phone rang at all the volunteer firemen's homes, it also rang at the station. And I had these instructions: I would pick up the phone, listen to the announcement, put it down, interrupt the radio programming that we had on the air, and

say, "The fire is located at 313 Locust Street. Please do not fol-low the fire trucks. The fire is located at 313 Locust. Please avoid that area." Then, after a discrete pause, I would say, "Are you properly insured? For a complete line of home fire insurance needs, call the Frubb H. Leech Agency."

Wait, it's not over. When the bell went off on the United Press International wire service ticker signaling what passed for an urgent or a bulletin in South Dakota—generally an-other highway fatality—I would again interrupt the program-ming, but now we had sound effects. I would hit a button. There would be a prerecorded sound effect that went like this: "BONG, BONG, BONG." In my best sixteen-year-old fu-neral tones, I would come on the air and say, "For whom the bell tolls, thirty-eight-year-old Jim Selachek of rural Gettas, South Dakota, was killed in a one-car accident tonight two miles south of Gettas. BONG, BONG, BONG. For whom the bell tolls, thirty-eight-year-old Jim Selachek." Then, after a discrete pause, I would say, "Are you properly insured? For a complete line of life insurance needs, see the Morgan T. Smith Insurance Agency."

So for those of you who are news directors and feel that you have commercial pressures now, you know nothing about for whom the bell tolls.

By 2002, Brokaw developed that talent for understated, wry humor and anecdotes that seems to be the birthright of the re-gion. So often when we think of prairie men, from Abraham Lincoln to Harry Reasoner, we think of how much we have en-joyed them because of a light, humane sense of humor.

Brokaw attributes his first major break in broadcasting to the weakness of the current anchor, rather than to his own still-developing skills. He was hired in 1961 as a part-time weather-man and backup anchor at KTIV, the NBC affiliate in Sioux City, after a stretch as a reporter with the CBS affiliate in Rapid City. But by the early 1960s, he had a basis for a career cover-ing major political figures after covering the 1956 presidential campaign from Yankton and the 1960 campaigns in Rapid City. He also earned a political science degree from the University of South Dakota. In addition, he served as Boys State Governor of South Dakota in an organization that was a popular American Legion public policy program of the time that brought high school juniors from across the state together for a week of debates and seminars. Following a successful start in South Dakota, Brokaw made his first step into a wider world of "big city" television when he applied for work in Omaha.

Job Hunting and Fishing

Brokaw recalled the story of his hiring in his RTNDA address:

> If many of you go back to your newsrooms and dig deep into your files, you will probably find one of those applications there. Especially if you are one of those stations that ended your job opportunity ads in the back of RTNDA journals and *Broadcasting* magazine with, "Good hunting and fishing opportunities in the area."
>
> I managed to find a man in Omaha, Nebraska, by the name of Mark Gottier, who would see me for an interview. He took me to lunch at the worst greasy spoon in downtown Omaha, and I thought my career was over before it began. Two days later, he called and offered me a job: ninety dollars a week as a general assignment reporter. I held out for a hundred bucks.
>
> He said, "That's fairly outrageous. You came here begging for a job, I've offered you one, and now you want a ten dollar raise before you begin." And I said, "Mr. Gottier, you don't understand. I'm marrying the daughter of a physician in my hometown. I have to be able to go to him and say, 'I'm making a three figure salary as I marry your daughter.'"

Gottier learned early on what we, as an American audience, learned much later: people just *liked* Tom Brokaw. He could ask for the outrageous and find a way of making the request so that it sounded okay.

Brokaw attributed his rise from general assignment reporter to news editor to ineptness with a camera. "I was, conceivably, the worst man ever to hold film in his hands. And the Houston Fearless Film Processor terrified me no end. So, they made me a news editor. I did the morning cut-ins, and the noon news, and the Saturday night news for the princely sum of one hundred twenty-five dollars."

Brokaw left the Midwest after only a few years. He was hired as the eleven o'clock anchorman at WSB Atlanta in 1965. "I've often thought I should go back to Atlanta, go on the air, and apologize to the good people of that community for having given them the news as a twenty-five-year-old Yankee anchor in the midst of the civil rights revolution that was going on in their community. And I learned more in Atlanta about another culture and another way of life and the great social conflict that was exploding across the South."

Brokaw, however, missed out on the opportunity to cover the rise of Jimmy Carter because just as Carter was elected to the Georgia State Senate in 1966, Brokaw was offered a job by NBC. He moved to the network that has been his home ever since. However, because the job was at KNBC, Los Angeles, he missed out on Carter, but he jumped right into the story of another legendary president's rise. In 1966 Ronald Reagan made his first run for political office and won the governorship.

Former President Reagan is one of the more lionized of our presidents, inimitably associated with the successful conclusion of the Cold War and a conservative turn in social and taxation policies widely approved in the country as a whole. It's not widely remembered that Reagan's tenure as California governor was, especially in his first term, a time of real confrontation and tough politics. Reagan was hated widely, especially by younger Californians. It was a real baptism for a twenty-six-year old reporter in Los Angeles one year removed from Omaha. Brokaw was in the city of the 1965 Watts riots and just a few miles removed from Reagan's ranch to the north of the city and his political base in Orange County.

Brokaw became known for asking tough questions of the governor, even at the risk of being confrontational. When Reagan was caught flying in a jet that he said he sold to save the taxpayers money, in the days after the governor raised that state's sales tax, and when *Washington Post* columnist Drew Pearson called Reagan a homosexual, Brokaw was in the governor's face looking for a response.

It was an education not only for Brokaw, but for viewers and network executives as well. Brokaw, even in those days, had an ability to charm even when being tough. In fact, the two often went hand in hand—strong credentials indeed during the angry era of the 1960s, when politics took an ugly, almost brutal turn.

But Brokaw brought more than style to the job. Somewhere in his career, he became a good technical reporter. He was solid at moving stories along and, more importantly, able to handle some of the most mundane but critical aspects of the reporter's life; he made sure he could get the film, get it to the lab, and get it on the air. Those were different days of television news. Television used film and had off-duty police motorcycle officers drive the film back to the station, so by the time the reporter fought traffic, the film was processed and ready to edit.

The days were long and full of the frustrations of traveling and racing against deadlines, but, even in his mid-twenties, Brokaw developed a reputation for keeping up with seasoned Los Angeles reporters. Because of his anchoring experience, he picked up an assignment as the Sunday night anchor at KNBC. Because KNBC is an owned-and-operated NBC affiliate, Brokaw was offered occasional network assignments, which he gladly accepted.

His biggest break at that time was the opportunity to cover the 1968 political conventions. The 1968 political season was perhaps more focused on California than any before or since. On the Democratic side, the race to succeed Johnson was incredibly close and undecided leading up to the California primary in June. The primary was won by Robert Kennedy, who was assassinated shortly after his victory speech.

On the Republican side, there was far less drama, but of the three main contenders for the Republican nomination, two were Californians: Richard Nixon and Ronald Reagan. Both had their California political base in Southern California. Young Brokaw had a considerable advantage in covering the season and the conventions because of his years covering Reagan. Also, he was able to draw on a long-standing interest in politics.

Brokaw was a quick study and a success, and he received more assignments for the 1972 conventions. It was at the convention in 1972 that Brokaw remembers John Chancellor saying to him, "It's time for you to move east and be a grown-up."

And east he went. One year later, in 1973, he became NBC's White House correspondent and was front and center for Watergate. It was perhaps the best time in history to be a White House correspondent. It is possible that the exposure that Watergate provided for White House correspondents Dan Rather at CBS and Tom Brokaw at NBC was the source of their eventual elevations to anchor. It was a time when the credibility of journalism was at an all-time high because of the Watergate crisis and the role of the Fourth Estate in getting the story out.

Today and Tomorrow

By 1976, both Brokaw and Rather were on the move. Brokaw was asked to move over to the *Today Show* with Barbara Walters, where he replaced Jim Hartz. Although Walters only officially was co-host for a few years, she became the soul of the highly successful, highly profitable program. When the ratings started to slip, Hartz took the blame. But although Brokaw immediately brought stability to the show, which had been lacking stability since Hugh Downs departed in 1971, Walters herself left for the evening news anchor job at ABC. After a pairing through the summer with Betty Furness, Brokaw was teamed in the fall of 1976 with the twenty-five-year-old phenomenon Jane Pauley, who already had served as evening news anchor at WMAQ, the NBC affiliate in Chicago.

The pairing of Brokaw and Pauley proved to be a major success, and the *Today Show* returned to its traditional leadership position in the ratings. But Brokaw felt that the *Today Show* did not have the hard-core news elements to which he was accustomed. He wanted more, much more. Brokaw said, "I wanted to get back to what I did, which was covering politics and international news."

He continued on *Today*, however. Then, because questions about the future of the NBC evening news arose as John Chancellor aged and NBC slipped in the ratings competition with Cronkite at the resurgent ABC, Roone Arledge approached not only Rather, but also Brokaw. Arledge was determined to bring *World News Tonight* into the number-one position. Brokaw remembered:

> Roone Arledge [ABC] made a big pass at me, and it was the first time that somebody talked openly about me anchoring one of the evening news broadcasts. That was pretty heavy stuff because I had just turned forty when that happened. I was very tempted to go to ABC with Roone. I thought he had some exciting ideas, but a man by the name of Vern Bradshaw had taken over NBC, and he had known me from California. We were not friends, but he had known me from my work out there. He was determined to hang on to me, and

Roger Mudd had it in his contract that he would be the successor to John Chancellor.

It's Getting Muddy

By 1982, Rather was appointed successor to Cronkite, and with Chancellor getting ready to retire, there was considerable speculation about Mudd and Brokaw. The latter recalled:

> Roger very generously came to me and said I'll share this with you if you'll stay. In some part because Roger wanted to stay in Washington and was not keen about moving to New York. We really had hoped that we could put together this new two-man show. That was an exciting but daunting time. I often look back on it and thought we probably plunged in, in a way, and didn't think enough about how we were going to make this work between the two of us, what our interests were, and how we were going to make it different enough to make it a coherent broadcast. It was solid in terms of information and what we put out there, but, in some ways, it was less than the sum of its parts.

The Mudd and Brokaw experiment ended within a year, and Brokaw was named solo anchor in 1983. He reflected modestly on the experience of reaching the top of his profession:

> I set out to only be a reporter, and the essence of reporting was finding the information that is essential to the story and putting it in a form that people can understand it and be engaged by it. That has become the essential rule of an anchorman on a daily basis. You just have a much broader canvas, obviously, on which to do all that. There are many more selections to make. It's not just the work of a sole reporter, and you become, in some cases, the catalyst, in some cases, an editor, some cases, you play a supporting role instead of the primary role. I always think of myself as a reporter. When I come to work every day, I always see the news from the ground up, not from the top down, at least I try to. It's how

we build it during the day, so when it gets on the air, when I'm out there reporting it, it's reflecting the reportorial instincts that I have that we shape that day.

By late 1983, when *World News Tonight* and the NBC *Nightly News* both became solo anchor jobs, the fraternity of network evening news anchors was reduced to three. It was the first time since 1956 that all three networks placed solo anchors in the slot. The competition was essentially between the big three throughout the 1980s, and Brokaw more than held his own. For long periods, he held the ratings lead. But with the broadcasts so similar in overall structure and the anchors deeply experienced as reporters, ratings depended, to some extent, on their personalities. Often, ratings depended on the quality of the local lead-in. Overall, the competition was extremely evenly matched during the 1980s and into the early 1990s. The crisis in Eastern Europe during the late 1980s and early 1990s, plus the Gulf War, gave a certain advantage to Peter Jennings. He had, after all, served many years as chief European correspondent for ABC News, spent ten years based in London, and had significant experience in the Middle East.

Yet it was an event in Europe that proved to be the highlight of Brokaw's career; he covered of the fall of the Berlin Wall. He said:

I was the only one there. That was a thrilling and unsettling time. I knew I was going to be the only one there that night. CBS, NBC, and not even CNN had anyone live on the air. We had the only satellite path out of Berlin. I was standing in front of the Brandenburg Gate. The great symbol of Communist oppression was crumbling behind me.

I came on the air to do the NBC *Nightly News*, and it became an instant special, in effect, and we stayed on the air all night long. It was the fact that I got it right. Kept it in context, and I had helped move the story. Earlier in the day, by getting an interview with a key German official, in which he

acknowledged to me flatly that they were going to allow people to go out to all the exits in the wall, and we were able to
get that on the air. That was the real affirmation that they
had made this decision, even though it turns out they were
not clear about the consequences of this. So, that was an
enormously important night for me personally. It's one I look
back on with great pride.

It's a story he was born to tell. First, Brokaw had, from an early
age, excelled at taking advantage of the technical aspects of reporting, the actual problem of managing to be at the right
place at the right time, with a satellite hook-up. It was the
same sort of ability to get on the air that put Murrow on the
map in the 1930s, when he supervised the coverage of the Anschluss. Or Rather's ability to get reports on the air at CBS in
1963 at the time of the Kennedy assassination.

"Fear and Adrenaline!"

But even more than technical reporting, Brokaw's calm demeanor is well suited to crisis journalism. The descriptors "hot-
head" or "prima donna" are just not associated with the man.
His mid-key presentation is excellent when the public perceives a crisis and looks to one of its favorite anchors. Anchors
are not only a news source, but also a certain calm in the
storm. We often treasure emotional moments from our anchors, such as Cronkite's tears at the Kennedy assassination
and Reynolds's outburst in the 1981 Reagan shooting, but we
value anchors' poise even when we know that the anchors'
pulses must be racing. Brokaw admits that the allure of the big
story, the big challenge, is wrapped up in the excitement of
having a corner seat at historic events:

Fear and adrenaline! I'm serious. I've said to people before
that if you stop and said to yourself, "Okay you're addressing

the entire country on a matter of critical importance or of historic consequence, and they are looking to you in ranch houses in northwestern Montana, in country clubs in Dallas, in towers of power on Wall Street, all across America, they've got their screen on, and you're the one who's conveying that to them, you can get paralyzed by that. But, if you have a kind of general sense that that's what's going on, and you want to get it right for them, and you don't want to embarrass yourself—there's vanity involved—it's just hard to describe the feeling. Adrenaline is a very powerful drug under those circumstances. All the synapses are firing.

It all came together for Brokaw during September 11, 2001, when the resources of the network news operation were called upon as never before. For the first time, the big story was happening in New York, and the television masts and satellite dishes that crumbled with the World Trade Center buildings were an integral part of the New York communications system on which the networks depended. Brokaw said:

> About 9-11, all three of us [Brokaw, Jennings, and Rather] have said the same thing. It took everything that I knew as a professional journalist and for someone who's lived for sixty-plus years to get through those days. I mean, it really took everything I've learned personally in my life and professionally in my life to get through that time and to do it in a way that seemed to have some impact on our audience based on the mail and the calls and the other input that we got.

September 11, 2001, represented another watershed, for it was the first major domestic crisis covered in the years since the introduction of the twenty-four-hour news networks. It is essential to remember that broadcast news itself was born as a serious profession out of the crises of the 1930s and the onset of World War II. The dominance of the network evening news was firmly established by the Kennedy assassination and Vietnam, when the public's appetite for information no longer was satiated by the daily newspapers. PBS news was born out of Watergate, and CNN became an international phenomenon with the Gulf War.

The "Brokaw Law"

Brokaw has commented extensively on the problems posed by the advent of so much television news product. He calls his view the Brokaw Law of Spectrum Physics:

> When I was a young man coming into this business, when night fell on America, there were really only two real news planets that lit up the skies: CBS and NBC. Then a third one was added: ABC. Then CNN came along, and then we had another planet. Then it happened, we had the big bang, as a whole new universe was created with Fox News, MSNBC, and all the other all-news channels around the country, and expanded local news. That gave rise to rise to what I describe as the new law of physics. Some piece of information will get sucked into it at 5:30 in the morning, and it may be an offhanded remark by some talk show person somewhere, or maybe just a rumor that's floated out over the Internet. It gets passed around by the morning talk shows, by the *Today Show*, GMA, and then it gets picked up by the local news, and no one really knows what the origin is.
>
> It begins to take shape and gains weight as if it really has consequence, and, by four o'clock in the afternoon, I'm having to deal with this, and it's giving me a migraine headache, and I'm saying, where in the hell did this come from?
>
> That's one of the dangerous consequences of this huge machine that's operating now. All these new gravitational forces that exist in this new universe means that stuff gets in there that gets acted on very swiftly, and passed on, and begins to mutate before your eyes without you knowing quite where it came from.

One of the by-products of the Brokaw's Law of Spectrum Physics is the perception of a liberal bias in the news media.

The fact that stories get traction and move quickly across network after network to be picked up, dissected, and re-reported, as Brokaw argues, leaves the news media open to charges of bias when the stories themselves have a liberal leaning. The airwaves get blanketed by them.

Bernard Goldberg wrote in *Bias* that Hunter Thompson, a journalist and author, "has come up with something honest and brilliant". Thompson said, "The television business is a cruel and shallow money trench, a long shallow plastic hallway where thieves and pimps run free and good men die like dogs." Brokaw doesn't see it that way. "One of the reasons that I think that journalists get tagged with the label of liberal is that we tend to cover social appeal. We cover change, that's the essence of news, what's new, what's different, what's changed or what should be examined. We also cover those dark corners of America that don't get much attention."

But Brokaw concedes that there is a connection between perceptions of bias and his own Spectrum Theorem because network news increasingly treads in the troughs of unsubstantiated news and punditry. "Even the discerning viewer must be confused," he told the RTNDA in 2002, "by this meteor shower of information that is unsubstantiated, especially when it is accompanied by those journalists who appear on one medium as reporters, and a moment later on another medium as commentators and as pundits."

More than that, Brokaw is concerned by the problems of creating and balancing a modern broadcast. In Cronkite's day, the anchor was, in essence, the managing editor of the "front page of the news". The commentator, if there was one, such as Eric Sevareid or Howard K. Smith, served, essentially, as an editorial page editor. Today, all three networks largely have jettisoned the commentator's role or diminished it substantially. All three of the current anchors largely continue to create that "front page of the news" quite successfully as a journalistic exercise. But they have considerable difficulty attracting audiences of the size to which network owners became accustomed in Cronkite's day.

The Need for News

As networks combat slipping ratings with sensationalism, Brokaw is concerned about the power of journalistic ethics to provide a boundary of propriety. Journalistic ethics are supposed to provide those boundaries, but unrestrained competition makes them difficult to enforce. Brokaw said:

> The various news media do not have the time and space to do what television does best, which is transmit experience, in the words of Reuven Frank, the founding father of the *Huntley-Brinkley Report*. Those Californian freeway chases are the maddening hypotheses of the transmission of experience. But what he expected in the transmission of experience and in the coverage of news, however unsavory the topic, was that the fundamental tenets of journalism would have application. Election night, 2000, was a painful reminder of the absolute need for persistent vigilance and the maintenance of standards in a climate of competitive pressures.

Brokaw acknowledges the challenges posed by the explosion of new media, but he adds, "I think there will always be a place for the network news if we continue to produce it well, and do the stories that are important and relevant to their lives, and use the resources that the network uniquely has. We make big commitments to big stories that are important to people."

He is less certain about the role of evening news anchor. His remarks on the future of news are almost exclusively from the point of view of the national reporter and on the importance of the national report. There's very little that can be said for sure about Brokaw's beliefs on the importance of the news anchor;

stating such beliefs would require Brokaw to comment on his own importance, which doesn't seem to be part of his makeup.

Perhaps what makes a successful anchor is a lack of a sense of self-importance. Brokaw has forty years of news experience and more than twenty years at the anchor desk, but he speaks with the personal ego of a weekend reporter from Los Angeles. At the same time, Brokaw recognizes that the American public places an enormous—if sometimes unspoken—amount of trust in the national news media. He said, "After almost forty years in this profession now . . . I have one enduring and primary conclusion. Our viewers—the American people—take us seriously, and we fulfill our most fundamental obligation to them and our place in this system of governance when we return the favor."

Anchoring creates a mysterious relationship. Anchors join us in our homes for one half hour each night in a completely impersonal relationship. However, in some immeasurable way, a relationship is formed. Inevitably, the anchors we like are often similar to the people whom we choose as wise friends and valued counselors; we choose journalists in whom we feel we can place our trust. We also choose those in whom we recognize some character trait that is quintessentially American because anchors interpret the American experience for us. True, Tom Brokaw travels to Riyadh, but it is the American experience of Riyadh that he communicates.

It is not surprising that viewers respond well to the poised, low-key South Dakotan with a decent sense of humor. He is a midwestern, decent, well-read fellow who never talks down to viewers and never appears to think too highly of himself. He is just the sort of journalist viewers might enjoy having over to dinner—which, of course, is how so many people experience the news. They have Tom Brokaw over for dinner and listen for twenty minutes or so while he reports what went on in the world.

What is next for Brokaw? In June, 2002, he announced his retirement from the NBC anchor chair effective in 2004. Why 2004?

> You know how old I'll be in 2004? I'll be just shy of sixty-five. I've done this for a long time, and I love doing it. But, there are other things I love doing as well. Writing books is one of them. I just screened a documentary called, *They Took the Money and Ran.* It's about Enron and Global Crossing. We did a whole hour on it. It took four months to shoot, and it came about because of some instincts that I've developed. I kept thinking this story is just going to get bigger and bigger. We've got to do a whole hour on it. It was very satisfying to do that. So, I'm not going to go away, but life is about regeneration constantly and going off to do other things. . . . My wife insists that I am going to miss it terribly, but I don't know.

Chapter SIXTEEN

Connie Chung

Associated Press

Before Connie Chung, only half of the network evening news anchors ever changed networks, and none of them ever did it more than once. Only three—Harry Reasoner, Barbara Walters, and Howard K. Smith—did it while at the peak of their careers, and, in each case, they headed to ABC for more freedom, more opportunity, and more money.

Connie Chung's frequent career changes and the force of her considerable personality have combined to make her one of the most talked-about anchors of all time. Observers of the news scene who delight in "inside" stories endlessly have been fascinated by her many and often startling moves. Stories written about her often focused on the business side of news, examining her difficulties rather than her triumphs and comparing other anchors with Chung. Endlessly and famously, she has been compared to her husband, the well-regarded local anchor Maury Povich, who moved to Fox in the 1980s and became one of the first tabloid journalism phenomenons with *A Current Affair*. Those who avoided that comparison primarily compared her with Barbara Walters.

It makes sense on the surface. Chung and Walters have much in common. Both are best known for celebrity interviews, both worked at ABC in the 1990s, both left prominent jobs at NBC in search of anchoring opportunities, and, together, they form the complete membership of the "female network news anchor" club. Chung and Walters were the only two female anchors to be given a regular slot on the network evening newscasts. But these are surface comparisons between the two anchors. Chung's career path, in fact, reveals more and more of the continuing influence of Chet Huntley, the celebrated NBC anchor of the 1950s and 1960s.

It was said of Chet Huntley and David Brinkley that they were the first modern anchors, coming as they did on the heels of John Cameron Swayze and the *Camel News Caravan*. This was primarily a tribute to their broadcasting style, but, in Huntley's case, he set a precedent that only recently has been followed with great success. Huntley was the first among all the anchors to leave the national scene for a local one. None of the other anchors ever worked in local broadcasting again once they reached the national desk.

Why did Huntley do it? Exposure and opportunity. It seems that he didn't care about any unwritten rules about staying on the national correspondent level. And, without question, it was his work with ABC in Los Angeles that gave him the exposure, the following, and the experience that led to success as an evening news anchor for the network.

Sunset Boulevard

Connie Chung was the first anchor since Huntley to go into local news from national news and then back again. Her path led her directly from anchoring KCBS, then known as KNXT-TV and located on Sunset Boulevard in the late 1970s, to anchoring the Saturday night news for NBC in the mid 1980s. From that point forward, as the most visible woman among the network anchors, it seemed inevitable that she eventually would land a seat at the anchor desk for the evening news.

Although Chung's career path followed a pattern first tried by Huntley, there was a sea of change between their times— not only in network news, but in the country. Chung started her career in 1971 with CBS, a year after Huntley's departure from the scene. What was different?

Back in the 1950s, when Huntley was in local news, local was still king on the West Coast, coast-to-coast hookups were not yet established, and network news did not reach all the way to Huntley's base in Los Angeles. By the time Chung anchored in Los Angeles during the 1970s, she was the lead-in to the national news. A gap had opened in the intervening years—a Berlin Wall separating local and national news had fallen.

To look at any local broadcast versus any national broadcast, it is apparent very quickly that in local news, personality matters. At the sports, weather, and anchor desks, local news people always strive to establish personality, to capitalize on a relationship with viewers. Local news personalities are expected to be active members of the community. In short, local anchors learn to build and keep a following. They learn to connect to such an extent that none but the most dynamic of foreign correspondents, who tell us about the most remote and mystifying events, can dream of achieving the same connection.

So many of the great anchors made their reputations as national or foreign correspondents. Typically, they did so in the midst of a great crisis that focused viewer attention: Murrow, Smith, and Daly during World War II; Chancellor in Berlin during the crises of the early 1960s; Rather during the Kennedy assassination and Watergate periods; Brokaw during Watergate; Jennings during the Yom Kippur War of 1973 and the Israeli-Egypt peace accords. In the long stretches between crises, local anchors have greater opportunities to develop a rapport, to build and keep an audience. That was the opportunity handed to Huntley and Chung.

But when Huntley arrived at NBC headquarters in New York in 1956, there were only three networks, and a fifteen rating wasn't too hard to come by. Today, a fifteen rating puts any program into Nielsen's top ten. Audience is harder than ever to come by.

Given the cost of sustaining a network news operation and the difficulties of building and sustaining a viable audience, both the advantages and disadvantages of an anchor personality like Connie Chung are evident. First, her ability to connect with viewers is widely written about and admired. Her focus on event interviews—often featuring a confrontational, attention-getting personal style—generates big ratings and, at the same time, a credibility problem among some peers and critics.

Chung's strengths and weaknesses, combined with her lack of on-air chemistry with co-anchor Dan Rather, led her to strike out into news magazine territory when she returned from an extended absence in the late 1990s. Perhaps in her CNN *Connie Chung Tonight* program she has found not only her niche, but a new direction for news. Critics continue to carp at her interview subjects and interviewing style—most notably, a closely watched event interview with Congressman Gary Condit in 2001—but her ability to generate attention is undeniable.

Magazine or "personality" programs, such as Connie Chung's, *Shields and Novak*, or *Crossfire*, are hugely popular with the twenty-four-hour cable networks. They are cheap, can be promoted to a specialized following, can be juggled in the schedule, can be cancelled or expanded without prompting hysteria, and can focus in on any set of issues, topics, or styles. What's not to love from a star's perspective?

The stars of yesterday—Dan Rather, Harry Reasoner, Walter Cronkite, Howard K. Smith, John Chancellor—all moved into the anchor slots on the evening news. It's far less likely that stars automatically will go that route today. They launch magazine shows, which provide better salaries, better profits, more personal journalism, and more of a personal following.

For a traditional newscast, we see less star journalism and more emphasis on moderator skills and news reading ability. Brian Williams of CNBC offers an excellent example of this trend, but it comes very much from the moderator model perfected by Jim Lehrer on PBS and a succession of excellent news readers who succeeded in putting CNN Headline News on the map.

It is likely that the traditional anchor prospect, such as a Connie Chung, will opt for magazine shows and leave the evening news to an anchor from the moderator or newsreader school.

Face to Face with Maury

Connie Chung was born on August 20, 1946, in America. She was the youngest of ten children born to parents who came to the United States from Nationalist China in 1945. Her father was an officer in the Kuomintang (Nationalist) Party's Intelligence Agency. The Chungs remained in the United States, became citizens, and raised their youngest daughter here.

"I wanted to be my father's son to perpetuate the family name," she said, showing a fierce familial loyalty and devotion to her parents and to her Chinese heritage. She devoted herself to her studies, which were strongly emphasized in her household.

Like Douglas Edwards, she was entranced by news at an early age, but, in her case, she was the first anchor to grow up in the television era. Her model was the television correspondent.

Her family lived in Washington, D.C., and she, like most locals, showed an inordinate interest in politics and national issues. She combined this with her passion for journalism and earned a degree in journalism from the University of Maryland in 1969. She was the first anchor to go through the 1960s as a student. When John Chancellor was arrested on the floor of the 1964 Republican convention, she was in high school. When Dan Rather was punched out and assaulted at the 1968 Democratic convention, she was ready to start her senior year in college.

Many of her classmates celebrated graduation with a summer trip to Woodstock in 1969. Chung, instead, ambitiously worked to join the ranks of the journalists. She won a job immediately at WTTG-TV on the copy desk, then moved over to news writing. WTTG was one of the old DuMont network stations, along with KNXT, where Chung worked from 1977 to 1983. It was a Metromedia station when she joined and a proving ground for many journalists. It was the starting point also for Maury Povich, who pioneered the talk show *Panorama* there in the late 1960s.

She joined CBS News in 1971 as a national correspondent based in the Washington bureau. She was one of the few Asian American or female correspondents and was the only "double minority," a distinction of which she made light, referring to herself as television's "best-known yellow journalist". She traded not on her looks or gender, but on an aggressive style and considerable ability—not unlike her future co-anchor Dan Rather, who was also based out of CBS Washington during these years. They were excellent years for aggressive national reporters. She covered the McGovern presidential campaign, the 1972 Democratic National Convention, and Watergate. She reported from the Middle East and Moscow on Nixon initiatives; ironically, the one major Nixon story she missed was the opening to China.

In 1977, she took the local anchor slot at KNXT in Los Angeles in 1977. She was certainly not the first national correspondent to "go local"; it happens all the time. But she was the first to go local and then come back as an evening anchor. To her credit, as stated in her official biography from CNN:

> In 1983, she joined NBC News as a correspondent and anchor. Her assignments at NBC included anchoring the Saturday edition of the NBC *Nightly News*, NBC *News at Sunrise*, NBC *News Digests*, several primetime specials, and a news magazine. While at NBC News, she often served as a substitute anchor for NBC *Nightly News*. She was a floor correspondent at the 1984 political conventions and a podium correspondent during the 1988 conventions, and provided political reporting and analysis during the presidential campaigns and elections.

In 1989 Chung returned to CBS news as anchor and correspondent on *Saturday Night with Connie Chung*, also anchoring the Saturday edition of the CBS *Evening News*. In 1990,
she became the anchor and senior correspondent for the
Emmy Award–winning CBS News primetime series, *Face to
Face with Connie Chung*. During this time, she conducted a series of exclusive interviews, including the first and only national television interview of Joseph Hazelwood, the captain
of the *Exxon Valdez*, and the first interview with L.A. Lakers
star Magic Johnson after his announcement that he was HIV
positive. She was also the first network television correspondent to report on the controversy over testing rapists for
AIDS, for which she earned the American Bar Association's
1991 Silver Gavel Award.

The "Bitch" Incident

In 1993, CBS was in third place, with Tom Brokaw and Peter
Jennings pulling way ahead of Dan Rather. CBS, in an effort to
gain publicity and boost the sagging numbers, put Connie
Chung at Rather's side. She became the second woman to hold
the job.

When it was announced that she would take that chair, she
later told *Mediaweek* magazine about Walter Cronkite's advice
to her. "Walter sang me a little sea chantey. The verse ended,
'Just watch your back with Dan, dear, just watch your back
with Dan.'"

Rather declines to remark on those three years. But Connie
was more candid when talking with Larry King some years
later:

> CHUNG: I have this way of only remembering the good times,
> which is really strange. But I can only remember good things
> that happened, which, I don't know, it sounds, like, Polyanna-
> ish, but it's true. I once bought an old car back after I sold it
> because I missed it so much, and I had forgotten that it never

ran. It was a British racing car. You know, because I just wanted it back. I could only remember what was good about it. Now, I'm not comparing Dan Rather to a British racing car, but what I'm saying was it was a good time, that sense that those two, fulfilling years covering the major stories that our nation faced internationally and reporting the news from the anchor chair. It was what was Walter Cronkite's chair. I think that was quite an experience.

Every night on the set, Rather reportedly made comments and faces. It became tense between the two. He patronizingly advised her on ways to sharpen her journalism skills. If Rather wanted to find a way to get her out of the way—which may or may not have been the case—he could not have asked for a more tailor-made incident than the one that happened on January 5, 1995. Chung did her interview show, *Eye to Eye*. Newt Gingrich had just taken over as Speaker of the House and seemed to be on many politicians' hit lists. She sat at a table across from his parents, Bob and Kathleen:

CHUNG: These are some of the things that are said about your son: "a very dangerous man."

KATHLEEN GINGRICH: Never.

CHUNG: "Visionary."

KATHLEEN: Yeah.

CHUNG: "Bomb-throwing guerilla warrior."

KATHLEEN: No.

CHUNG: "Abrasive."

KATHLEEN: That could be.

BOB GINGRICH: Especially if you don't like him, then he becomes very abrasive.

KATHLEEN: Yeah, but who doesn't like him?

BOB: Yeah, right.

CHUNG: Which brings us back to the battlefield. It's shaking up as the political heavyweight title fight. And it's expected to run two bruising years. Do you think that Bill Clinton and Newt Gingrich can ever become friends?

BOB: I don't think so.

CHUNG: Mrs. Gingrich?

KATHLEEN: I don't think so either.

CHUNG: What does Newt tell you about President Clinton?

BOB: The only thing he ever told me was that he's smart, that he's an intelligent man. That he's not very practical, but he is intelligent. That's all he's ever told me.

CHUNG: Mrs. Gingrich, what has Newt told you about President Clinton?

KATHLEEN: Nothing. And I can't tell you what he said about Hillary.

CHUNG: You can't?

KATHLEEN: I can't.

CHUNG: *(leaning forward)* Why don't you just whisper it to me. Just between you and me.

KATHLEEN: *(leaning in and whispering)* "She's a bitch."

CHUNG: Really? That's the only thing he ever said about her.

KATHLEEN: That's the only thing he ever said about her. I think they had some meeting, she takes over.

CHUNG: She does?

KATHLEEN: Oh yeah, yeah. But when Newtie's there, she can't.

The reaction was fast and furious. CBS said that the remark was off the record. CBS News President Eric Ober told the *Washington Post*: "It's a legitimate, very good interview that has unfortunately been reduced to one five-letter summary."

But if it was off the record, why did Chung use it? Many journalists asked that and questioned her journalistic integrity. Questions were raised that never came up when Drew Pearson broke the story in 1943 of General George Patton slapping an enlisted man, a story on which John Charles Daly famously sat.

Excepts of the interview ran all over CBS from the morning show to the *CBS Evening News*, so by the time it ran on *Eye to Eye*, it was too late. CBS had to do damage control.

Chung's take was a little different, as she told Larry King:

> KING: How did you deal at the time with the criticism? We all get it in this business, when they wrapped you over the Mrs. Gingrich interview and—you've been a potshot—they've taken potshots at you frequently. Do you handle that well?
>
> CHUNG: Of course not. I go home and tell my husband, it's awful. It's a terrible day. It won't wash away in the bathwater. Then, the next morning, I'm still thinking about it, but that, looking back, of course, I thought was terribly unfair. I think people who did actually see the interview didn't feel as if I was being unfair to Mrs. Gingrich. And, truly, where is Newt Gingrich now?

The relations between Chung and Rather came to a head on April 19, 1995, when the Federal Building in Oklahoma City was bombed. Rather came in from vacation to anchor the coverage from Oklahoma City. Enraged by Chung's presence and the air time she got, Rather made a series of intensely critical comments about Chung to numerous CBS staff members off the record, but the story was circulated widely throughout the network by personnel who overheard him.

Everything went from bad to worse for Chung, so she left CBS. She adopted a child and stayed at home to develop a syndicated talk show with her husband, Maury Povich, whom she married in 1984. Povich anchored the early hit for the fledgling Fox Network, the American version of the long-running Australian news magazine show, *A Current Affair*. (The show's distinctive percussion bridge between segments became known in the industry as the "Ka-Chung".) In 1991, he left the show and returned to his roots as a talk show host just as the talk shows heated up in syndicated ratings. There was talk about

Chung and Povich hosting a show together. Before that could happen, ABC came knocking and hired her to report for *Prime Time Live* and *20/20* and to fill in as anchor when needed. She played back-up to Diane Sawyer, Barbara Walters, and Peter Jennings, and was viewed as a potential competitor to Walters and Sawyer. It was a time in which Sawyer and Walters were involved in head-to-head competition for celebrity interviews at ABC.

Good News and Bad News

For Chung, it was the best of times, it was the worst of times. One of the best times was her Salute to Excellence Award from the National Association of Black Journalists for "Justice Delayed," an investigation into the murder of Ben Chester White in 1966. As stated in her official biography from CNN:

> As a result, the U.S. Justice Department opened the case after more than three decades and announced the indictment of Ernest Avants for the murder. He had lived as a free man since his acquittal on state murder charges in 1966. "Justice Delayed" has won a number of other awards, including the 1999 Chicago International Television Competition's Silver Plaque for Investigative Reporting, the 1999 Communicator Award's Crystal Award of Excellence, and the United States International Film and Video Festival's first place Gold Camera Award.

During the same season, she won the Amnesty International Human Rights Award for her report from Bangladesh about acid burnings of young women by sexually rebuffed young men.

The worst of times came in August, 2001, with her interview of Congressman Gary Condit. The nation watched. There was a media circus like no other surrounding the disappearance of intern Chandra Levy. Chung landed the interview:

CHUNG: Congressman Condit, do you know what happened to Chandra Levy?

CONDIT: No, I do not.

CHUNG: Did you have anything to do with her disappearance?

CONDIT: No, I didn't.

CHUNG: Did you say anything or do anything that could have caused her to drop out of sight?

CONDIT: You know, Chandra and I never had a cross word.

CHUNG: Do you have any idea if there was anyone who wanted to harm her?

CONDIT: No.

CHUNG: Did you cause anyone to harm her?

CONDIT: No.

CHUNG: Did you kill Chandra Levy?

CONDIT: I did not.

CHUNG: Can you describe your relationship? What exactly was your relationship with Chandra Levy?

CONDIT: Well, I met Chandra . . . last uh, October. And um, we became very close. I met her in Washington, D.C.

CHUNG: Very close, meaning . . . ?

CONDIT: We had a close relationship. I liked her very much.

CHUNG: May I ask you, was it a sexual relationship?

CONDIT: Well, Connie, I've been married for thirty-four years, and uh, I've not been a . . . a perfect man, and I've made my share of mistakes. But um, out of respect for my family, and out of a specific request from the Levy family, I think it's best that I not get into those details uh, about Chandra Levy.

Viewers who watched this famous interview when it was aired live may have shaken their heads and wondered why she kept asking the same question over and over again. It was clear that

Condit had a rehearsed answer from which he would not stray. Chung's relentless questioning ate up most of the thirty minutes she was given to talk to Condit, and, when it was over, virtually no new information emerged. News directors will tell you that a good reporter will always break new ground in a story, and, in this case, there was no earth-shattering revelation. The interview is now used in newsrooms as an example of how not to conduct an interview.

The question has been asked frequently: why does this bright, able journalist focus on anchoring opportunities and celebrity interviews instead of the magazine format where her considerable reporting skills shine through? Further, it's an open question why ABC had Sawyer, Walters, and Chung all chase the "big" interview of the day. It pointed out a lack of coordination; three different programs in the same news division competed with each other for the same interviews almost on a daily basis. Shortly thereafter, Chung left ABC to join CNN.

Her career tour has taken her to CBS, NBC, ABC, CNN, and a short tenure at WTTG, which is now the Washington Fox affiliate. She has had a unique experience among the anchors. She is also unique because she came back after her Huntley-esque departure from CBS in 1995, famously announcing, at the time, a desire to concentrate on her family and having a child.

Several anchors had prominent post-anchoring careers: John Cameron Swayze, John Charles Daly, Edward R. Murrow, David Brinkley, Douglas Edwards, Walter Cronkite, and Harry Reasoner most prominent among them. But Chung, Brinkley, and Reasoner were the only ones to carry on a high-profile news career at a rival network. Like Reasoner, Chung is best in the magazine format where her talent for reporting has won her a following, and, like Brinkley, she is an excellent anchor of her own program. Her interviews have been varied, from disaster victims to George Lucas, from Pakistan in the aftermath of Daniel Pearl's murder to Rome in the wake of the sex abuse scandal.

But her main project debuted on CNN in 2002: *Connie Chung Tonight*. The title is evocative of the old style of naming network news after the anchor (*Douglas Edwards and the News, Edward R. Murrow and the News, John Daly and the News*), but the angle of the show has more in common with *The Point* or *Larry King Live*. Like the latter shows, it shapes the broadcast around the talent of the newscaster, rather than focusing the newscaster around the role. *Connie Chung Tonight* is infinitely less expensive to mount than the evening news, more personal to her, potentially more profitable, and designed for the fragmented audiences of today.

That was until the Iraqi War broke out. CNN went through a management change in early 2003, when Walter Isaacson resigned. Chung was one of Isaacson's hires. In this industry, when the person who hired you is out, you may be next. That was the case in late March of 2003. With the war with Iraq less than one week old, CNN decided it had had enough of Chung's show and canceled it. Chung was asked to stay, but she declined. Some observers credit a remark that Ted Turner made to Canada's *Globe and Mail* just a few weeks before, calling Chung "just awful" as having something to do with her show's demise.

Killing the Evening News?

The rap on Chung is that she "lost" the anchor job. The counterargument is that she "found" the right format—the coming format. Who's to say that she is in a worse position now than she would have been if she were saddled with the CBS *Evening News* working alongside an aging Dan Rather with an alarmingly aged viewership that may well represent the last devotees of the old ways of news? She became known for her incompatibility with Rather—for a forced chat at which neither of them seemed good. Had she stayed, she would have been the presumptive heir to the anchor slot when Rather retired.

Chung would have had the dubious honor of performing the old CBS round-up with a group of correspondents no longer resident in their respective foreign capitals. They would have been good reporters thrown hastily onto airplanes to Beirut, Moscow, or Riyadh to do exotic stand-ups, which, in all probability, would have been warmed-up commentary from American sources abroad. In short, she would have had the traditional anchor role and format without the resources which previous anchors had when they first ascended to the role. Her situation would have been more in line with the early days of Douglas Edwards than the early days of Rather or Cronkite—other days when the hopes for the broadcast far surpassed the resources.

More than that, Chung would have been a continuing source of controversy because of the ratings. Today, we know that the ratings continued to decline and that CBS fell to a distant third place by the millennium. But then, such results would have been ascribed to Chung's performance by many people. She might have been blamed, in part, for the demise of the evening news if an enterprising CBS executive pulled the plug altogether. Of course, none of that ever happened, and eventually, she moved to Atlanta and joined CNN for a short stint on the air for the twenty-four–hour news network.

Despite the cancellation of her CNN program, she has a niche, a following, and an undeniably distinguished track record. If you take Jennings's formula that the anchor is primarily an editor, sometimes a writer and celebrity, and add in something about being a dogged interviewer determined to get to the bottom of a story, then you may have in Connie Chung a vision of the next big thing.

Chapter SEVENTEEN

Robert MacNeil and Jim Lehrer, PBS

Courtesy of PBS

The *NewsHour with Jim Lehrer* long has been considered an oasis in the network news landscape. The only hour-long newscast, it has almost sixty minutes of coverage versus the twenty-two afforded the commercial networks. The result is a greater depth of coverage of major stories without loss of breadth, more time for correspondents to do feature material, more time for interview subjects, and more time with newscast regulars, such as panelists, essayists, and correspondents, as well as the anchor. In short, it's the sort of broadcast people say they want, but can't do on the commercial networks because of ratings pressure.

Dan Rather framed the problem in his landmark 1993 speech for the Radio-Television News Directors Association:

> Make nice, not news. This has become the new mantra. These have become the new rules. The post-Murrow generation of owners and managers have made them so. These people are, in some cases, our friends. They are, in all cases, our bosses. They aren't venal. They're afraid. They've got education and taste and good sense, they care about their country, but you'd never know it from the things that fear makes them do—from the things that fear makes them make us do.
>
> It is fear of ratings slippage if not failure, fear that this quarter's bottom line will not be better than last quarter's—and a whole lot better than the same quarter's a year ago. A climate of fear, at all levels, has been created, without a fight. We—you and I—have allowed them to do it, and even helped them to do it.
>
> Now you would be absolutely justified in saying to me right now, "Excuse me, Mr. Big Shot Anchor Man, but what the hell do you expect me to do about it? If I go to my boss and talk about TV as a weapon, and why don't you take *Current Affair* or *Hard Copy* or *Inside Edition* off the air next week and let me put on a tell-it-like-it-is documentary about race relations—I know they're gonna put me on the unemployment line, and I'll be lucky if they don't put me on the funny farm."

So why does the *NewsHour* attract such a famously low audience? Approximately 1.4 million households and 2.7 million viewers tune in each night—a monster audience for a magazine or newspaper, but not even close to a minimum "table stakes" in the television news business. Undeniably, those who watch the celebrated *NewsHour* are well-heeled and well educated—

exactly the sort of people who tend to be generous with contributions at pledge time. But the broad public never has embraced the *NewsHour* or its predecessor, the *MacNeil-Lehrer Report*.

The anchors and executives behind the broadcast profess not to worry about the ratings—their focus is on a quality newscast. But the fact that the *NewsHour* wins so many awards and receives so much praise from inside and outside of the industry, yet doesn't connect with the public, raises questions about the very assumptions of broadcast news. Can any thoughtful broadcast find a network-sized audience? Or, possibly, do we openly admire the *NewsHour*, but secretly find it boring, too long, or irrelevant? Are we, the public, too busy for the news?

The *NewsHour*'s ratings problem is troubling because the show embraces so many concepts that were considered key to the network broadcasts in their hey-day. It was supposed to be an alternative or a supplement to the network news, but the audience that has been leaving the networks steadily since the 1980s hasn't crossed over. Why?

The *NewsHour* is on PBS, of course, and that creates difficulties of awareness—but after twenty-six years on the air and PBS's 99 percent national coverage, surely that cannot be considered an issue. Presumably by now almost everyone who conceivably could be regarded as a serious news watcher is aware of the *NewsHour*.

It is more than a case of a broadcast with a small audience. It is a broadcast with a narrow audience. The complaints about the *NewsHour* are few, for it is just as generally admired as it is generally ignored. But those who do try to explain its small audiences point out that the content is too dry, too-many-white-folks, too long, and too deeply rooted in the concerns of Washington, D.C., to appeal to a broader section of the country.

Are the criticisms true? Why is it that the public asks for a more substantive, informative newscast, yet steadfastly refuses to watch the one that is out there?

The broad expansion in viewer choices is certainly a factor. The average television viewer has ten to twenty times as many channels as the average viewer of a generation ago. The presence of six twenty-four–hour news networks is certainly a major factor in forcing the major networks, as well as PBS, to offer effective alternatives to "always available" heading services, such as CNN *Headline News*.

However, the major factor appears to be the analog, linear nature of television itself. Unlike newspaper subscriptions, which are presold, television news must grab its audience on an "opt-in basis" every night. Yet network news is utterly unlike newspapers, which allow the reader to skip stories and sections and to choose topics. In network news, the storyline is as fixed as a movie's and is unchangeable. One unappealing story in a newspaper does not decrease readership; one unappealing story in a news broadcast can lead to channel surfing with a remote control.

This is where the proliferation of channels can have a devastating affect. In 1967, the average viewer was unlikely to own a remote control. He or she flipped on the VHF dial from channel two to four, five, or seven. Viewers found three evening news broadcasts before stumbling onto alternative programming on channels nine, eleven, or thirteen. Today, for example, channel surfers leaving PBS may run into the Hallmark channel or HBO. A viewer surfing from CBS may run into HBO or the QVC home shopping channel. A channel surfer may pass through thirty-nine stations to traverse from PBS to *Headline News*. It is increasingly rare for a viewer who surfed out of the news because of a weak story ever to come back in during the same broadcast.

This viewership leakage dramatically changes television ratings, whereas it rarely hurts print readership. Typically, readers' interests shift to alternative stories, or readers already are committed to receive the next issue. And a focus on in-depth reporting carries a greater danger of "turning off" viewers; to "turn the page" so to speak, on television, viewers must change the channel.

The question becomes not one of the excellence of the *NewsHour*, but of relevance. Should public television, a commercial-free haven that provides a financial shelter for alternative programming, be devoted to programming which, by and large, the public does not consider an attractive alternative? More so, should it carry a format which dictates viewer choices through the device of a "major story of the day" when one of the mandates for public television is to broaden the available television product and bring in "turned off" viewers? Would the *NewsHour* better serve the public interest with a format that made news viewership broader, rather than offering a more in-depth broadcast?

These are troubling questions for the *NewsHour* and for public television. They are all the more troubling because of the fabled quality of the program. Would it matter to the broad body politic if it went away? Is it the best national newscast that just happens to be ignored, or is it just an unbelievably well-made national edition of a local Washington newscast? After all, the *New York Times* and the *Wall Street Journal* have national editions. What would a truly national alternative "public" broadcast look like?

The Robin Landed in News

Robert "Robin" MacNeil was born in Halifax, Nova Scotia, in 1931, during the Great Depression, a period that had a devastating impact on the Canadian Maritime provinces. "I'm one of those people who is forever stamped by the Depression. You'll find this with Jim Lehrer, too. It's a degree of caution, and a little of you can't believe the good times are going to last, so you'd better be careful."

He fell into the news business in the early 1960s when, as a struggling young playwright in London, he took a job with the London bureau of Reuters. He then was hired by NBC as weekend relief for correspondent John Chancellor. MacNeil's first major story was the construction of the Berlin Wall in 1961. He was assigned to Havana in 1962 because, as a Canadian, he could travel to and from Cuba. As the crisis worsened, he was placed under house arrest by the Cuban government. He said:

> I was sweating it for a few days. The American planes were coming in very low, and we thought the place was going to get bombed. We were forced guests for nine days. Then we were let out, and I was arrested again, sent to jail for a few days, and deported. The main thing I got out of that, besides a lot of colorful stories, was a box of cigars that I gave to correspondent Sander Vanocur, who gave it to Press Secretary Pierre Salinger, who gave it to President John Kennedy. So Kennedy got a box of Cuban cigars from the Cuban war.

Following his release, he covered national politics and was in Dallas on November 22, 1963, to cover Kennedy's Texas visit. Instead, he found himself covering an assassination. When the shooting started, MacNeil needed a phone. As it turned out, when he did reach NBC headquarters, an unthinking staffer placed him on hold and never came back to the phone. MacNeil was unable to file his story, and CBS got the edge in on-the-scene coverage. Before he placed that call, however, MacNeil looked for directions. He ran into a young, slim, dark-haired man coming out the Texas School Book depository; MacNeil was given directions, it appears, by Lee Harvey Oswald.

He continued as a national correspondent for NBC and *Huntley-Brinkley* until 1967, when he moved quickly in and out of a weekend anchor assignment. Ironically, for a man who became best known for serving twenty-three years as an anchor, he quit because he didn't like anchoring. Instead, he returned to England until 1972. On loan from the BBC, he covered the 1972 American presidential election campaign for PBS. He teamed up with former NBC colleague and fellow Cuban prisoner, Sander Vanocur. MacNeil said:

> We got a lot of flak from the Nixon Administration. There were memos from Bob Haldeman saying, "We've got to get rid of these guys, or they'll start another liberal network," or something. They spread all kinds of stories about us at public television, and it was really bad. At the end of the year, Sandy left because he was much better known than I was and was the target for much of this.

The 1972 campaign coverage immediately transitioned into 1973 Watergate coverage, and MacNeil was joined by a WETA in Washington journalist, Jim Lehrer. They provided forty-seven days of the most extensive Watergate coverage on television and were reunited in 1975 as the co-anchors of what was then called *Robert MacNeil Report with Jim Lehrer.*

The style of the show was eerily reminiscent of the *Huntley-Brinkley Report*, MacNeil's old haunt. MacNeil was in New York: Lehrer was in Washington. They used the same, "Good night, Robin. Good night, Jim" closing. In this case, what was friendship between Huntley and Brinkley was replaced by true, best friendship between MacNeil and Lehrer. "We really are each other's closest friends. The *Report* became an institution amazingly rapidly because we had fitted into a niche right after the network news shows in a kind of dead half-hour of network time. We used to advertise, 'Watch Walter Cronkite, then watch us.'"

Stepping Up to the Plate

Jim Lehrer was born in 1941, in Wichita, Kansas. He is part of that large group of television anchors that hails from the "anchorland" of the Missouri and Mississippi watershed. A baseball hopeful who didn't quite make the grade, he turned to sportswriting as a back-up when his high school teachers noticed his flair for writing. After serving as editor of the high school paper and earning a B.A. in journalism from the University of Missouri, he served as a Marine infantry officer from 1956 to 1959. After leaving the service, he joined the *Dallas Morning News* as a reporter.

He moved to the *Dallas Times-Herald*, and there he, like MacNeil, Dan Rather, Cronkite, Chet Huntley, David Brinkley, and others, was caught up in the Kennedy assassination coverage. In fact, it was during his interview with a Secret Service agent that the fateful decision was made, given the dry weather that day, to remove the protective bubble top from the president's limousine.

Lehrer stayed with the *Times-Herald* through the mid-1960s. He worked his way up to city editor, when, unexpectedly, he sold a screenplay he wrote on the side. He pocketed the money and decided to try his luck as a full-time writer and novelist.

During his writing sojourn, he did consulting work for Dallas public television. Eventually, he was awarded a Ford Foundation grant for a new type of public television–based public affairs program, the success of which brought him to WETA in Washington as a public affairs correspondent. When Sander Vanocur stepped back from the PBS Watergate coverage, Lehrer stepped in.

The premise of the newscast was simple: thirty minutes, no commercials, one story. It was an immediate success in terms of public television's credibility, and it became, along with *Nova, Masterpiece Theater*, and *Sesame Street*, one of the Big Four programs on public television. All four remain signature shows for the network.

The goal of the show was to "provide a window on the federal government" and has been criticized over the years for being too narrowly focused. But it won virtually every journalism award available.

In 1983, Les Crystal joined the *Report* and was instrumental in preparing the program for its debut as the nation's first hour-long newscast. Crystal was one of the leading lights of NBC News, the former Chicago bureau chief of the *Huntley-Brinkley Report*, and became the producer and executive producer of the PBS newscast its last two years. One of Crystal's most important assignments was as vice president for affiliate news. He transformed the relationship of news feeds between the network and the field. It served him well in the patchwork quilt of public television, where the relationship of PBS to local stations is profoundly different; the network acts more like a syndicator of locally produced programming than commercial networks do.

Believing

MacNeil and Lehrer were joined by a talented roster of correspondents, analysts, and essayists, such as Mark Shields, Paul Gigot, Judy Woodruff, Charlayne Hunter-Gault, Doris Kearns Goodwin, Roger Rosenblatt, and Michael Beschloss. The *NewsHour* is notable among broadcasts for its cool style, inclusionary interviewing technique, the absence of lens-hogging correspondents making fatuous statements on the steps of the Capitol, and more awards than can fit in a large display. Even MacNeil's retirement in 1995, which prompted a refocus of the show around Lehrer and the Washington bureau, did not detract from the reputation of the newscast.

But where are the viewers? *Los Angeles Times* television columnist Howard Rosenberg said:

> They were far and away, hands down, any cliché you want, the best newscast on TV. It's not even close. [But] as much as I love the show, the ratings are the commercial equivalent of nobody's watching—an estimated 2.5 million viewers per night. I don't know whether the broad cross section of viewers doesn't want a newscast like that, or we're so accustomed to what we're getting now that any story longer than ninety seconds makes us very fidgety and nervous.

Adding more mystery to the missing viewers is the credibility of the newscast. Said MacNeil about Lehrer, "He has inherited the Walter Cronkite mantle as the most trusted man in America." Lehrer has become the de facto moderator of choice for the presidential debates, handling the chores in both 1996 and 2000.

The public was surveyed recently on which broadcast they would believe if they received conflicting reports of the same news story. Forty-two percent chose the *NewsHour*, making it the most trusted program by two points over CBS. When the others were eliminated and CBS and the *NewsHour* were pitted against each other, the *NewsHour* came out ahead by 37 percent to 26 percent.

The *NewsHour with Jim Lehrer* provides the most compelling evidence that, by 2001, the United States broadcasting industry finally perfected an award-winning, trusted, meaningful, in-depth, evening newscast with a low budget that was capable of sustained achievement over time. It's the broadcast that would have blown away the competition in 1960, and now hardly anyone tunes in. What was conceived as an experiment in public television is essentially an achievement in elite television;

the shelter that PBS was supposed to provide from commercial pressure has, instead, become a refuge from the need to be watched by an alternative selection of the public. It is the strangest of all broadcast television paradoxes.

Lehrer would be the first and most vehement to disagree, however. When MacNeil left the broadcast, he said to the staff:

> We know who we are and what we are doing. We know what we believe. We believe the audience is at least as smart as we are, the news and the people who make it and analyze it are as important as we are. We believe it is possible and important to be fair. We believe the news is not just a product to be packaged, hyped, and sold; it is also the vehicle on which an informed public keeps our democracy fired up and viable.

Part Four

The Challenge of Cable News

Chapter EIGHTEEN

Associated Press

Even more than Bill Paley is associated with CBS, even more than David Sarnoff is associated with NBC, we associate Ted Turner with CNN. One of the reasons for this is the undeniable fact that Ted Turner makes for excellent copy. He makes news wherever he goes and is probably the best-known player in any number of dramas, from the launch of the Superstation to the attempted takeover of CBS, from his marriage to Jane Fonda to the dramas played out at AOL Time Warner. He has come far since his days as "the mouth of the South", but Ted Turner continues to be a singular personality.

But when the discussion turns around to Cable News Network, there are more fundamental reasons why no other personality is so closely associated with the network. It is also because of the singular absence of a defining anchor to personify the news division. The absence is deliberate and makes this the most distinctive chapter in this book, for it is the chapter about "No Anchor". Instead of profiling a monumental star like Murrow, for CNN, one can profile only comets: a thousand points of anchoring light in the Turner news system, flitting across television screens during the singular events with which they were associated. These are the reporter-anchors and the interviewer-anchors who kept us spellbound from Cape Canaveral to Baghdad, Waco to Lockerbie, Rockingham to Riyadh, Grenada to Ground Zero.

And so we associate Bernard Shaw with the Persian Gulf War, Larry King with the rise of Ross Perot, and Aaron Brown with September 11, 2001. But no personality expresses the whole except perhaps Turner, and then mostly concerning the early days. We think of Turner's vision: the all-news-all-the-time, all-around-the-world, for-breaking-news-watch-us universe of Cable News Network.

There are so many angles to Ted Turner that charting his story is best accomplished not with a linear thread, but with the slashes, circles, Xes and Os with which John Madden charts the fortunes of the Atlanta Falcons—a team that Turner owned. Turner was the owner and skipper of the America's Cup–winning yacht, *Courageous*, and the former husband of Jane Fonda. He is a cable entrepreneur and founder of so many networks that it would take a page to list the acronyms. Known as the "mouth of the South", he is a quixotic citizen-statesmen whose Goodwill Games represent one of the most interesting private peace initiatives by an American philanthropist since Andrew Carnegie offered Kaiser Wilhelm II a twenty million dollar check to pull out of World War I.

Turner is the world's largest private landowner, whose massive holdings in South America's arid, barren Patagonia should stand as a definition in *Webster's Dictionary* for the phrase, "long-term land vision". He is the largest single shareholder in the world's largest communications corporation, AOL Time Warner, and a legendary survivor of its tumultuous boardroom. He is the man who made *Gone With the Wind* an annual television event and brought us the World Wrestling Federation every week. Turner owns the World Series–winning Atlanta Braves. He was the black knight in a hostile takeover attempt of venerable CBS, and a New Mexico rancher who gave one billion dollars to the United Nations.

He is the man who declined to criticize Saddam Hussein, but has described Rupert Murdoch as "a Nazi". He is the man who went a step beyond Kissinger's, "power is the ultimate aphrodisiac," when he likened voting for the AOL Time Warner merger to the first time he made love. Turner is an ardent environmentalist and alternative-fuel enthusiast, who maintains a hunting regimen. He's a cowboy boot–wearer whose movie catalog includes the glittering films of Greta Garbo, the arch comedies of Lubitsch, and the musicals of Gene Kelly.

But of all the larger-than-life things Ted Turner has said and done, there is one thing that people will point to as his singular achievement—as they did in 1992 when he was named *Time* magazine's Man of the Year. In 1980, he established Cable News Network, known to everyone as CNN.

CNN's ratings in the United States number four hundred thousand or so households on a normal news day. It spikes during breaking news, but, otherwise, it posts numbers which, even in this era of scattered audiences, are thin. It even trails Fox News in the ratings tundra occupied by the three cable news networks. Its evening audiences are dwarfed by even the smallest of the three network news programs. It has anchors, but so many of them have such small personal followings that they, by and large, blend into a seamless whole along with the lead reporters and the talk hosts. It faces new criticism for becoming "talk radio with pictures", "losing its commitment to news", "abandoning its original premise", and "failing to live up to its promise" and trades along with the rest of AOL Time Warner at an appalling discount from its 1999 share price.

Yet CNN remains more than an international icon. It is a money-making machine as a news network, pulling in an annual profit of more than two hundred million dollars. It has an as-yet-untouched international reach and reputation. It has spawned more competitors in the news field than the networks faced in more than fifty years. It competes successfully in the United States, Europe, and Asia. Its United States audiences compare favorably overall to the Big Three networks if taken over a month, and, in terms of world audience, it is an unchallenged news leader. Its programs, designs, and organization are envied and emulated all over the world.

It did so many things differently from the Big Three networks and went so far away from the "star anchor" format that it merits serious consideration not only as a credible ongoing competitor to the Big Three, but as, in the eyes of many, their Ghost of Christmas Yet to Come.

From Billboards to Boardrooms

To paraphrase CNN's biography of him, Ted Turner was born Robert Edward Turner III in Cincinnati, Ohio, on November 19, 1938. George Washington made it to the Ohio River and the Ohio Valley first, becoming the largest landowner in the region in the process. Steve Spielberg made it later, born there in 1946. Somewhere on a straight line between Washington and Spielberg is Turner: part citizen-statesmen, part dreamer, part unsurpassed entertainer, part builder of bright new things, part steadfast leader in dark times, part champion of great causes, part mogul. The brashness, however, is pure Turner.

After leaving Brown University, Turner got married three different times and had five children, according to his official CNN biography. It also details the start of his career, noting that he started out as an account executive at his father's Turner Advertising Company, where he sold roadside billboards, but following his father's death in 1963, he took over as president and chief operating officer.

Among media moguls, he has much in common with Rupert Murdoch—both suffered the early loss of their fathers and inherited a troubled business at a tender age, and both subsequently stabilized and then transformed their businesses into international giants.

In 1970, Turner purchased WJRJ-Atlanta, Channel 17, a small, struggling, UHF station and renamed it WTCG, for parent company Turner Communications Group. Through careful programming acquisitions, Turner guided the station to success. In December, 1976, WTCG originated the "superstation" concept; it transmitted via satellite to cable systems. Turner figured out that the Atlanta Braves had to play someone new every week, and, with a national distribution, he owned a national sports broadcast for a fraction of the cost.

In 1979, the company changed its name to Turner Broadcasting System, Inc. (TBS, Inc.) and the call letters of its flagship entertainment network to WTBS. With his superstation innovation, Turner set up a platform to deliver to local cable companies, and the idea of broadcasting twenty-four–hour news on a national level was born. On the surface, the idea makes sense. If WTBS can work in entertainment and sports, why not distribute news on the same basis? But the idea is fantastic in its logistics, scope, format, in everything. How do you fill twenty-four hours? How do you get the footage and the people? How do you put it together? How do you get the viewers? Most importantly, how do get the world to cough up twenty-four hours worth of filmable, interesting news every day?

"They said it couldn't be done" or "they all laughed" begin many an entrepreneurial tale and not a few direct-mail promotions, but it was an understatement in this case. News executives didn't think Turner was going to fail. They *knew* it. The question was the scope of the catastrophe. Would there be anything left of Turner's empire to buy cheaply, or would there be nothing left but old stationery, some advertising trinkets, and the tatters of a great man's ego after he walked unknowing into a broadcasting Vietnam? They wondered if he had completely lost his mind. More than one company, famously including Time Inc., ruminated on the concept of a twenty-four–hour news network, studied it, and fled screaming into the corporate night. It couldn't be done.

Turner hired a few old hands, a lot of just-out-of-college talent, rented a basement in the Progressive Country Club, bought a bunch of computers and video equipment, and they set to it.

Broadcast Video reported the opening days:

> Turner had hired Reese Schonfeld, founder of a successful news cooperative for independent TV stations, to help him build CNN and Schonfeld had immediately recruited Burt Reinhardt, a TV news veteran, to be his second in command. . . . To make sure CNN's set would pop with the process of newsgathering, Schonfeld had had it built right in the newsroom. It was an idea that would later be widely imitated, but that at the moment, was the source of endless confusion during rehearsals.

"In the early days at CNN," a staffer remembers, "it was a 'family' sort of operation. Uncle Ted was there and accessible. He was in the newsroom frequently, talking to his pioneering crew of newsies. . . . It was palpable, the feeling that this was a new kind of operation that was destined to become the 'world's most important network'."

Breaking Tradition

There are so many ways that CNN broke the mold, and one was obvious from the first second—the news set was right in the middle of the newsroom. It was unheard of, but it worked. Other major differences are CNN's absence of film and, given its de-emphasis on anchors, an ironic rise in the emphasis on personality. CNN is talk, and it is little surprise that the nation's talk master, Larry King, holds down a nightly slot. Unlike the networks, where a large flock of correspondents contribute pieces of the great narrative delivered by the high priest of the network, the anchor, contemporary CNN features numerous programs hosted by journalists offering points of view and the constant bickering of a crowd of talking heads.

Most importantly, the anchors are not the stars and hardly the managing editors. Guests on the CNN studio tour ask, "What do the anchors do when they are not on the air?" They are told, "They can research background facts for an upcoming interview, scroll the wires, go over the upcoming scripts, and get any questions answered." They are integral to the broadcast, but not in anywhere near the same manner as a major network anchor who works as the editor of the broadcast right up to news time. CNN anchors work longer broadcasts and are hugely influential in the give-and-take of interviewing. They are journalists on camera, rather than newsreaders who rule the news through commanding and controlling the script on the Teleprompter.

CNN is notable also for the heavy use of voice-over and third-party footage; live video and sound tends, with the international coverage, to feature graphics (e.g. maps) combined with voice or long stand-ups by correspondents when they engage in give-and-take interviews with CNN Atlanta anchors. The hermetically sealed, magazine-like story that is so much the signature of the major networks, featuring the star correspondent framing a story with a voice-over, dramatic footage, and a handy wrap-up sermon at the end is much less in evidence. There are also no points for beauty in CNN's coverage, and no award of Miss Congeniality for happy talk amidst the news. The most celebrated instances of CNN coverage are celebrated less for how CNN covered it than the fact that CNN covered it at all.

The immediate effect of launching CNN was a lot of grief from launch-era bloopers and huge financial losses stemming from miniscule advertising and cable revenues. As if financial and critical tsunamis were not enough, CNN attracted two avid admirers: ABC and Westinghouse. The admiring companies liked the niche so much that they leaped in with a well-financed and competing joint venture.

They announced two networks under the name Satellite News Corporation (SNC) and both were immensely threatening. The second would compete directly with CNN; the first would be a headline news service. Turner had every reason to fear ABC's news operations, which included not only the revamped network under Arledge, but six owned-and-operated local stations who could feed breaking news. Turner also had every reason to loathe Westinghouse, which, at the time, was the single largest cable operator in the country and could guarantee strong distribution. On paper, they should've wiped Turner out.

They failed. Turner launched CNN2 (now CNN Headline News) immediately and got on the air before SNC could launch. But competition costs. Beating competition costs blood. So Turner went from losing a lot of money to losing a ton of money. Losses in the first three years reached $275 million, making the success story of CNN not only one of loyal viewers, but extremely loyal bankers. But they succeeded in getting CNN2 on the air in four months.

It was a bloody price war. SNC launched with 2.6 million subscribers, double that of CNN2, but Turner leveraged years of contacts in the cable operator industry and created an "affordable pricing" policy for ad time that would've made Crazy Eddie proud. He put CNN2 into the lead and SNC into an early grave in late 1983.

Turner Wants More

Turner's other initiative failed; he tried to buy CBS in a $5.4 billion junk-bond financed hostile offer. The move was part of his expansionist strategy to gain as much distribution and product as he could lay his hands on. The attempt so offended Bill Paley that he turned to Lawrence Tisch, the CEO of Leow's, for a rescue. Tisch went on the board, sailed into the CEO slot, and ousted Paley before the old CBS chieftain could say "double-cross".

Tisch initiated severe cost-cutting at CBS that resulted in the elimination of practically the whole of the CBS foreign bureau structure. ABC and NBC imitated the cuts in similar moves, thereby handing Ted Turner and CNN the opportunity to become the definitive source of international news. CNN opened select bureaus in Beijing and other major world centers and moved into profitability, then into historic profitability. In the end, Turner owned what he would have bought CBS to gain, only without the junk-bond debt that the deal would have entailed. Turner subsequently took on the debt, anyway, to fund his entertainment expansion, which faltered so badly at first that it nearly sank his company.

Along the way, CNN pioneered a technique that reverberated over the next fifteen years of broadcast history. CNN formed a separate company called Newssource and partnered with commercial television stations throughout the country. It was a type of news exchange. The television station got CNN's national and international pictures, and, in return, CNN got local breaking news. CNN soon became a vital news source for local television stations, and CNN was able to charge for the services, giving Turner another revenue source.

Load-distribution was a Ted Turner specialty. Cable operators provided him an entry to the market in 1976 when he wanted to go national. It was left to other, less imaginative people to take on debt, buy stations, and build networks the very expensive, old-fashioned way. The Atlanta Braves provided him with a national sports broadcast contract, with 162 games or approximately five hundred hours of prime time (or nearly prime) programming that appealed to eighteen- to fifty-four-year-old men—a tough audience to find, as any broadcaster will tell you. Other, less imaginative people bought national rights from cartels like the Major League.

In 1985, Ted Turner and his team again took CNN into the international arena with a new concept. It was part "since we're neighbors, let's be friends" political philosophy and part unique, visionary entrepreneurism. Turner decreed that CNN would not cover "foreign" news—it would cover "international" news. It would be the world's news network that fed news to the world *via* America, not exclusively *for* America.

CNN was positioned to be the network of all news and of all nations. Cooperative efforts were made with networks in other countries for news footage. It was a good neighbor, good cost-control policy for CNN: make people happy to get their news out, and get some news in return for less than the cost of Georgia peanuts. To be sure, there was resulting confusion and concern about the sources and accuracy of reports that were generated. More often than not, however, the concern was from government-sponsored news organizations.

As Atlanta Turns, So Does the World

The great appeal of CNN in the early days from its headquarters in Atlanta was its breaking news. The majors were loathe to break in on entertainment programming for "flash" news and quick to return to it. For CNN, of course, news was the programming, and the more they milked out of an event, the better. Often, the coverage continued on CNN when the other networks switched back to *Password* and *Guiding Light*. CNN not only became the obvious "go to" channel when news was breaking, it increasingly was recognized as the "stay with" network. For example, the ratings showed strong spikes during the gripping, two-day drama of rescuing two-year-old Jessica McClure from a Texas well shaft.

That was also the case when the *Challenger* launched in 1986. CNN was the only network that captured the tragic explosion live, and it stayed with the story long after the networks had shown the ugly plume of smoke, mourned the loss of the seven astronauts, and gone back to *As the World Turns*. It was CNN again in 2003 when it was the first to air video to the nation of the shuttle *Columbia* streaking to its demise across the Texas skies. Again, seven astronauts were lost tragically, and CNN stayed with the story long after the network stations returned to programming. Unlike in 1986, CNN was joined in 2003 by Fox News Channel, MSNBC, and others.

CNN planned extensive coverage of the Sino-Soviet summit of 1989, so key anchorman Bernard Shaw was on hand when one million students took to the streets in Beijing and coalesced in Tiananmen Square. It was reported that the White House followed Shaw's reports from the square. His team, in CNN style, kept with the story right through the thick of the protest and into the shooting and became part of history when Chinese authorities came to shut down their broadcast. An ensuing tussle resulted in the eventual shutdown, but not before CNN figured out a way to broadcast video over secret phone lines. It carried footage of the massacre that followed in the square.

CNN covered the fall of Communism in eastern Europe, the fall of Gorbachev and the rise of Yeltsin in Russia, and, most famously, the Persian Gulf War and the air strikes against Iraq. They covered the war, immortally, from Baghdad itself, duplicating Edward R. Murrow's broadcasts from the London Blitz, except CNN had the far more daunting task of reporting from hostile Baghdad rather than friendly London.

Peter Arnett, the CNN reporter in Baghdad, recalled:

> I volunteered to cover the Baghdad story when the January 15th deadline ticked by for two reasons. The first was that for CNN to realize its promise to become the communicator of the future, as the voice of the emerging global village, it would need to be in Baghdad. Most of the world had decided that Saddam Hussein should be forcibly removed from Kuwait. I felt that we had the responsibility to cover the implementation of that resolve as widely as possible, and that included watching the bombs falling in Baghdad and telling where they hit. The reason I stayed was that I was convinced that the press billet in Baghdad, the Al Rashid Hotel, would not be targeted by the Allied side. I had no promises from the Pentagon to that affect; I just wanted to believe it.

Peter Arnett went back to Baghdad in 2003 to cover the new Iraqi war for MSNBC and National Geographic. He went on Iraqi television after the war started, and, in an interview, he stated:

> Clearly, the American war planners misjudged the determi-
> nation of the Iraqi forces. . . . And I personally do not under-
> stand how that happened because I've been here many
> times, and, in my commentaries on television, I would tell
> the Americans about the determination of the Iraqi forces,
> the determination of the government, and the willingness to
> fight for their country. But me, and others who felt the same
> way, were not listened to by the Bush Administration . . . that
> is why now, America is re-appraising the battlefield, delaying
> the war maybe a week, and rewriting the war plan. The first
> war plan has failed because of Iraqi resistance. Now they are
> trying to write another war plan.

The White House, the Pentagon, and the American public were upset that Arnett not only said the war was not going well, but he did so in front of the Iraqi people. Critics argue that it gave some Iraqis a sense that they could win the war and encouraged them to fight harder. That night, Arnett was fired by MSNBC and National Geographic and became the source of much criticism for what he said.

Changing the Television Landscape

There's not the slightest shadow of a doubt that the viewers who saw the Persian Gulf War broadcasts saw and felt the war in a way utterly unlike anything they saw anywhere else or at any time before that. The reporting by John Holliman, Bernard Shaw, and Arnett really was anchoring—what did they report? Shells over Baghdad? Everyone knew that city was under fire. The men brought the war home to us not because of what they showed us or said, but because of what they did. Their reports from underneath a table without a camera assured us that they were alive. Like the best of Edward R. Murrow, it was vivid. Like the best of Walter Cronkite, it was true.

The image that CNN painted blends the anchor and reporter

roles. We see anchors reclaiming their reporter status by chasing stories in Europe and elsewhere. We also see reporters such as CNN's Christiane Amanpour receiving the focus and promotional push once exclusively given to anchors. A generation ago, we saw a sea of change in the anchor role: anchoring and commentary were separated, as in the Murrow model. Now, with CNN field reporting, reporting and anchoring are fused. In the newsroom, the nonreporting interviewer and anchor has returned.

The anchoring role is changing, partly because of logistics. There are too many fronts from which a sole anchor must report. The true anchoring role in modern days is not editing, as in the Cronkite world, or reporting, as in the Rather and Murrow nexus, or even serving as a commentator as Chancellor, Reasoner, and Smith were born to do. The true anchor role—a product of satellite technology—is interviewing. The concerto of reports from the field is giving way to a symphony of interviews. Why have one anchor coordinate reports on twenty subjects, when you can have one anchor coordinate twenty interviews on one hot subject? Add a headline service from a newsreader for an overall perspective on what's happening, and you have a one-hour newsfest from a modern network.

This technique made its spellbinding debut during the O.J. Simpson drama in 1994. CNN viewers saw one Ford Bronco for one hour of drama, followed by hours of back story and commentary to piece together the events. Thousands of experts explained what they thought happened, finger-pointers assigned blame, investigators fouled-up the forensics, and the stunning courtroom drama recreated an event that was never on television in the first place and upon which the basic facts never were agreed.

The pattern was repeated for crisis after crisis, the death of Princess Diana, for one, and, even more famously, on

September 11, 2001. Where once there was the dream of 24/7/365 coverage, now we have 24/7/365 recaps plus "reaction from the White House". The first instance of such extended coverage occurred after the Kennedy assassination, when the news just wouldn't sign off and the public just wouldn't turn off the television. Something changed that day; people reached out to the news not for news itself, but for reflected feeling, to witness and deal with grief and shock, and to watch the news played out in the reactions of anchors.

CNN coverage today is personality shows driven by anchors' followings, Larry King's, for example. The shows are format driven, not news driven. The aim is not reading news script, but talk, perspective, and reflection. Only half the coverage is traditional anchor reporting.

Is it a trend, or is it CNN? Fox News launched a similar format, and MSNBC went in the same direction. The three networks are intent on building up their stables of reporters who can anchor in the field and newsreaders who can anchor at the desk. There's less emphasis on editing, more emphasis on directing, more immediacy, and plenty of made-for-the-small-screen headshots. There is field video for the headline service and opinion on the main service. Such changes appeared first in magazines, where general interest long ago gave way to special interest. The trend can be noted in radio, as well; Larry King, Rush Limbaugh, and Don Imus have worked from perspective, personality, and interviewing for years. When you think about the early days of radio, Edward R. Murrow was a commentator with a viewpoint and a very large audience, much like Rush Limbaugh is today.

Interviewing is increasingly a staple form of the anchor's art, and the news is increasingly seen by the public as a dry commodity. All the money is in field anchoring, desk interviewing, personality, and showing the news by showing it happening to the people. All of it presented in the highly stylized, rhythmic language of the anchor, for that is the thing that does not change. The speech of the anchor in is short sentences and a low register, with frequent changes in pace and stress, but rarely in tone. The warm smile and eyes do not change, nor does the use of colloquial speech and time and place cues.

In the end, we have lost our memory of the voice, the pause, and the face of Edward R. Murrow, but his cadence and register are the legacy he handed down to all the anchors. His style will remain in news people's tool chests, no matter what shape the presentation of the news takes.

Chapter NINETEEN

Since 1995

Beginning in 1995, the three evening news anchors, Dan Rather, Peter Jennings, and Tom Brokaw settled collectively into an eight-year run at the top of the network news pyramid. In fact, the period between 1983 and 2003, excepting the two-year period at CBS when Rather shared anchoring duties with Connie Chung, can be seen as a twenty-year period of unprecedented stability. Although David Brinkley served for more than twenty years as an anchor and Walter Cronkite served just short of twenty, there never was a period with such continuity.

The anchors themselves, taken as a group, are arguably the most distinguished trio ever to serve at the top at the same time. They consistently—and often brilliantly or courageously—upheld the traditional anchoring role and values as set down by the legends such as Edward R. Murrow, Cronkite, and Brinkley. Their newscasts are models of "front page news" as established by Cronkite; their use of the round-up techniques is assured and polished—even if discerning viewers have noticed a steady reduction in the ranks of the foreign correspondents. Their collective judgment on news selection and balance, as the managing editors of the newscasts (a hallmark of the anchoring role), is generally unquestioned. They are, by and large, considered to be the leaders of their industry and give noted addresses at industry conclaves, such as Radio-Television News Directors Association and Foundation (RTNDA). Rather's fiery 1993 address, in particular, recalls the intensity of Murrow's 1958 address. Each man works hard to keep up that unique perspective of the evening news anchor:

they have corner seats to many of the great events of the age, and yet they must interpret them for, and on behalf of, the common viewer.

Like the great anchors of the previous generation, the current trio made forays into book writing. For example, Brokaw wrote the bestseller, *The Greatest Generation*. Also, the big three lent their names and talents to a wide variety of news specials and additional series. For example, Rather notably returned to a correspondent's role with *60 Minutes II* and *48 Hours*.

Given this glittering collective record, their ratings record is a paradox: they presided over the greatest erosion in network evening news ratings ever. By the standards of the 1960s and 1970s, their ratings and market share generally are acknowledged to be a disaster. Yet there has been far less public rumbling about changes and reshuffles of the anchoring assignments than ever before. In every previous instance that an anchor showed an overall and sustained decline in audience, a change was made—often in a brutal or preemptory manner.

The next change in anchoring assignments is not due until 2004, when Brian Williams is scheduled to take over for Brokaw. Neither Jennings nor Rather have given any firm indication of a retirement date, despite the fact that already both are past the age at which Cronkite gently was nudged out the door.

The best way to begin to resolve the ratings paradox is to understand that the anchors are a sort of eye at the center of a news hurricane. Their long tenures give a veneer of stability to what otherwise has been a twenty-year period of unprecedented change in the national news landscape. These changes fundamentally altered the national news organizations and fragmented the national news product so completely that the network evening news became an increasingly small jewel in the crown of the network news operations.

Additionally, the last twenty years brought such a revolution in communications technology—unprecedented even when measured against the incredible era between 1925 and 1950, when radio and television news were born—that the very premise of a national news audience, which gave rise to the evening news in the first place, was undermined almost completely. As we look back on the twentieth century and divide it into quarters, we can see that the second quarter of the century marked the rise of the anchors, the third quarter was their period of greatest impact, and, in the fourth quarter, the changes in society and technology ensured a steady collapse in the audience and prestige of the evening news.

Based on the level and composition of their ratings, and understanding that the current anchors built significant personal followings that will not automatically flow over to their successors, it is arguable that the evening news broadcasts have become an anachronism and should be scrapped as soon as the current generation of anchors retires.

Looking back, the current anchors inherited a "news landscape" during the late 1970s and early 1980s that was virtually unchanged since ABC moved to a thirty-minute evening news broadcast in 1967. In fact, it changed very little in its overall structure since the mid-1950s. All three networks featured thirty-minute broadcasts, anchors in New York, round-ups of reports from Washington, reports from various domestic and foreign correspondents, and, typically, were leavened by commentary by the anchor or a former anchor personality. The average viewer in 1978, when Peter Jennings returned to the anchor desk after an eleven-year hiatus, experienced the news in a way that was largely unchanged for a generation.

In 1978, there were approximately ninety hours of news

programming per week in major markets, counting the morning shows, news magazines, local news, the Sunday programs, and the evening news itself. The average television news consumer was faced with a choice of approximately thirty featured news personalities, including anchors, hosts, and feature correspondents such as the reporters on *60 Minutes*. Straight news—subtracting the Sunday shows and the news magazine programs—accounted for approximately forty hours per week. The average viewer chose from ten anchor personalities on four networks. The unchallenged focus of viewers and the networks was the evening news.

In 1978, no more than twenty news personalities on the networks were promoted as, or considered, household names. Six were the major anchors of that day: Cronkite, John Chancellor, Brinkley, Jennings, Frank Reynolds, and Max Robinson. Others were: Mike Wallace, Rather, Harry Reasoner, Howard K. Smith, Roger Mudd, Barbara Walters, Hugh Downs, Brokaw, and Charles Kuralt. Perhaps another three or four came from magazine or morning shows.

By 2003, news programming rose to more than 1,170 hours per week in major markets, an increase of more than 1000 percent. The average viewer is now faced with a choice of more than one hundred featured news personalities and anchors. Straight news accounts for more than 670 hours of programming per week, and the average viewer chooses from more than fifty anchor personalities on thirteen networks. The average network news promotion focuses on building the images of at least one half-dozen major personalities for each network. The personalities' draws are the single-most important factors in keeping their programs profitable and on the air.

Today, the list of household names is arguable because the news product is so diffuse. It is not always entirely clear who can be considered a major personality. It is fair to say that regular news watchers recognize at least one half-dozen local news anchors as stars and at least fifty major (i.e. extensively promoted) national news anchors, hosts, and correspondents.

The major stars include the anchors, morning shows hosts such as Katie Couric and Diane Sawyer; the correspondents and hosts at *60 Minutes, 20/20,* and *Dateline*; Jim Lehrer of PBS; and a corps of news personalities from the cable networks who often defy labels: Larry King, Judy Woodruff, Aaron Brown, and Paula Zahn. Others include: Brian Williams of CNBC, Brit Hume at Fox News, a gaggle of news and political pundits from the *McLaughlin Group,* plus the personalities of *Crossfire* and its descendents, including: David Gergen, Pat Buchanan, and Chris Matthews; journalists with their own programs, such as Greta Von Sustern, Wolf Blitzer, and Bill O'Reilly; quasi-news personalities such as Maury Povich; and a range of personalities from George Stephanopoulos to Charles Osgood and Tim Russert of the Sunday morning programs. There are doubtless others that should be added to that distinguished list, not the least of which are the corps of correspondents, which include heavily promoted personalities such as Sam Donaldson and Cokie Roberts.

The most significant development was the introduction of CNN in 1980, with 168 hours of news programming, which more than doubled the total weekly news product and ultimately proved the viability of twenty-four–hour cable news operations. There are now six twenty-four–hour cable news networks: Fox News, CNN, MSNBC, CNBC, CNNfn, and CNN Headline News. Each one provides more news programming in a week than a typical network produced in a year in 1978.

One of the unintended results of the expansion of news programming is a devaluation of the individual news product. Faced with shoestring budgets and fractional ratings, programs are designed around central personalities. Even when tracking major stories, there is a tremendous increase in the amount of "fill" time on network news: unsubstantial updates, repetitive interviews, and an endless parade of pundits and experts offering an explosion of analysis and opinion. Today, each network has fewer international and domestic bureaus than it did in 1978, despite an enormous expansion in the overall amount of programming.

What is the effect on news viewership? Not surprisingly, overall viewership is up substantially, but individual, successful programs have micro-ratings that would have landed them in the dustbin of history only twenty years ago. Fifteen years ago, a rating of five or less, even in a pre–prime-time slot on a weekend, caused a great deal of discussion at major market network affiliates about the viability of a given program. Today, a five rating at any cable news network for any single program is considered to be an historic achievement.

A closer look at the ratings tells an even more remarkable story. The demographic group of those people fifty-five years and older—those born before the baby boom—watch more television today between 4:30 P.M. and 7:30 P.M., the "news hours," than the corresponding group of people fifty-five years and older did in 1979. The catastrophic drop-off is in viewers born after 1945.

Brokaw chose his subject well for *The Greatest Generation*; because he chose the generation that survived the Great Depression and fought the Second World War, he covered and lauded the backbone audience of the network news. To the extent that they are the essential loyalists who give the evening broadcasts any audience at all, we can understand why the networks are reluctant to change the anchors. Networks know that the problem is not, ultimately, viewer attrition; it is the wholesale inability of evening news programming to attract baby boomers and Gen X-ers in large numbers to the product in the first place. This problem was evident even in the 1960s, but, at the time, it was not understood that younger viewers who did not adopt the network evening news habit in their twenties would never, taken broadly as a generation of viewers, adopt the habit at all.

In fact, an in-depth look at the ratings suggests that the popularity of the anchors and of the evening news format is limited to the pre-1945 generation. Their appeal was never strong with the baby boomers (and even more limited among the younger generations now entering their prime news consumption years). The startling conclusion may well be that the evening news was only a transitory phenomenon that had more to do with the particular needs and outlook of the generations born between 1900 and 1945 than anything else.

When we look closely at the different worlds faced by the generations born before 1945 and those born afterward, we typically look at the changed political landscape or the changes in the public culture. However, perhaps the most profound change has been an overwhelming explosion in personal communications. Of which, the arrival of the Internet is the best known, but hardly the only major development.

In 1929, at the dawn of broadcast news era, there were an estimated 45.25 billion private messages exchanged in the United States (phone calls, letters, and telegrams), or an average of 368 per person per year. By 1999, that number rose to an estimated five trillion private messages (phone calls, e-mails, faxes, letters, and instant messages), or an average of 17,857 per person per year. That is a staggering increase. During the past seventy years, the rate of communication has grown approximately 2.5 times faster than the economy, and that indicates an enormous growth in the complexity of American personal and business life. This increase is little studied and less understood, but it is a vital component in understanding the perspective of Americans born after 1945 in relation to public information, such as magazines, newspapers, radio, and television.

According to a Yankelovich survey, Americans now spend seventy-seven minutes per day managing voice mail, cell phone, pager, and e-mail messages—a completely new usage of time since the Cronkite era. Although much of that time comes out of the workday, we also face home lives with more complexity and less time.

Psychologists have studied the impact of information overload. Not surprisingly, it adds stress, and it has a depressive effect. A landmark study by researchers Levine and Burgess concluded that the negative emotions called up by stress and depression actually hinder memory and recall. So we find ourselves in an information "death spiral": the more information with which we are overloaded, the less likely we are to comprehend it, draw conclusions from it, know it, or enjoy it. Moreover, an earlier clinical trial showed that depressed individuals, when viewing news film, counted more actions in a short film clip than non-depressed people, which suggests that as information overload affects us, we see more and more information, which reinforces the information overload itself.

Individuals know the phenomenon well. They come home after work and crave moments of privacy and time to chill out. Those people know well that a meeting with friends or half an hour of peace and quiet are often the only tonics for coping with feeling besieged and overwhelmed by tasks and information. In a world where private communications have increased one hundred-fold and the average American's personal message load has increased by a factor of fifty, the public faces a daily information overload that leads them to tune out the news—especially news programming scheduled during those after-work hours of recovery.

But tuning out is a transitory phenomenon for most people— we all have to get up in the morning and face the grind again. There is a section of the population that has tuned out national and international news in a more comprehensive fashion. It is difficult to measure the size of this problem by analyzing television ratings because television ownership has steadily increased in the lower-socioeconomic section of the population. That section has lagged behind in news consumption with every news medium for generations.

The more worrisome phenomena are the other two traditional strategies used by individuals to cope with information overload. The first is a relatively well publicized, but minor phenomenon. Certain sections of the population now gather their news through digital media—via the Internet rather than analog media such as radio, television, or newspapers. Gathering news via the Internet is a close cousin of the phenomenon of organizing a library or filing cabinet when faced with an overflow of books or files. Certain sections of the population cope with information overload by aggressively managing the inflow through Yahoo! or MSN news pages. The information is channeled and organized by digital media and files that allow them to store and retrieve a massively large set of information.

The people who prefer digital news tend to be well-educated information junkies who see innovations such as hypertext and the combination of print and video as a means of better organizing their information. It leads them toward higher news consumption, but they have, in many cases, all but abandoned traditional media. The number of people in this category is quite small.

The second strategy for coping with information overload is halfway between tuning out and going digital. When faced with information overload, most people simply become much more selective in their media consumption; they tend to focus intensively on specialized subjects of interest and make less of an attempt to keep up with the general culture. They abandon the attempt to develop a command of general knowledge. A survey of American sixth graders found that only 20 percent of them could successfully identify the United States on a world map, yet we are often astonished by our children's mastery of the immense detail of the world of Harry Potter, Pokémon, and the like.

Most Americans fall into this category of coping with information overload via specialization. Increasingly, we are a nation of specialists. In the realm of information, we have seen the closing or wholesale decline of the majority of general-interest magazines of an earlier generation, yet there is a small but successful magazine devoted to every breed of dog recognized by the American Kennel Club. Top 40 has been splintered into innumerable formats. Television has splintered into hundreds of channels. In every major market, there are now more than one hundred fifty channels available via digital satellite—a total of more than three thousand hours of daily programming from which to choose. In 1970, the average major market viewer had less than three hundred hours of programming.

To break through this clutter, programming itself became increasingly audacious, and news programming, in particular, latched onto attitude and bias as a means of survival. The best-selling book, *Bias: A CBS Insider Exposes How the Media Distort the News,* by Bernard Goldberg, discusses a liberal political bias at CBS News. Reviewers noted the glee evident in Goldberg's chapters as he detailed not only the private acknowledgment of bias by network personnel, but the furor—and near cover-up—

that he launched at CBS when, as a staffer, he had the audacity to write in the *Wall Street Journal* about it.

Yet one of CNN's enduring hits is *Crossfire*, a veritable temple to bias. It pits pundit-journalists such as Michael Kinsley or Bill Press "from the left" against pundit-journalists such as Pat Buchanan or Robert Novak "from the right" with guests caught—fortunately or unfortunately—in the crossfire. Goldberg's book is about the phenomenon of hidden bias, but more and more successful news programs reflect more and more attitude, angle, and open bias and find an audience.

In short, commentary and style are making a comeback. The balanced, authoritative, dispassionate, "that's the way it is," style of anchoring that proved so successful for Cronkite is proving less successful in an environment of information overload with a massive increase in programming choices. Commentators, being more candid, tend to have problems finding a mass audience, but are proving to be more successful in the current era. Commentators are also cheaper to produce than in-depth, in-the-field journalism, and eat up more air time.

Overall, the news landscape reflects an increasing tribalism, something we see in the culture as a whole. Increasingly, programming is built less around original reporting and more around personalities (e.g. news personalities like Bill O'Reilly or personality-driven interview programs such as *Larry King Live*) or perspective (e.g. *Crossfire* or *Evans and Novak*) to build a steady, devoted following of viewers. Pat Robertson's consistent following remains a model for many shows. When the substance of a broadcast is less on reporting than interpretation, the role of the anchor changes into one of moderator, interviewer, and, typically, a commentator also.

The primary difference between the viewers born before 1945 and those born later is their attitude toward tribalism and the national culture. By and large, the first generations of the twentieth century rejected regionalism and embraced a national culture like no other generation before them. Innovations in transport and communications made a national culture possible on a new level, and the mobility of the population scrubbed out many regional dialects, regional consumer product brands, and sectional politics. The generations born before 1945 were the customers of national media. They embraced national and international news as soon as it hit the airwaves. They were the originators of thousands of letters written to television entertainment personalities mistaking their shows for real life. There has been no group of generations like them before or since.

But they are aging and declining in numbers. What replaced them is the generation of Woodstock—a generation raised on a diet of Vietnam and Watergate. That generation has a far darker, more conspiratorial, suspicious attitude when it comes to the news. The next news-consuming generation will be a mystery until it reaches the prime news years. For it is the generation of *Smells Like Teen Spirit*. "Entertain us!" cries Kurt Cobain in that seminal Nirvana anthem. It is a generation with an entirely different perspective on television and news, a generation for whom the line between reality and fiction in entertainment is becoming utterly blurred, but in an entirely different way than the previous generations. Viewers before 1945 often mistook fictional programs for reality. Today, the viewers embrace reality shows in which real people live fictional and highly stylized experiences, which are presented as reality and graphically documented by the cameras.

It was that audience that first supported reality shows on MTV—shows that are anything but reality, but rather are monuments to an exhibitionism that delights the coming generation. It is not clear how they will get their news, but, assuredly, the generation that accepts and embraces a completely staged, framed experience as a show about reality—a generation hugely interested in the edge where fiction meets reality—will be hard pressed to accept the traditions of Murrow, Cronkite, and "that's the way it is".

It is difficult to speculate what future events might unfold and how the role of anchoring will change. It is fair to assume that the current generations of viewers will continue to expand their private communications networks through more e-mail, instant messages, chat, phone calls, and file exchanges than ever before. It is also fair to say that there will be a convergence of devices such as television and computer over the next twelve to fifteen years. Computers will continue to evolve from desktop units, and computer-based communications will be networked throughout the home to a family of devices that can bring video, sound, and text.

The fairest speculation is the viewers increasingly will have the option to become the managing editors of their own broadcasts, choosing digitized reports on demand, or packages of reports, rather than tuning in to a scheduled analog feed of thirty minutes of news plus commercials. Analog feeds may well be restricted to news events, such as war, catastrophe, the death of a popular personality, when the fragmented national news audience reassembles for a brief period of time. Then, the public's insatiable appetite for news bits can be satiated by the resources of a major news organization.

The astonishing coverage of the Iraqi War offered some insight and confirmation of the changes taking place among viewers. In previous national crises, network news ratings rose 10 to 15 percent, but combined viewership for the ABC, NBC, and CBS evening news fell 5 percent during the first three weeks of the 2003 war. Ratings for MSNBC, FOX, and CNN rose by 179 percent. Overall cable viewership of the evening news remains substantially higher than the average audience for the cable networks, but the cable networks are, of course, broadcasting over twenty-four hours. Their "viewer hours" now swamp the big three networks. "This is a war being fought in front of us in real time," Teya Ryan, general manager of CNN/US, told the Associated Press. "You don't want to wait until 6:30 or seven o'clock to get the news. It's happening now, and I think people are compelled by that."

Though the cable news networks developed a system of real-time anchoring and round-up reporting during the Persian Gulf War, the round-ups presented by the networks in 2003 were dazzling in comparison to those in 1991. Images from the Al-Jazeera network provided the sounds and images of U.S. bombs in Baghdad, as well as the impact of the war on the civilian population and the reactions of the Iraqi leadership. In addition, embedded reporters with videophoned reports from "hot" spots made reporting more immediate. The initial coverage of the advance into Iraq electrified the nation, as embedded reporters such as CNN's Walter Rodgers provided live footage of the advance from forward-scouting units, so that even President Bush used the networks to follow developments. "This is a reporter's war, not an anchor war; this involved a series of very profound individual vignettes," CBS News President Andrew Heyward told the New York Times.

The war also confirmed a shift in the way the public watches and perceives anchors. A pioneering study, "War in Iraq: Perceptions of Media Coverage," by BBI Systems and Emerging Interest detailed viewers' perceptions of the war coverage. The most surprising result of the survey is that CNN's Aaron Brown and the FOX News team of anchor personalities, such as Bill O'Reilly, had higher percentages of viewer preference than Brokaw, Jennings, or Rather. They also received far higher percentages of positive or neutral comments than the big three did.

The network news operations made calculated decisions not to invest heavily in Iraq War coverage compared to the cable networks, either in air time or resources. Presumably, the thinking was that, as was the case with the Persian Gulf War, the gains made by cable news would disappear with the end of the war. There is some evidence that the prediction came true; cable news was down almost 10 percent in prime time for the third week of the war. The evening news telecast that fared best during the war was Tom Brokaw's, which increased viewership despite substantial declines at ABC and CBS. It does not seem to be a coincidence that NBC, with MSNBC and CNBC, is the sole network with a cable network arm. The implication is that the evening news is drawing strength from the cable networks, rather than lending strength to them.

Problems remain with the cable news broadcasts, such as questions about the ability of embedded reporters to give balanced and accurate reports, questions about the extent to which networks are used to distribute propaganda, and questions about early declarations of victory. But whatever the problems, the American audience gained an intimate and immediate experience of the Iraq War like no other war before it, and the public continues to turn to anchors around what Jennings called "the electronic campfire" in times of public crisis. The role of the networks, and in particular the evening news broadcasts, were diminished by the war, but the phenomenon of anchoring and our dependence on news organizations and anchors has been strengthened greatly.

Whatever the future brings, it is clear that the era of the anchor personalities—when the focus of our attention and respect was on the occupant of the New York desk of the nightly evening news—is quite possibly, perhaps even probably, at an end. Evidence of this accumulates all the time, but was exemplified by the coverage of September 11, 2001, and the coverage of the 2003 Iraqi War. We saw how a major, national news event of the first magnitude could be covered by the cable news networks and local broadcast stations. What we will see in the following chapter, "September 11, 2001," is a situation where the anchors added to the overall excellence of the day's broadcasting, but were in no way central to the coverage in the way that we understood the anchor role to be at the time of the Kennedy assassination. The absence of the anchors in 1963 is unthinkable; the absence of the anchors in 2001 would have been undesirable.

How We Experienced

Chapter TWENTY

September 11, 2001

When Tom Brokaw, Peter Jennings, and Dan Rather ascended to their anchor chairs between 1978 and 1982, 95 percent of Americans who watched network television news preferred to watch the big three. PBS's broadcast was widely available, but seldom watched. CNN's telecasts were new and hard to find on cable systems. The other cable networks had not arrived, and the Internet was the obscure playground of a handful of academics, government workers, and defense contractors.

"I don't think journalism is changing," said Peter Jennings, as the rising popularity of the cable networks began dangerously to erode the big three's share of market. "What's changing is access to journalism. I both envy the cable news networks in one respect, when there's a really great news day, but, boy, I sure feel for them when there's nothing going on."

By the close of 2000, the big three's shares tumbled to 60 percent, and by the close of 2001, they eroded to 47 percent. For the first time, a majority of viewers preferred to get their news from cable news networks.

As September 11, 2001, dawned, the three major networks were in the midst of the ratings slide when the attacks on New York City interrupted broadcast reception throughout the city. Ultimately, the disruptions disconnected New York from the big three because the local stations, WCBS, WNBC, and WABC ran their own local coverage. It is the most significant example since World War II of how news distribution would function without the network news.

	2001	**2000**
CNN	18.2%	14.4%
Fox News	14.2%	7.5%
MSNBC	10.4%	8.0%
CNBC	9.7%	11.4%
HLN	<u>7.0%</u>	<u>5.9%</u>
	59.5%	47.2%
NBC	16.8%	26.7%
ABC	14.0%	18.2%
CBS	<u>9.5%</u>	<u>7.7%</u>
	40.3%	52.6%

Source: CNN and Nielsen Galaxy Explorer 1/01–12/30/01 and 12/27/99–12/31/00. Does not include broadcast prime time magazine programs.

Broadcasting and Cable magazine did a remarkable job of piecing together what the New York City audience actually did see that morning:

8:45 A.M. A plane crashes into the north tower of the World Trade Center (WTC) in New York.

8:49 CNN: Obviously, a very disturbing live shot of the WTC, and we have unconfirmed reports that a plane has crashed into one of the towers.

8:52 WTTG: We'll go to a live picture from New York City. A plane has crashed into the WTC. We don't know whether this was an accident or some sort of planned incident.

9:01 WABC (eyewitness via phone): It looked like a normal plane going over the city, and then, all of a sudden, a turn to the left, and it slammed right into the WTC.

9:03 A.M. A second plane crashes into the WTC's south tower.

9:03 CNN: We've got an explosion inside. This would support the probability . . . that the fuselage was still in the building.

That could cause a second explosion such as that. We're getting word that perhaps a second plane was involved, but let's not even speculate on that point, but perhaps that may have happened.

9:06 CNN: Eyewitness says a small plane—it looked like a propeller plane—came in from the west about twenty to twenty-five stories from the top and appeared to crash.

9:07 WABC: I don't know if perhaps some type of navigation system or some type of electronics would have put two planes into the WTC within—it looks like—eighteen minutes of each other.

9:08 CNN (airing feed from WNYW-TV New York): Some people said they thought they saw a missile, so we might keep open the possibility that this was a missile attack.

9:10 CNN (Ira Furman, former National Transportation Safety Board spokesman, on phone): Absolutely inexplicable. There shouldn't be any aircraft in that area. It's just not possible for a pilot during the daytime to have taken a course that would put it right into the WTC. A second occurrence within a few minutes is beyond belief.

9:12 WCBS: Thousands of pieces of what appeared to be office paper came drifting over Brooklyn about three miles from Tower One, according to a witness.

9:14 WTOP: Clearly, this has been a morning of extremes for us here. This is the most serious of circumstances that we're monitoring in New York. Earlier today, it was euphoria in this town as we all celebrated what appears to be word from Michael Jordan that he is going to be returning to the National Basketball Association and playing his next season with the Wizards. Obviously, our coverage of that will continue at its appropriate time.

9:15 AP: The FBI is investigating reports that the two crashes are the result of foul play.

9:15 CNN: President Bush is informed in Florida and cancels the rest of his schedule.

9:17 WABC: LaGuardia and Kennedy airports are now closed.

9:18 WCBS: The UN has been evacuated as a precautionary measure.

9:26 WABC: Many people see those twin towers as an example of American capitalism and as an example of American might and power. They are a very strong and very vulnerable symbol to the rest of the world—and the U.S.—and that may be why they were targeted this time. Osama bin Laden is the former Afghan freedom fighter—a billionaire by all accounts—who is maybe number one on America's list of terrorism exporters. He springs immediately to mind.

9:30 CNN (President Bush makes a statement in Florida): Today, we've had a national tragedy. Two planes have crashed into the WTC in an apparent terrorist attack on our country. Terror against our nation will not stand.

9:31 CNN (on-screen graphic): SOURCES TELL CNN ONE PLANE WAS AN AMERICAN 767 FROM BOSTON.

9:32 WNBC (eyewitness via phone): The second plane was a larger plane because the explosion from the second plane was tenfold larger than from the first plane. May God be with all those people because this is going to be a tough day for all of New York.

9:33 WABC (phone call from man in the WTC): I'm stuck on the eighty-sixth floor of Tower No. 1 on the east side. I heard a noise, felt the whole building shake, and the glass on my floor was blown from the inside out, and the interior core of part of the building collapsed.

9:34 WCBS: A no-fly zone has been established over Manhattan.

9:36 CNN (on-screen graphic): ALL NY AREA AIRPORTS CLOSED. Information we now have is that there are at least one thousand injuries.

9:36 WNBC: To New Yorkers, try to get out of that area to let the emergency crews do what they need to do because there clearly are still people trapped up there, and fire fighters and emergency crews still need to do a lot of work.

9:40 A.M. A plane crashes into the Pentagon.

9:43 AP: An aircraft has crashed into the Pentagon, witnesses say. The West Wing of the White House is being evacuated amid terrorist threats.

9:43 WTOP: We're going to interrupt the [CBS Radio News] coverage and bring it closer to home. We have some indication of fire and smoke at the Pentagon right now. We've gotten calls from people who live and work around the Pentagon, who have told us that they have seen something that they have described as an explosion.

9:43 WTTG: There are reports of a fire at the Pentagon. You can see the thick, black smoke. This is no trash fire, folks, so obviously something has happened. [To producer]: Do we have any indication that a plane was involved here?

9:43 CNN: There's a huge plume of smoke from the west side near the helicopter landing zone. The plume of smoke is enormous; it's a couple hundred yards across.

9:45 CNN: We're also getting reports that there's a fire on the Mall in Washington.

9:46 WTOP: We're hearing from a caller who says she is eyewitness to another hit here in town; the USA Today building may also be on fire in addition to the Pentagon.

9:48 WTTG (terrorism expert from American University): It is a well-planned, concerted attack on the U.S. as the world's superpower, particularly, I would assume, because of the role it plays in the Middle East, in its hostility toward Iraq, Iran, and other Arab countries, and its support, obviously, of Israel.

9:49 AP: The Federal Aviation Administration has shut down all aircraft takeoffs nationwide.

9:50 CNN: Bridges and tunnels into New York are closed.

9:51 WTTG: Metro is shutting down its trains, possibly concerned that Metro might somehow be used in this.

9:54 WCBS: A number of people were apparently jumping from windows. We saw at least five or six. The people who were standing there were absolutely horrified to watch this. Many people started screaming, many people started crying. There were people hugging each other, and, every time they saw a person jump to his death, there were people who were just grabbing hold of each other and sobbing and wiping their tears.

9:56 CNN (on-screen graphic): CAPITOL, TREASURY, WH EVACU-ATED. This has all the appearances of an extremely well-coordinated and devastating terrorist attack.

9:56 WNBC (terrorism expert): This has all the worst-case scenarios put together into one. When you think of the psychological trauma that this is going to cause New Yorkers and to Americans, it's monumental, it's off the map.

9:59 A.M. The south tower of the WTC collapses.

9:59 WTOP: After the WTC was hit, the Pentagon's antiterrorism unit went into action. The first thing it did was dispatch military aircraft to what is now a no-fly zone over Manhattan. These fighter aircraft, armed with guns and missiles, have direct orders to divert and, in a worst-case scenario, to shoot down any plane that seems bent on crashing into something else.

10:00 AP: An explosion hits another building near the WTC.

10:01 WABC: The attack on the WTC in February of 1993 was designed to bring down the towers. It appears that, this time, one of the towers is down.

10:01 WCBS: Generally speaking, for a building to collapse in on itself like that, it would seem to indicate—obviously, this is just early speculation—that there could have been an explosion, a bomb planted on the ground, that would make the building collapse in on itself.

10:02 WTTG: The 14th Street and Memorial bridges are shut down.

10:06 CNN (on-screen graphic): WITNESSES SEE PEOPLE JUMPING FROM WTC TOWER. Some of the Secret Service patrolling the perimeter of Lafayette Park directly across the street from the White House have automatic rifles drawn.

10:07 A.M. A plane crashes in Somerset County, Pennsylvania; a portion of the Pentagon collapses.

10:09 WTOP (reporter near the White House): Another explosion has just occurred. We don't know where it happened, but it sounded like a cannon going off, and now we're seeing big billows of black smoke in the direction of the Pentagon. It's sort of organized chaos. A lot of people have had the presence of mind to whip out the old video camera and take pictures of whatever is going on here.

10:12 CNN: There's a report of an explosion on Capitol Hill. [Five minutes later, a congressional correspondent says there was no explosion, but that "the speaker and other leaders have been evacuated to a secure location."]

10:15 WNBC: St. Vincent's Hospital is preparing for the possibility of many more people arriving. They have what looks like a trauma center set up on the street, on the sidewalk of 7th Avenue.

10:16 WTOP: We've just been told that all government offices are closed, and people are advised to go home. They obviously want to get people out of the downtown area and away from federal buildings, which, presumably, are still targets.

10:17 WTTG (U.S. Capitol Police spokesperson): Ten minutes ago, we ordered a mandatory evacuation of the Capitol and all the House and Senate office buildings. We are taking extraordinary precautions to protect the leadership of the Congress.

10:19 AP: The State Department is evacuated due to a possible explosion.

10:21 WABC: People [near City Hall] were running out of the smoke. The street now is just littered with shoes as people literally ran out of their shoes to escape the smoke and debris. There are pieces of the plane on Church Street . . . what look to be large pieces of the fuselage and this, amazingly, was about three blocks away from the scene.

10:22 WCBS: Doctors . . . expect thousands of people to be affected by smoke inhalation in and around the WTC because of that building falling in.

10:22 WTOP: A plane went overhead . . . some sort of jet, maybe it was a military plane. But everywhere you looked, people were looking up into the sky with concern and fear on their faces that this might be another incoming terrorist attack. Just mind-boggling.

10:23 AP: A car bomb explodes outside the State Department, senior law-enforcement officials say.

10:26 WTTG: We're told there is another aircraft that has been hijacked and is twenty minutes outside Washington, D.C.

10:26 WNBC: Looking up at the top of the building, at a rate of about one every five minutes, you see people that are jumping from the top of the building. It is an absolutely harrowing scene.

10:28 A.M. The north tower of the WTC collapses.

10:28 CNN: Good Lord. There are no words. This is just a horrific scene and a horrific moment.

10:28 WCBS: You're looking at what there is of the Manhattan skyline. The two most prominent landmarks—the WTC—now reduced to a pile of ash and rubble, smoke billowing above the city.

10:29 WNBC: They're gone. The WTC is no more.

10:29 CNN: There were several people that were hanging out of windows right below where the plane crashed when, suddenly, you saw the top of the building start to shake and people began leaping from the windows.

10:34 WABC: If you are a child watching and you do not have a parent there, I don't know what to advise you, if you can understand this. This is just so tragic that it's ridiculous to try to talk through this.

10:37 AP: A large plane crashes in western Pennsylvania, officials at Somerset County airport confirm.

10:43 CNN: All federal office buildings in Washington are being evacuated.

10:43 WTTG: There are now fighter jets in the air as the situation continues to unfold here at the Pentagon. There are unconfirmed reports that they are concerned about Camp David as well.

10:48 CNN: Military officials anticipate a second aircraft arriving at the Pentagon. [At 11:04, it reports: No second plane ever materialized.]

10:49 WTTG: All museums and public attraction in the District of Columbia have been shut down.

10:51 WTOP: A senior law-enforcement official gave information that is now being contradicted. We are now being told that the Federal Protective Services says there was no car bomb at the State Department.

10:52 WCBS: We're hearing from intelligence sources that there were actually eight planes hijacked and that five are still in the air. The Air Force and military intelligence are scrambling to try to take these planes out of the air before they can do any damage.

10:58 WCBS: At Newark International Airport, there are officers with shotguns blocking the road leading to Port Authority offices and the air traffic–control tower.

10:59 WTOP (reporter): I just drove in, and people are not paying attention to things like stop signs and red lights today. You have to be very careful . . . it's a very dangerous situation out there. [Reporter at Washington Monument: There's a big crowd of people around the pay phone. Nobody can get a cell signal out, nobody can get a cell phone call in.]

11:00 CNN: Mayor Giuliani urges people to remain calm and at home unless they're in lower Manhattan, in which case they should "get out and walk slowly and carefully . . . directly north."

11:03 WTOP (traffic reporter): It's pandemonium everywhere on the highways right now.

11:04 WNBC (NYU Downtown Hospital spokesperson): We've seen hundreds of people. Our entire cafeteria has been transformed into a triage area, and it is wall-to-wall people.

Using September 11, 2001, as a guide and example, we can look back on the coverage of the day and reflect on the cataclysmic changes it showed not only for the future of the country, but for the future of television news broadcasting. It is a remarkable portrait in many ways, especially because viewers were able to watch a colossal tragedy unfold before their eyes in the very backyard of the major networks. Viewers got a complete picture of the event, despite the fact that what New York saw was local coverage supplemented by major cable networks.

What is the role of the national network evening news? The contrast between the Pearl Harbor, the Kennedy assassination, and the World Trade Center disasters is important to consider. All were national catastrophes of the first magnitude. The central action unfolded over periods of less than two hours. But Pearl Harbor and the Kennedy assassination happened essentially off camera, and no live coverage of the events was available.

Our experience of Pearl Harbor on December 7, 1941, was almost entirely through the medium of radio and from reports generated and read out of the New York network headquarters. On-site reporting was extremely limited due to distance, the lack of broadcast facilities and personnel in Hawaii, and an immediate clamp-down on local reporting by military officials. The story spread extremely slowly, and the reports featured extensive recapping, rather than substantive updates. Initially, the reports were presented in the form of bulletins. Only later in the day did they take the form of continuous coverage. The anchors were indispensable because they were not only a focal point for news delivery, they were a focal point of newsgathering as reports were fed in to New York. Moreover, our collective national memory of the experience is indelibly associated with the words and tone of the anchors themselves. Extended coverage via film and newspaper rapidly developed late on Sunday and into Monday, December 8, 1941—but at the flashpoint, at the point when we as a nation first learned about Pearl Harbor, America was being anchored by the anchors.

By 1963, television supplanted radio as the primary network news distribution medium, but the anchors also played a central role in the reporting of the Kennedy assassination. Although there were news crews on the scene, there was no live coverage of the Kennedy motorcade and no crew was filming during the shooting. The first reports came in from the field via telephone, and no visual information was available for hours. News crews were not permitted into the hospital or near Air Force One, where the action shifted in the effort to save the president and to move President and Mrs. Johnson and Mrs. Kennedy back to Washington, D.C.

There is perhaps no single image that better sums up the Kennedy assassination than Cronkite's report of the president's death. And although all Americans over the age of six would forever remember where they were when first told of the assassination, our experience of the president's death was primarily, like Pearl Harbor, something experienced through the ears rather than through the eyes. We heard about it second- or third-hand. Most of us found ourselves turning to the informed voices we could trust—and those were the voices of the evening network news anchors.

On September 11, 2001, we had, for the first time, a national tragedy played out on live television. Such a statement is not intended to diminish the significance, say, of the 1986 *Challenger* disaster, but September 11, 2001, was an event out of all proportion to everything that came before it. The tragedy was experienced visually—news watchers actually saw the collapse of both towers, and CNN was on the air with live pictures only four minutes after the first jet crashed into the north tower and fourteen minutes before the second jet crashed into the south tower. Also, the attacks were on the air as a live story well before anyone at the networks had a firm grasp on the storyline. We experienced the visual material and attempted to grasp the significance in virtually the same time frame as the networks and even the government did. There was no need for a Walter Cronkite to inform us about the collapse of the south tower—we all saw it at the same time. In fact, viewers of CNN saw it before anchor Aaron Brown did; he was delivering a rooftop broadcast from midtown Manhattan as it happened, and the camera was pointed at the World Trade Center in the background. In order to look into the camera, Brown had to look away from the WTC as the south tower collapsed behind him.

By the time the network anchors were on the air—and they were on quickly—much of the story already had played out in front of our eyes. The anchors excelled in helping us to understand the background information so that we could develop an understanding and context for the event, but the broader question on everyone's mind—what next?—was something no one could answer. A nation that was comforted by anchors on November 22, 1963, went to sleep on September 11, 2001, confused and frightened, if it went to sleep at all.

When the network evening news ran on November 22, 1963, there had been only a few hours of bulletins during the day. Because there were few televisions in offices during that era, many Americans received their most comprehensive briefing on the crisis during the news hour. By contrast, virtually every broadcast and cable network ran constant coverage of the crisis throughout the day on September 11, 2001. Indeed, many entertainment cable networks, such as Comedy Central, switched their coverage over to feeds from the news networks. The average American cable-connected home had access to more than four hundred hours of continuous coverage by the time the network evening news was anchored by dozens of personalities (local, cable, and network), including Brokaw, Jennings, and Rather. By the time of the scheduled evening news, the main attacks were over and few comprehensive answers were available regarding the terrorists, their backers, or their next plans.

The September 11, 2001, attacks demonstrated that the device of scheduled evening network news broadcasts is increasingly unsuitable for anchormen. Anchors now appear to be caught between the proliferation of twenty-four–hour television news and detailed news via the Internet. Whether it is a slow news day or a colossal tragedy such as September 11, there seems to be little incentive for viewers to wait for a scheduled news presentation. Therefore, anchors, instead of deriving recognition from the evening news, appear to be building their images through books, other news programs, and network promotions. They apply that "brand awareness" to the task of keeping the evening news ratings afloat.

Yet, for each of the big three anchors, it was to be a workday like no other. Afterward, they reflected on the emotion and the adrenaline of a day that touched and challenged the New York–based broadcasters like no other tragedy did before.

Tom Brokaw

"During September 11, I was very conscious of that all day long. I didn't want to break down on the air. I was surprised, and, frankly, I'm a pretty emotional person, and I was worried that there would be episodes that would crash through whatever barriers I put up. By and large, I, through the day, I kept control of my emotions, and I think I had some help by this adrenaline pumping and this laser-like intellectual focus—I had what I was doing. There was so much information, it was all new, and it was coming from unexpected places, and I just had to work as hard as I possibly could. So I didn't have time to get emotional.

"A couple of times there would be something that happened

unexpectedly and would catch me unaware. One man was on the air with a telephone, and he began to break down as he described leaving Tower Two, and they were way up high, and there were people in motorized wheelchairs at the entrance to the stairs and they weren't going to be able to get down. I have particular empathy for people who are confined to wheelchairs with spinal injuries because I live such an active life, and they're generally so brave, and I thought my God, the end came this way for them. That was a hard moment."

Peter Jennings

"I was thinking about the story—what was happening to the country, what was happening to the people? I think that, in many respects, those people who were anchoring on that day and subsequently—and this is particularly true for people who had lots of experience, I would not have wanted to do this if I had not had a lot of experience—were so focused on what was happening to other people that, in some way, we were insulated. We were insulated from the emotional trauma of it that so many of our friends and fellow citizens were having who were not engaged in something.

"I watched the HBO program months later about September 11th. I was in tears before it was halfway finished. But, on the day in question, there was simply no time for tears. The magnitude of it was so enormous. One minute you were trying to find out what was going on in Washington, what was going on overseas, how would the U.S. respond? I could spend an hour talking about the many datelines that we dealt with hour after hour after hour. I refer to myself and others like me as editors because what an editor does on an occasion like that is to try to lay the table hour after hour, so that people with strengths in a variety of areas, like intelligence, law enforcement, the fire department, the political arena, in all those arenas, so you can lay it out and have it make sense to people."

Dan Rather

[Note: Rather appeared on the Late Show *with David Letterman some weeks after September 11, 2001, and became emotional when talking about the coverage.]*

"When you have a cataclysmic event, a calamity on the scale of September 11th, I know that the audience overwhelmingly and, in general, recognizes that it's inhuman to expect everyone, every second of every day, in every way, on that story not to, at some point, have their emotions show through. About the *Letterman* program, it was an entertainment program, not a news program. Perhaps it was ill-advised of me to go on. I didn't think so then, and I don't think so now, but I don't have any argument with anyone who thinks it was, but that was a case of 'I wasn't on a news program'."

What Happens If You Subtract the Evening News from the Equation?

The role of the evening news also comes under scrutiny, for the pace of news distribution has been on a steady increase in the United States for almost two centuries. Because the Internet brings major news stories into environments in a relatively unobtrusive, yet comprehensive fashion, is there any need to catch the 6:30 broadcast? The continuous coverage of September 11th and the ratings spikes throughout the day reinforce the common-sense awareness that the public will not wait for the evening news on major stories.

The evening news seems, in retrospect, too late for major stories like September 11, 2001, and too short at twenty-two minutes for complex ones like Watergate. It requires the presumption of a large band of common interest that just does not exist in today's culture. It depends on an appeal to a person who does not suffer from information overload and welcomes another analog, linear source of images, sound, and perspective. It also depends on a large band of viewers forming a personal relationship with an anchor in an era when fewer and fewer people even form a relationship with a next-door neighbor. Further, given the increasing pooling of newsgathering efforts, the difference between, say, ABC and CNN coverage is open to question.

It is fair to conclude that the outlook for the network evening news is decidedly gloomy. It is unreasonably optimistic to expect the broadcasts still to be around in ten years, when the analog generation will form only a tiny percentage of the overall audience and will be of marginal interest to sponsors.

The Future News Landscape

Predicting the demise of the network evening news is far less complex than predicting exactly what type of news structure will follow it. But several trends are clear. Viewers continue to form relationships with anchor personalities. However, the relationship will become more localized and specialized by age groups or interests. It is fair to speculate that there will be hundreds of anchors in the future who have narrow, specialized, yet loyal audiences. A current example today is Jim Lehrer. Individual news broadcasts will have smaller audiences, but the overall news audience will increase through the specialization of broadcasts—"now, something for everyone." And in the coming years, viewers may focus more on their national relationships with anchors who specialize in interviews and magazine stories, which show a continuing strength in prime time. Current examples include Jane Pauley and Barbara Walters.

The much-hyped convergence of Internet and broadcast devices will occur within the next decade, and digital television will, in all likelihood, vary between a basic, all-video service and a premium edition that offers a combination of Internet and television elements. Television broadcast elements may well be linkable, similar to the links we know from Internet pages. We may find ourselves linking not only between pages, but also between channels. A viewer watching a story may well have a clickable link to another network-owned channel that offers alternative coverage (e.g. coverage of the story from a foreign perspective, background on the story, or even lighter fare, such as links back to the headline service, sports, or entertainment stories).

In time, bias will not increase, but, increasingly, it will be better disclosed and understood through the packaging of services. CNN's *Crossfire* is an example: the political bias of the journalists is disclosed in the opening remarks of the presenters. This style hearkens back to the days when newspaper names like the *Democrat-Gazette* or *Journal-Republican* disclosed political leanings.

Increasingly, networks likely will become packagers of content, rather than originators of it. It is clear that original coverage by the competing news organizations will continue, although news organizations continue to produce lower percentages of their coverage independently, relying increasingly on "pool" sources (especially for foreign news). Specialist organizations will continue to develop as intermediaries. Reuters is a good current example. But pools should be expected to expand from story-sourcing (such as AP bulletins) and pooled newsgathering to include sourcing of amateur video, press conference feeds, professionally filmed footage, reaction from the White House, live interviews with witnesses and by-standers via cell phones, and expert opinion.

Whatever the shape of news to come, anchors continue to prove their value because they tell stories. And the storytelling device draws viewers in just as it did in the days of Homer and Herodotus. The anchors are presenters, but, essentially, they are storytellers and bards who traffic in fact rather than fiction. Their study and mastery of storytelling devices, cadence, tone, and personal style will allow them to survive not only the evening news broadcasts, but the very networks which gave life to anchoring.

Anchors, in fact, gave life to the network news. Bill Paley's round-up, the mechanical device of switching back and forth between New York and other cities around the world, always brought viewers home to one personality. That person combined great reporting skills with a talent for getting through to people and an affection for the bully pulpit. As newsgathering and news distribution became more digital, however, the mechanical reasons for an anchor's existence faded away. They are there because we like them. We like the focal point, their integrity, and their measure of independence. We see them at network headquarters providing probing interviews. And even if the simple, spoken summary of the news becomes the province of the text portion of the screen in the style of CNN *Headline News* or the TV Guide Channel, they will remain the anchors as we have always known them.

The first test of changing the anchor guard at one of the big three networks will come in 2004, when Tom Brokaw hands over the reins to Brian Williams, which is the plan as of the writing of this book. When Williams takes the chair at NBC and Jennings and Rather are replaced as well, the new loyal audience will seem like a pittance compared to what it was when the big three took those same chairs in the early 1980s.

Who is the next great anchor? Will there be one? Are Jennings, Brokaw, and Rather the temporary occupants of an enduring throne, or are they the last emperors? Perhaps what we have seen is that what defines an anchor is less in the personality of the occupant of the Teleprompter Throne and more in us.

As a public, we make decisions, expressed through the ratings, that certain journalists no longer just anchor newscasts—in fact, they anchor America. We turn to them in times of crisis as well as for their steady, scheduled broadcasts. Two elements make for a complete anchor, and both are products of trust. To be a complete anchor, a journalist must be trustworthy and actually have the trust of the public.

The second element is not present now—especially in the generations born after 1945. In this era of information overload, it is unlikely that these conditions will be present again soon. However, when technology makes it possible for the networks to do a better job of linking and orchestrating their coverage so that we may move seamlessly through a complete news service instead of flipping from channel to channel, that single focus of the news organization may well come into vogue again.

Suggested Reading

Alan, Jeff. 2001. *Responsible Journalism: A Practical Guide for Working and Aspiring Journalists*. Chicago: Bonus Books.

Bibb, Porter. 1997. *Ted Turner: It Ain't as Easy as It Looks: A Biography*. Boulder: Johnson Books.

Brinkley, David. 1997. *Everyone Is Entitled to My Opinion*. New York: Ballantine Books.

Brokaw, Tom. 2002. *A Long Way from Home: Growing Up in the American Heartland*. New York: Random House.

Chancellor, John. 1990. *Peril and Promise: A Commentary on America*. New York: HarperCollins.

Cronkite, Walter. 1997. *A Reporter's Life*. New York: Knopf.

Daly, John Charles. 1982. *Terrorism: What Should Be Our Response*. Washington, D.C.: AEI Press.

Fensch, Thomas, ed. 1993. *Television News Anchors: An Anthology of Profiles of the Major Figures and Issues in United States Network Reporting*. Jefferson: McFarland and Co.

Gilbert, Allison, ed. et al. 2002. *Covering Catastrophe: Broadcast Journalists Report September 11*. Chicago: Bonus Books.

Huntley, Chet. 1968. *The Generous Years: Remembrances of a Frontier Boyhood*. New York: Random House.

Jennings, Peter. 2002. *In Search of America*. New York: Hyperion Books.

MacNeil, Robert. 1968. *The People Machine: The Influence of Television on American Politics*. New York: HarperCollins.

Matusow, Barbara. 1983. *The Evening Stars: The Making of the Network News Anchor*. Boston: Houghton Mifflin Co.

Murrow, Edward R. 1989. *This Is London (Witnesses to War)*. New York: Schocken Books.

Rather, Dan. 1995. *The Camera Never Blinks Twice: The Further Adventures of a Television Journalist*. William Morrow and Co.

Reasoner, Harry. 1981. *Before the Colors Fade*. New York: Knopf.

Smith, Howard K. 1996. *Events Leading Up to My Death: The Life of a Twentieth-Century Reporter*. New York: St. Martin's Press.

Walters, Barbara. 1983. *How to Talk with Practically Anybody About Practically Anything*. New York: Doubleday Books.

Bibliography

INTRODUCTION

December 7, 1941

Accounts of Pearl Harbor abound, but oral histories with a connection to the media coverage of December 7, 1941, are surprisingly hard to track down. As this chapter was intended to show how the Pearl Harbor story was communicated, a variety of sources, from first-hand accounts at Pearl Harbor to accounts from the White House, CBS, and in the country were selected. An excellent resource is the Naval Historical Center, part of the Department of the Navy, available at *www.history.navy.mil/*. The oral history of Pharmacist's Mate 2nd Class Lee Soucy, who served aboard the battleship USS *Utah*, is available on this site.

Hugh Lytle's story was recounted in obituaries following his death in December, 2001.

Chester Burger's story from CBS headquarters is available from the Institute of Public Relations at *www.instituteforpr.com*.

Clarence Raulston's recollection of Pearl Harbor is located at *www.clarenceraulston.htmlplanet.com/Side%20Notes.htm*.

The story of "Wild Bill" Donovan and James Roosevelt at the Polo Grounds, as well as substantial amounts of background information on the late-night meetings between Donovan, Edward R. Murrow, and President Roosevelt, is recounted in the controversial, but valuable, *Day of Deceit: The Truth About FDR and Pearl Harbor* by Robert Stinnett (Free Press, 1999). *Day of Deceit* was also an invaluable resource in establishing a timeline of events at the White House on December 7th, although the timeline was compared with information in *Edward R. Murrow: An American Original*, by Joseph Persico (McGraw-Hill, 1988), the definitive Murrow biography. Persico's book and *In All His Glory: The Life of William S. Paley: The Legendary Tycoon and His Brilliant Circle* by Sally Bedell Smith (Simon and Schuster, 1990) were useful in providing further background information on Murrow's invitation to the White House, which coincided with the December 7th attack.

Clark Bane Hutchinson's invaluable oral history from July 18, 1997, is recorded at the Social Security Administration Web site at *www.ssa.gov/history/fbane.html.*

I Can Hear It Now, an LP edited by Edward R. Murrow and Fred Friendly for Columbia Records, includes actual radio recordings from December 7th, including recordings of John Charles Daly announcing the attack over the CBS network, complete with his unusual pronunciation of Hawaii.

It should be noted that the oral and personal histories were recorded (typically) decades after Pearl Harbor; individual witnesses disagreed about the timing and duration of the attack, as well as the nature and duration of radio bulletins and reports of the day. We have taken care to select the most representative accounts, but, in some cases, the narratives contain small errors of fact (such as Clarence Raulston's recollection that Jack Benny was preempted that night) that were retained because they are integral to the narratives and quotes selected.

CHAPTER ONE

Edward R. Murrow

The standard biography on Edward R. Murrow is the massive, magisterial, and thoroughly enjoyable *Edward R. Murrow: An American Original,* by Joseph Persico (McGraw-Hill, 1988). *Murrow: His Life and Times* by A.M. Sperber (Freundlich Books, 1986) is an excellent resource also. Two other earlier Murrow biographies are available: *Prime-Time: The Life of Edward R. Murrow* by Alexander Kendrick (Little, Brown and Company, 1969) and *Edward R. Murrow: Broadcaster of Courage* by Robert Lichello (SamHar Press, 1971).

Information on Murrow's habits, interests, and hobbies came from short biographical materials written by Murrow for network promotional and informational use. The materials were provided to the authors by CBS archivists. Information on Murrow's early life and the impact of the Pacific Northwest and Ida Lou Anderson on his consciousness was supplemented by a research trip to Washington in the summer of 2002.

Background information on Elmer Davis is available at *www. coutant.org/davis.html.*

Bernard Devoto's comments on the war and the post-war period are collected in *An American Retrospective* (*Harper's* magazine, 1984).

Tom Brokaw quoted Reuven Frank in an interview conducted for this book in the summer of 2002.

For background information on the rising threat of Nazi Germany, as well as some invaluable background on William L. Shirer, *The Rise and Fall of the Third Reich: A History of Nazi Germany* (MJF Books, 1998) has become a beloved classic of history. Shirer also wrote three other books about his years in Berlin between 1934 and 1941: *Berlin Diary: The Journal of a Foreign Correspondent, 1934–1941* (Budget Book Service, 1995), *This is Berlin: Reporting from Nazi Germany, 1938–40* (Overlook Press, 2002), and *The Nightmare Years: 1930–1940* (Little, Brown and Company, 1984). Shirer is the source of most of the information regarding the coverage of the Anschluss crisis, the remainder coming from archival material at CBS.

The remarkable story of Max Jordan is recalled in the excellent essay, *Max Jordan: NBC's Forgotten Pioneer*, by Elizabeth MacLeod available at *www.midcoast.com/~lizmcl/jordan.html*. MacLeod is the author of many invaluable essays regarding the early history of radio, and more about her remarkable, scholarly work and archives is available at *www.old-time.com/mcleod/*. Her analysis of the *I Can Hear It Now* recordings showed that Fred Friendly and Edward R. Murrow "doctored" part of the historical recording in order to increase the dramatic effect.

For information on Murrow's Boys, we relied on the outstanding *The Murrow Boys: Pioneers on the Front Lines of Broadcast Journalism* by Stanley Cloud, et al (Houghton Mifflin Company, 1996), not only an invaluable historical document, but also a truly fine read.

Background on the relationship between William S. Paley and Edward R. Murrow, as well as on the character of William S. Paley, was primarily provided by the definitive Paley biography by Sally Bedell Smith, *In All His Glory: The Life of William S. Paley: The Legendary Tycoon and His Brilliant Circle* (Simon and Schuster, 1990). Additional information was provided by two Paley lieutenants at CBS, who chose not to be identified. Paley's memoirs also provided background for the story of Paley's gala dinner for Murrow in the fall of 1941 after Murrow's triumphant return from London.

For background material on the beginning of the Second World War, Winston Churchill's memoir, *The Second World War* (Mariner Books, 1986) and William Manchester's masterpiece, *The Last Lion: Winston Spencer Churchill, Alone 1932–1940* (Little, Brown and Company, 1988) were consulted, as well as *Old Men Forget* by Duff Cooper (Rupert Hart-Davis, 1953). *Old Men Forget*, one of the most readable autobiographies in the language, is the source for Hillaire Belloc's stanza about Neville Chamberlain.

Background on Orson Welles and the impact of the *War of the Worlds* broadcast is widely available; a short essay at *www. transparencynow.com/welles.htm* provides an excellent overview.

Harry Hopkins's memorandum to President Roosevelt concerning Murrow is excerpted from *Murrow: His Life and Times* by A.M. Sperber (Freundlich Books, 1986).

Murrow's broadcasts from London on August 24, 1940, and September 21, 1940, are archived at *www.authentichistory.com/audio /ww2/ww2_1938-1941_04.html*, although the Authentic History site dates the second broadcast as occurring on September 20th.

Murrow's biographers are an excellent source for the background on the CBS management changes in the 1940s and on the influence and character of Ed Klauber and Paul White.

Background on the relationship of Fred Friendly and Edward R. Murrow and *See It Now* is best detailed in *Air Time: The Inside Story of CBS News* by Gary Paul Gates (Harper and Row, 1978). Gates is the coauthor with Dan Rather of *The Palace Guard* (HarperCollins, 1974).

The relationship of Don Hewitt and Edward R. Murrow is described in *Tell Me a Story: Fifty Years and 60 Minutes in Television* by Don Hewitt (PublicAffairs, 2001). An excellent excerpt of the book at *www.publicaffairsbooks.com/books/tel-exc.html* details the relationship of *60 Minutes* to *See It Now* and *Person to Person*, as well as the background on John Lardner's description of the two programs as "high Murrow" and "low Murrow".

The McCarthy broadcast is documented in the Murrow biographies, as well as in *Air Time: The Inside Story of CBS News* by Gary Paul Gates (Harper and Row, 1978). An essay by Joseph Wershba for *Eve's* magazine (*www.evesmag.com*), titled, "Edward R. Murrow and the Time of His Time," provides more background.

The Radio-Television News Directors Association provided the transcript of Murrow's 1958 RTNDA address.

Murrow's personal papers were donated by Janet Murrow to Mt. Holyoke College, South Hadley, Massachusetts. The main collection of Murrow photographs is held at Washington State University.

The quotation from Plato's *The Republic* is from the conclusion of Book IX, translated by James M. Lane for use in this book.

CHAPTER TWO

Douglas Edwards, CBS

The primary information on Edwards's early life, career, interests, and hobbies came from short biographical materials written and distributed by CBS between 1945 and 1980 and provided to the authors by CBS archivists. The materials also were the source for audience figures for Edwards's programs, including the unaudited claim to thirty-four million viewers per week in the 1950s for *Douglas Edwards and the News*.

Background information on Edwards's relationship with Edward R. Murrow and the CBS war correspondents during and after WWII is contained in *The Murrow Boys: Pioneers on the Front Lines of Broadcast Journalism* by Stanley Cloud, et al (Houghton Mifflin Company, 1996).

There are numerous sources for stories regarding the 1948 conventions in Philadelphia; *www.ushistory.org/gop/history/avery1-48.htm* gives an outstanding overview of the main events and mishaps. Zachary Karabell's *The Last Campaign: How Harry Truman Won the 1948 Election* (Knopf, 2000) is an invaluable additional source of facts and anecdotes.

Walter Cronkite's interview with Jeff Alan for this book provided additional background information on the transition from Edwards to Cronkite in 1962.

Quotes from Charles Kuralt, Don Hewitt, and Howard Stringer are from the CBS archives.

CHAPTER THREE

John Cameron Swayze, NBC

Background information on the Swayze family and pioneer days in Hope and Atchison, Kansas, was researched via Internet-distributed genealogy sites, *World Almanacs* of the period, and a 1997 essay by Larry Potter on early Hope, published at *www.ku.edu/heritage*. Background on the Orpheum circuit came from *Harpo Speaks!* by Harpo Marx, et al (Freeway Press, 1961)

Background information on experimental television in Kansas City, including the quotes from C.C. Jones, is published at *www.earlytelevision.org*.

Reuven Frank's quotes, and the material regarding the *Camel News Caravan*, is published at *www.tvweek.com/topstorys/111201earlydays.html*.

An invaluable resource for general information about Swayze's career was a short essay by Elizabeth McLeod published at *www.members.aol.com/jeff99500/am11.html*.

Barbara Matusow's *The Evening Stars* (Houghton, 1983) also provided an excellent summary of Swayze.

There are numerous sources for stories regarding the 1948 conventions in Philadelphia; *www.ushistory.org/gop/history/avery1-48.htm* gives an outstanding overview of the main events and mishaps. Zachary Karabell's *The Last Campaign: How Harry Truman Won the 1948 Election* (Knopf, 2000) is an invaluable additional source of facts and anecdotes.

Sources for statistical information about television ownership are from the *World Almanac* of the period.

CHAPTER FOUR

John Charles Daly, ABC

There is no standard biography of John Charles Daly, and information on his early life is quite sketchy. Background information on the coverage of December 7, 1941, comes from CBS Radio logs published at *njcc.com/~tomkle/otrc.htm*, a National Public Radio interview with Robert Trout, and an essay on Daly by Elizabeth McLeod. Afternoon program logs for December 7, 1941, came from CBS and NBC (which owned ABC—known as the NBC Blue Network at the time).

Producer Mark Goodson provided the background material for the blacklist period. His papers are housed at *warren.dusd.net / ~ dstone/Resources/11P/NYTM_Goodson.htm*.

The observer quoted regarding the quality of *What's My Line?* is Steven Lance. He recalled the program in a 1999 essay, "Big Game Hunting," published at *www.tv-now.com/lance/hunting.htm*.

A primary source of information on the early days of ABC is the ABC archives and FCC and congressional testimony.

Background on Leonard Goldenson was supplemented by background information from Bob Thomas's biography of Walt Disney, *Walt Disney: An American Original* (Hyperion, 1994).

Primary source material concerning Daly's departure from ABC is from *richardleacock.com*. Daly's later career was profiled in *Voice of America* press materials, as well as PBS promotional material for his specials in the 1970s.

CHAPTER FIVE

Chet Huntley and David Brinkley, NBC

Primary background material for David Brinkley is from his outstanding memoir, *David Brinkley* (Knopf, 1995). Chet Huntley also wrote a moving memoir, *The Generous Years: Remembrances of a Frontier Boyhood* (Random House, 1968), but Huntley's autobiography is limited to his childhood. Brinkley also wrote a memoir of his WWII days called *Washington Goes to War* (Knopf, 1988), which is a source for his wartime anecdotes. Additional quotes from his early career and hiring as NBC co-anchor are from an interview conducted over NPR by Joel Brinkley, including Brinkley's comments about President Kennedy. Additional background information is available in *Air Time: The Inside Story of CBS News* by Gary Paul Gates (Harper and Row, 1978).

Information on the *Huntley-Brinkley Report* ratings are from Neilsen and were reported in various media of the period.

Program information from the 1950s comes from *TV Guides* of the periods.

Technical background, e.g. use of "Chet" or "David" as an artifice designed to advise New York when to switch signal to Washington and vice-versa, is from Brinkley's memoirs, as well as from the

Museum of TV and Broadcasting's summaries of the program and anchors at *www.Museum.TV/index.shtml*.

Brinkley's memoirs are the primary source for information about his relationships with Presidents Kennedy, Johnson, and Nixon. Additional background material on the Nixon Administration period was available from: *The Haldeman Diaries: Inside the Nixon White House* by H.R. Haldeman (Putnam, 1994), *The White House Years* by Henry A. Kissinger (Little, Brown and Company, 1979), and *The Palace Guard* by Gary Paul Gates and Dan Rather (Harper and Row, 1974). Additional background information on the Kennedy assassination came from William Manchester's *The Death of a President* (HarperCollins, 1967).

Sound clips of Vice President Agnew's Des Moines speech of November 13, 1969, are available at *www.historychannel.com/*.

Comments about the impact of the *Huntley-Brinkley Report* by Dan Rather, Tom Brokaw, and Peter Jennings are quoted from individual interviews conducted by Jeff Alan for this book.

Background on Roone Arledge is available at *www.Museum.TV/index.shtml* and from multiple obituaries written at the time of his death in the fall of 2002.

CHAPTER SIX

Walter Cronkite, CBS

A primary source for information about Walter Cronkite is the original interview conducted by Jeff Alan for this book. Other sources are: *Cronkite: His Life and Times* by Doug James (JM Press, 1991) and Cronkite's memoir, *A Reporter's Life* (Knopf, 1996).

Additional background material on CBS News is from *Air Time* by Gary Paul Gates (Harper and Row, 1978). Barbara Matusow's *The Evening Stars* (Houghton, 1983) is an excellent resource for information about Cronkite, also. *In All His Glory: The Life of William S. Paley*, by Sally Bedell Smith (Simon and Schuster, 1990) is excellent background material for the corporate politics at CBS, especially during the 1970s and Cronkite's role on the CBS board of directors.

Don Hewitt's memoir, *Tell Me A Story*, offers insight into the origin of the term "anchor" and on the early career of Cronkite, as well the launch of the *CBS Evening News with Walter Cronkite*.

The Oliver Quayle and Company surveys on the most trusted public figures in America is available at: *www.tamu.edu/univrel /aggiedaily/news/stories/02/101802-6.html*.

Additional background material on Cronkite and CBS, including comments by Harry Reasoner, were provided through the CBS News archives and by former CBS staff members who chose to remain anonymous.

President Johnson's assessment of Cronkite's influence at the time of the Tet Offensive is available in a number of Johnson biographies and confirmed in *A Reporter's Life*. Lloyd George's assessment of Neville Chamberlain is quoted from Manchester's *The Last Lion* (Little, Brown, 1988).

Background on Cronkite's early life and career in Kansas City is contained in his memoirs. One of the most remarkable of oral histories devoted to the media is one from Margaret Richards, archived at *npc.press.org/wpforal/richint.htm*. It is an invaluable resource for understanding the culture and work ethic of United Press International in Kansas City in the 1930s and 1940s. Cronkite's memoirs and an interview for *The Russia Project* by Reese Erlich offer background on his post-war work as a foreign correspondent.

Jim Hamilton's book about the Writing 69th is titled, *The Writing 69th* (Green Harbor Publications, 2001).

Background on the 1952 election coverage is from Don Hewitt's memoirs, and additional background on the UNIVAC I computer can be found at *www.thocp.net/hardware/univac.htm*. Background material on Sig Mickelson, the decision to hire Walter Cronkite, and Cronkite's assignment him to the 1952 conventions was obtained from a tribute written about Mickelson by Bob Priddy for the RTNDA.

Cronkite's assessments of Truman and Eisenhower are from his memoirs.

Background information on 1962, the first year of the CBS *Evening News with Walter Cronkite*, including material on the Cuban missile crisis, is from the *World Almanac*. George Washington University hosted *An Evening with Walter Cronkite* on September 6, 2002.

Cronkite's memoirs are an excellent source for information about his relationships with the Johnson and Nixon Administrations;

further information came from an interview in the September, 1997, issue of *Midwest Life*. Background information on the Vietnam War and ratings during the 1960s is available in the *World Almanac*. The Neilsen ratings were reported in many media outlets of the day.

Cronkite's response to the CIA controversy in 1976 is detailed in his memoirs and in the Doug James biography.

CHAPTER SEVEN

Frank Reynolds, ABC

For basic background information on Frank Reynolds, an excellent primer is the citation and brief biography associated with his Presidential Medal of Freedom Award and his biography in the Indiana Media Hall of Fame. Also, his papers are archived in the Frank Reynolds Collection at Georgetown University and are the source for quotations from his letters to his viewers. Finally, Barbara Matusow's work, *The Evening Stars* (Houghton Mifflin, 1983), offers much insight into his personality.

The Vanderbilt University Television News Archive is the authoritative source of all evening news logs dating back to 1968. The extensive quotations from this log for August 5, 1968, are excellent reference material not only regarding Reynolds, but broadcasting standards and techniques of the day for all networks.

Lewis H. Lapham's comments on information overload are from his editorial outlined for *Lapham's Quarterly*.

Assessments of Reynolds's aggressive style are drawn from his letters, *Air Time* by Gary Paul Gates (Harper and Row, 1978), and are further demonstrated by his on-air remarks at the time of his replacement in 1970 and during the Reagan assassination attempt.

The definitive account of ABC News under Roone Arledge is *The House That Roone Built: The Inside Story of ABC News* by Marc Gunther (Little, Brown and Company, 1994). Michael Thompson's review of the book at *lavender.fortunecity.com/fullmonty/22 /alredge.htm* also is quoted in this chapter.

Background information on the Reagan assassination attempt is available from *Reagan: The Man and His Presidency* by Deborah Hart Strober (Houghton, 1998).

CHAPTER EIGHT

Howard K. Smith, ABC

Primary source materials for Howard K. Smith are his own highly readable memoirs: *Last Train from Berlin: An Eyewitness Account of Germany at War* (Phoenix Press, 1942), which covers his period as a foreign correspondent in Berlin until the outbreak of World War II, and *Events Leading Up to My Death: The Life of a Twentieth-Century Reporter* (St. Martin's Press, 1996).

Background material on Smith as a war correspondent and as one of the Murrow Boys is contained in the outstanding, *The Murrow Boys: Pioneers on the Front Lines of Broadcast Journalism* by Stanley Cloud et al (Houghton Mifflin, 1996). Background on Smith's relationship with Edward R. Murrow is also detailed in *Edward R. Murrow: An American Original,* by Joseph Persico (McGraw-Hill, 1988) and *Murrow: His Life and Times* (Freundlich Books, 1986).

Accounts differ regarding Smith's public confrontation with William S. Paley. Smith's account is in his memoirs, and a slightly different version (as well as background on Paley) is available in *In All His Glory: The Life of William S. Paley* (Simon and Schuster, 1990).

Transcripts of the first Kennedy-Nixon debate are available at *www.jfklibrary.org/60-1st.htm* in audio and *www.juntosociety.com /pres_debates/kennedynixon.html* in text form.

For background on Smith's time at ABC, we relied primarily on Smith's memoirs and *TV Guide* program listings. Program details for the ABC Scope series are available at *lists.village.virginia .edu/sixties/HTML_docs/Resources/Bibliographies/VN_on_TV/VN_ on_TV_01.html* and the Vanderbilt Television News Archive.

Notes on Smith's later career and his exit from ABC are primarily sourced from his memoirs and *The House That Roone Built: The Inside Story of ABC News* by Marc Gunther. (Little, Brown and Company, 1994).

CHAPTER NINE

Harry Reasoner, ABC

Background material on Harry Reasoner comes from *Before the Colors Fade*, his memoir (Knopf, 1981), *www.Museum.TV/index. shtml,* as well as *Air Time* by Gary Paul Gates (Harper and Row, 1978), which provides extensive details regarding his career at CBS.

Don Hewitt's *Tell Me a Story: Fifty Years and 60 Minutes in Television* (PublicAffairs, 2001) contains valuable background on *60 Minutes*. *The House That Roone Built: The Inside Story of ABC News* by Marc Gunther. (Little, Brown and Company, 1994) provides excellent insight on the 1970s at ABC News when Reasoner was anchor.

CHAPTER TEN

John Chancellor, NBC

Primary source material for John Chancellor was NBC biographical summaries and a recap of his career written by Sandy Smith at the time of the establishment of the John Chancellor Award for Excellence in Journalism by Ira Lipman.

Comments in praise of Chancellor by Tom Brokaw, Robert Mac-Neil, and others are sourced from the many tributes and obituaries published at the time of his death, including Tom Brokaw's tribute on the NBC *Nightly News*. Chancellor recorded an oral history of his time as director of the *Voice of America*, which is located in the Lyndon Baines Johnson Library at the University of Texas and available at *www.lbjlib.utexas.edu/johnson/archives.hom /oralhistory.hom/Chancellor/chancellor.pdf*. The history provides much insight not only into Chancellor's impressions of Johnson, but also his own character.

Transcripts of his *Face the Nation* interviews with Presidents Kennedy and Nixon and the fourth Kennedy-Nixon debate of 1960 are available online—the latter is at *www.jfklibrary.org/60-4th.htm*.

The story of John Chancellor at the 1964 conventions is widely quoted and was recounted in Tom Brokaw's tribute on the NBC *Nightly News* following Chancellor's death.

Background material on the *Day in the Life of the President* broadcast and President Nixon's favorable attitude toward John Chancellor is found in *The Haldeman Diaries: Inside the Nixon White House* by H.R. Haldeman (Putnam, 1994) and *The White House Years* by Henry A. Kissinger (Little, Brown and Company, 1979). The comments about Chancellor by President Nixon in 1973 are quoted from Stanley Kutler's *Abuse of Power: The New Nixon Tapes* (Free Press, 1997).

CHAPTER ELEVEN

Barbara Walters, ABC

Primary source materials for Barbara Walters are *The House That Roone Built: The Inside Story of ABC News* by Marc Gunther. (Little, Brown and Company, 1994), and archival and biographical material provide by NBC (*The Today Show*) and ABC news. Additional material on her early years in New York is available at *www .Museum.TV/index.shtml* and at *www.namebase.org.* Her connection with William Safire is noted in her biography, and Safire has confirmed his association with Jerry Finkelstein, former New York Democratic Party committeeman. Walters's close friendship with Roy Cohn is discussed in *The Autobiography of Roy Cohn* by Sidney Zion (Lyle Stuart, 1988).

Howard K. Smith's comments regarding Reasoner and Walters are discussed in his memoir, *Events Leading Up to My Death: The Life of a Twentieth-Century Reporter.* (St. Martin's Press, 1996).

Walters's interview with *New York* magazine about her transition to ABC was published in the April 6, 1998, issue and is available online at *www.newyorkmetro.com/nymetro/news/people/features /2433/.*

The *Columbia Journalism Review* article about the rivalry between Barbara Walters and Diane Sawyer over the Monica Lewinsky interview was published in the July–August, 1998, issue.

Background information on Frederick S. Pierce is available at *www.Museum.TV/index.shtml.*

CHAPTER TWELVE

Max Robinson, ABC

Primary source material for Max Robinson is *The House That Roone Built: The Inside Story of ABC News* by Marc Gunther. (Little, Brown and Company, 1994) and archival and biographical material provide by ABC News. Additional material on Robinson is available at *www.Museum.TV/index.shtml.*

Peter Jennings discussed Max Robinson in an interview with Jeff Alan for this book.

Source material for Robinson's early career at WTOP includes obituary material on Ray Hubbard and viewer correspondence with

Gordon Peterson, Robinson's longtime co-anchor in Washington. A sketch of Jim Snyder, who was influential in putting Robinson in a local anchor slot, is available at *www.geocities.com/dcbaltotvnews /wyman/*.

Background on Max Robinson's brief stint as a puppet operator is related in a story by Stephen Moorer and Donn Murphy at *kidshow .dcboomer.com/hal6.html*.

Additional material on the final days of Max Robinson can be found in a sketch of Robinson by Aaron Freeman, available at *www.afreeman.com/writer/max.html*.

An interview with Carol Simpson was a source for background material on the impact of Max Robinson and is archived at *npc.press.org/wpforal/sim7.htm*.

CHAPTER THIRTEEN

Peter Jennings, ABC

Primary source materials for Peter Jennings are *The House That Roone Built: The Inside Story of ABC News* by Marc Gunther (Little, Brown and Company, 1994), an interview with Jeff Alan for this book, archival and biographical material provided by ABC news, and *The Evening Stars* by Barbara Matusow (Houghton Mifflin, 1983). All otherwise uncredited quotes from Jennings come from the Jeff Alan interview.

Background material on Charles Jennings is available via the Canadian News Hall of Fame Web site. Further information on Elmer Lower's decision to hire Jennings is found at *www .Museum.TV/index.shtml*. Background information on ABC News and ABC Sports at the 1972 Munich Olympics is found in *The House That Roone Built: The Inside Story of ABC News* by Marc Gunther. (Little, Brown and Company, 1994).

Descriptions of specific broadcasts are found at the Vanderbilt University Television News Archive.

The *Rolling Stone* interview with Peter Jennings was published May 4, 1989.

CHAPTER FOURTEEN
Dan Rather, CBS

Primary source materials for Dan Rather are his memoir, *The Camera Never Blinks* (Morrow, 1976), and *The Camera Never Blinks Twice*, written with Mickey Herskowitz (Morrow, 1994). Other sources include biographical material supplied by CBS News and transcripts of his 1993 address to the Radio Television News Directors Association.

Jeff Alan recorded an interview with Dan Rather for this book, and all otherwise uncredited quotes from Jennings come from the Jeff Alan interview.

Additional background material on CBS News is from *Air Time* by Gary Paul Gates (Harper and Row, 1978). Barbara Matusow's *The Evening Stars* (Houghton, 1983) is an excellent resource for Rather, also. *In All His Glory: The Life of William S. Paley,* by Sally Bedell Smith (Simon and Schuster, 1990) offers insight on the transition from Walter Cronkite to Rather. Don Hewitt's memoir *Tell Me A Story* offers insight into Dan Rather's *60 Minutes* years.

Background material on the Kennedy assassination, including the appearance of the Zapruder film, is from *Death of a President* by William Manchester (Harper and Row, 1967). *The Palace Guard* by Dan Rather and Gary Paul Gates (HarperCollins, 1974) provides background on the Nixon White House during Rather's years as White House correspondent.

Broadcast logs are from Vanderbilt University's Television News Archive.

A short recap of the Rather-George Bush interview of January 25, 1988, is online at *secure.mediaresearch.org/news/mediawatch/1988/mw19880201p1.html.*

A list of Rather-isms from Election Night 2000 is online at *www.dol.net/~d.gaffney/rather.html.* The site, *Ratherbiased.com,* has a host of additional material, very little of it flattering to Rather, as well as a more complete survey of Rather-isms over the years.

An important resource for information about Dan Rather is *Bias: A CBS Insider Exposes How the Media Distorts the News* by Bernard Goldberg (Regnery, 2002). *Bias* was written by a former writer for

Rather. Another resource is *The Murrow Boys* by Stanley Cloud, et al (Houghton Mifflin, 1996), which profiles the relationship between Rather, Eric Sevareid, and Charles Collingwood, as well as Rather's attempts to represent the Murrow tradition at CBS.

CHAPTER FIFTEEN

Tom Brokaw, NBC

A primary source material for Tom Brokaw is his own boyhood memoir, *A Long Way from Home* (Random House, 2002).

Additional biographical material was provided by NBC News and an interview with Jeff Alan for this book. All otherwise uncredited quotes from Jennings come from the Jeff Alan interview.

Background material on Yankton, South Dakota, and the Yankton Sioux is from *Undaunted Courage* by Stephen Ambrose (Simon and Schuster, 1996).

Additional source material was Brokaw's 2002 address to the Radio-Television News Directors Association.

Biographical material was also available at *www.Museum.TV /index.shtml* and from a profile by Mark Miller for the April, 2002, issue of *Communicator* magazine.

CHAPTER SIXTEEN

Connie Chung

Primary source materials for Connie Chung are biographical materials provided by NBC News and ABC News, *www.Museum.TV /index.shtml*, and CNN. Additional profile material from 1999 is available at *Salon.com*.

The book *Bias* by Bernard Goldberg (Regnery, 2002) contains significant coverage of the period when Chung and Rather were co-anchors.

There are many sites and magazine articles offering analysis and opinion regarding Chung's Kathleen Gingrich interview in March, 1995; a superior discussion that puts the interview and Chung's subsequent departure from the anchor desk is *Boston Globe* magazine's report at *www.boston.com/globe/magazine/6-29/interview /523.htm*. Steve Wulf's *Time* magazine article was published May 15, 1995.

Background material on the relationship between Maury Povich and Connie Chung is available at *www.lifetimetv.com/shows /ip/portraits/9921/9921_bio_p2.html*.

CHAPTER SEVENTEEN

Robert MacNeil and Jim Lehrer, PBS

A primary source for information about Robert MacNeil and Jim Lehrer was biographical materials provided by PBS. Additional information came from *The Right Place at the Right Time* (Little, Brown and Company, 1982), Robert MacNeil's memoir that chronicles his experiences as a journalist, and Jim Lehrer's *A Bus of My Own: A Memoir* (Hawk Publishing Group, 2000).

Background material on the *News* report and *NewsHour* includes an outstanding essay by Jim Snyder in the winter 1995 issue of *Television Quarterly*, which also reported the survey in which 42 percent of the public chose the *NewsHour* as the most credible news broadcast.

A terrific profile at *www.emmys.com/whatwedo/halloffame/bios /macneil-lehrer.htm* includes the quoted material from *LA Times* columnist Howard Rosenberg.

CHAPTER EIGHTEEN

CNN

Primary source materials about CNN are the corporate history maintained at *CNN.com*, as well as several memoirs by CNN staffers.

A notable memoir is *Me and Ted Against the World: The Unauthorized Story of the Founding of CNN* by Reese Schonfeld and Chris Chase (Cliff Street Books, 2001).

There are several Ted Turner biographies, including *Ted Turner Speaks* by Janet Rowe (John Wiley, 1999), *Ted Turner: It Ain't as Easy as It Looks* by Porter Bibb (Johnson Books, 1997), and *Citizen Turner: The Wild Rise of an American Tycoon* by Robert Goldberg and Gerald Jay Goldberg (Harcourt, 1995).

Additional information was provided by current CNN staff members, who prefer to remain anonymous

In All His Glory: The Life of William S. Paley (Simon and Schuster,

1990) offers an excellent summation of Ted Turner's takeover attempt of CBS.

The Vanderbilt University Television News Archive is the source of all broadcast recaps. Peter Arnett's *Live from the Battlefield* (Touchstone, 1995) is a good recap of CNN's Gulf War coverage.

Electronic Media Online (*www.tvweek.com/special/121602notparents .html*) and *www.Museum.TV/index.shtml* both have excellent overviews of the battle between CNN and SNC (Satellite News Corporation) that led to the formation of CNN2, or CNN Headline News.

CHAPTER NINETEEN

Since 1995

Primary sources of information for the period since 1995 are the addresses by Tom Brokaw and Dan Rather to the RTNDA and interviews conducted by Jeff Alan with Dan Rather, Tom Brokaw, and Peter Jennings for this book.

For the sections on information overload, sources used to develop the statistics include the *World Almanacs* for 1930 and 2000, the Vanderbilt University Television News Archive, and *TV Guide*.

Ratings cited are from Neilsen as reported in various media.

The Yankelovich Partners survey was cited in issue 7.01 of *Wired*.

The Levine and Burgess study on depression and recall is cited at *www.uwinnipeg.ca/~epritch1/emocog.htm*.

The source for the statistic on American sixth graders is the *Harper's Index Book* (Henry Holt, 1987).

CHAPTER TWENTY

September 11, 2001

The definitive source of September 11th coverage analysis is the astounding work done by *Broadcasting and Cable* magazine, which reassembles the minute-by-minute coverage. The Vanderbilt University Television News Archive is an excellent back-up resource. Audience figures cited are from Neilsen and CNN.

Quotes from Dan Rather, Tom Brokaw, and Peter Jennings are from interviews conducted by Jeff Alan for this book.

Index

Index

About the Authors

Jeff **Alan** began his reporting career in radio while still in high school in 1968. During his first year as a reporter, he was an eyewitness to the assassination of Robert Kennedy and covered politics as a youth political reporter. His weekly beat reporting included former governor Ronald Reagan, Arizona Senator Barry Goldwater, and many others.

By the mid-1980s, Alan had received numerous awards and was hired to his first television news management position in northern Arizona. He began moving up in market size, first to West Virginia, then western Pennsylvania, Tennessee, Missouri, and Texas.

Alan has won more than fifty prestigious journalism awards, including the 2000 Emmy award for Outstanding Television News, the National Ed King Memorial Award for Outstanding Journalism from the Society of Professional Journalists, the Best Newscast in America Award, and the National Outstanding Community Service Award from the National Academy of Television Journalists.

Alan has directed news coverage of thousands of news stories, including the space shuttle *Columbia* tragedy, the crash of U.S. Airways flight #427, the Grand Canyon tourism air tragedy, the Jonesboro school shootings, the Pope's visit to Saint Louis, the death of Governor Mel Carnahan, and the Internet twins. Alan also anchored the news in Arizona, West Virginia, and Pennsylvania. He hosted his own weekly television talk program in Memphis and Saint Louis. He also produced award-winning television specials, documentaries, and weekly series.

Alan has taught a top-rated broadcast journalism course for four years at the University of Pittsburgh and lectured at colleges and universities nationwide. He is the author of *Responsible Journalism*.

James M. Lane has written five books and many magazine articles on media, technology, sports, and travel. He lives in Key Biscayne, Florida.